Documents
for the Study
of the Gospels

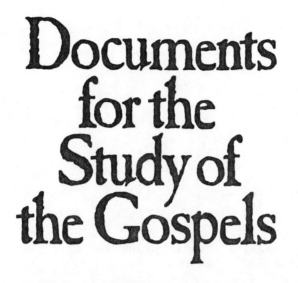

Documents for the Study of the Gospels

David R. Cartlidge   David L. Dungan

FORTRESS PRESS
Philadelphia

Published by William Collins Publishers, Inc.
Cleveland · New York · London

First published in U.S.A. 1980

First published in Great Britain 1980
by Collins Liturgical Publications
187 Piccadilly, London W1V 9DA

UK ISBN 0 00 599652 X

Library of Congress Cataloging in Publication Data
Main entry under title:

Documents for the study of the Gospels.

   Includes bibliographical references.
   1. Bible. N.T. Gospels—Extra-canonical parallels.
2. Rome—Religion. I. Cartlidge, David R. II. Dungan,
David L.
BS2555.5D62 1980   226'.06   79-21341
ISBN 0-529-05683-6
ISBN 0-529-05726-3 pbk.

Printed in the United States of America

For Florie and Anne

Contents

Preface

Although a collection such as this might have many different purposes, in our eyes it has essentially one basic purpose: to provide the educated reader with a better understanding of the way the early Christian portrayals of Jesus Christ called gospels arose, and what they might have meant to those who read them at that time. To this end we have felt it necessary first of all greatly to broaden the perspective on early Christianity by providing a number of little-known writings about Jesus Christ (some of them recently discovered), so that a more complete picture is available, representing the variety of ways in which Jesus Christ was portrayed during the first three hundred years. Accompanying this is a wide spectrum of contemporaneous Greek, Roman, and Jewish documents, which, hopefully, will convey a much more definite and comprehensive impression of the whole realm of Savior Gods who were already present when Christianity began, and over against whom Christians proclaimed their faith in Jesus Christ.

It is common practice to view the larger Greek and Roman environment, or even the varieties of contemporaneous Judaism, as a kind of "background" in opposition to which the early Christian Church sprang forth, radiating divine light as it proclaimed its unique message of Jesus Christ, Savior of mankind. Our hope is to enable the reader to go beyond this overly simple contrast between divinely-inspired Christianity and "pagan superstition" on the one hand, and "legalistic Judaism" on the other. As our collection makes evident, particularly with regard to the concept of Savior, the early Christians shared many of the religious concepts of their age. In fact, we would go on to suggest, although it is not within the purview of this book to demonstrate this claim, that it was precisely because the Christians shared so many ways of thinking and speaking with the other religious traditions of that age that it was able to communicate so effectively with them. Taking up the widely known concept of "Savior of the world" and creatively shaping it and charging it with the unique vitality of the incomparable figure of Jesus of Nazareth, the Christians immediately challenged the validity of every other "Savior of the world."

Although most of the texts in our book have been newly translated by us, we did rely on the assistance of colleagues for some of them, and it is our honor to acknowledge them here: Rev. Dr. Boyd L. Daniels, for his translation of the *Protevangelium Jacobi,* which he made on the basis of a fresh collation of the most important manuscripts; Professor Elaine Pagels, Barnard College, for her very helpful introduction and commentary on the Gospel of Philip; Professor Thomas B. Curtis, Princeton University, for his translation of Cicero's "Dream of Scipio"; Professor Ed Sanders, McMaster University, for translating the rabbinic parables and writing an introduction for them; and Mr. David Peabody and Mr. Frank Collison, Perkins Theological Seminary, for their text-critical notes and translations of portions of the *Oxyrhyncus Papyrus* 1381. We also wish to thank the editors of Judaica Press, New York, for their kind permission to include Philip Blackman's translation and notes of *Mishnah* Sotah 9.15.

Our indebtedness to our other friends and colleagues for their encouragement and helpful suggestions is very real to each of us, even if we cannot mention all of their names here. But three in particular must be singled out: Professor Helmut Koester, to whom we owe the basic inspiration for this collection, received during our graduate-school days at Harvard Divinity School; Professor Robert Funk, University of Montana, and Editor, Scholars Press, who initially encouraged us to publish our collection, and who endured the tribulations of two successive editions, as the collection gradually grew in size and scope; and Professor F. Stanley Lusby, Head, Department of Religious Studies, University of Tennessee, who has assisted and nurtured our labors through the years. We are especially pleased to have this opportunity of thanking him for all that he has done in making this book a reality—not least in providing Mrs. Joan Riedl and Miss Karan Dotson to help with the typing.

For the opportunity to revise the work completely, rechecking all of the translations and adding many new ones, we thank our sensitive and affectionate friend, Norman Hjelm, Vice President and Director of Religious Publishing for Collins Publishers. But it is to Ingalill Hjelm especially that we would like to express our appreciation for helping us to bring this great, ungainly pile of texts into the relatively sharp, clear-cut collection it is now, and for her hard work on the design of the whole book.

June 1979

DAVID R. CARTLIDGE
DAVID L. DUNGAN

Note on the Translations

Except for the selections mentioned in the Preface, all of the translations are our own. Our goal has been to provide a fluent English translation that remains as faithful to the words, style, and tone of the original as possible. But since translations always compromise the integrity of one or other of the languages involved, we have tended to lean toward readability on the assumption that technical research will be based on the original in any case. At the same time, if we have felt it necessary to add English words or phrases to the original to make the sense clearer, these are always indicated by being enclosed in parentheses (). Whenever the original text is in doubt, or when the original text has been altered or added to, those passages are always enclosed in brackets [].

The foreign words transliterated in parentheses relate to major early Christian concepts, such as *logos, sōtēr,* and *mythos,* or they are words referring to types of ancient literature, and have been included to shed some light on the question to what genres the Christian gospels belonged.

In regard to the use of capital letters when referring to Greek and Roman deities, we thought that it was hardly fair in a book of this sort always to capitalize the Christian's God, but never to capitalize the Greek's gods. So, rather than to place them all in lower case, which hardly seemed appropriate, we have used capital letters for them all.

Introduction

SAVIOR GODS
IN THE MEDITERRANEAN WORLD

> "For if there are so-called Gods, whether in Heaven or on the earth—indeed there are many such Gods and many Lords—but to us there is one God, the Father, . . . and one Lord, Jesus Christ" (Paul, 1 Cor. 8:5–6).

When Christianity appeared in the ancient Mediterranean world, there were indeed many Gods in the Heavens and many on the earth, occupying thrones, temples, shrines, and sanctuaries. The ordinary man or woman of that time had learned to be tolerant of the plethora of divinities, for each God had some special function or niche in the pantheon. Even more common was the tendency to group the deities according to function, giving the name of the Greek God of healing to the Egyptian deity of the same function, and so on. There were ancient deities whom people had worshiped longer than anyone could remember, and newer, more vigorous Gods who possessed the newest and most elaborate temples in the down-town areas.

In addition to these divinities there were the great emperors, the kings and regional potentates of one kind or another, who were also paid varying degrees of reverence. These are among the "Gods . . . on the earth" to which Paul referred. For example, the Provincial Assembly of Asia Minor passed this resolution regarding Caesar Augustus (ruled from 27 B.C. to A.D. 14) somewhere near the middle of his reign:

> Whereas the Providence which has guided our whole existence and which has shown such care and liberality, has brought our life to the peak of perfection in giving to us Augustus Caesar, whom it (Providence) filled with virtue (*aretē*) for the welfare of mankind, and who, being sent to us and to our descendants as a savior (*sōtēr*), has put an end to war and has set all things in order; and whereas, having become visible (*phaneis*, i.e., now that a God has become visible), Caesar has fulfilled the hopes of all earlier times . . . not only in surpassing all the benefactors (*euergetai*) who preceded him but also in leaving to his successors no hope of surpassing him; and whereas, finally, that the birthday of the God (viz., Caesar Augustus) has been for the whole world the beginning of the gospel

13

(*euangelion*) concerning him, (therefore, let all reckon a new era beginning from the date of his birth, and let his birthday mark the beginning of the new year).[1]

This edict, which was enacted around 9 B.C., is striking for its use of certain key terms—savior, gospel, and the promised era of peace—which also occur prominently in early Christianity.

That edict was promulgated throughout the Greek cities of Asia Minor shortly before Paul began his missionary work there. The following resolution concerning the Roman emperor Caligula was passed by the Ephesian City Council around the year A.D. 48, probably while Paul was actually there at Ephesus:

> The Council and the people (of the Ephesians and other Greek) cities which dwell in Asia and the nations (acknowledge) Gaius Julius, the son of Gaius Caesar as High Priest and Absolute Ruler, . . . the God Visible who is born of (the Gods) Ares and Aphrodite, the shared savior (*soter*) of human life.[2]

The custom of voting divine titles to living rulers was common, especially in the Eastern Mediterranean, where there were very ancient traditions of divine kingship. The famous Rosetta Stone, discovered near one of the mouths of the Nile in 1799, contains a lengthy announcement in flowery Egyptian style proclaiming the divinity of a Greek king of Egypt, Ptolemy V Epiphanes (210–180 B.C.). Issued in three languages around the year 196 B.C. at Alexandria, when the king was twelve years old, it says in part:

> In the reign of the young king by inheritance from his father, Lord of the Diadems, great in glory, pacifier of Egypt and pious toward the Gods, superior over his adversaries, restorer of the life of man . . . king like the sun, Great King of the Upper and Lower Lands, child of the Gods through the love of the Father . . . *living image of Zeus,* Son of the Sun, Ptolemy the immortal . . . priest of (the divine) Alexander (the Great) and the Savior Gods and the Benefactor Gods and the Gods of the love of the Father, the God visible, for whom thanks be given.[3]

Kings and emperors were not the only mortals to be paid divine honors. Famous ancient philosophers were also revered in this way. For example, the Roman poet, Lucretius (94–55 B.C.), wrote this lyrical

---

[1]F. C. Grant, *Ancient Roman Religion* (New York: Liberal Arts Press, 1957), p. 174.
[2]Ibid., p. 175.
[3]Quoted from Gilbert Murray, *Five Stages of Greek Religion* (New York: Doubleday; Anchor Books, 1955), p. 150; italics added.

praise for his philosopher-Savior Epicurus (c. 340–270 B.C.):

> Who has such power within his breast
> That he could build up a song
> Worthy of this high theme and these discoveries?
>
> No one, I believe, whose body is of mortal growth.
> If I am to suit my language to the majesty
> Of his revelations—he was a God,
> A God indeed who first discovered
> That rule of life that now is called *philosophy;*
>
> . . . whose gospel *(euangelion),*
> Broadcast through the length and breadth of empires,
> Is even now bringing soothing solace
> To the minds of men.[4]

There is even an occasional hint that some of these philosophers saw themselves as Gods and Saviors. The Greek philosopher Empedocles (fl. c. 450 B.C.) addressed his fellow citizens thus:

> Friends that inhabit (my) city . . . All hail!
>   I go about among you (as) an immortal God, no mortal now, honored by all as is meet, crowned with fillets and flowery garlands. Whenever I enter with these men and women in my train into flourishing towns, immediately reverence is given me. People follow me in countless throngs asking of me what is the best way to financial success, others desiring revelations about the future, while others, who have for many a dreary day been pierced by the grievous pangs of all kinds of sickness, beg to hear from me the word of healing.[5]

Examples abound from Hellenistic, Roman, and Jewish coins, inscriptions, epitaphs, and writings of every sort, that it was common to bestow the titles of "God" and "Savior and Benefactor of the human race." Grateful cities, provincial councils, the Roman Senate, and a wide spectrum of public and private religious assemblies granted this divine honor to kings, generals, statesmen, philosophers, poets, physicians, and even athletes.[6]

---

[4]Lucretius, *On the Nature of the Universe,* beginning of Book V; tr. R. E. Lathan (New York: Penguin, 1951), p. 171; italics in original.

[5]Quoted from J. Burnet, *Early Greek Philosophy,* 4th edition (London: A. & C. Black, 1930), p. 221f.

[6]According to W. L. Knox, *Some Hellenistic Elements in Early Christianity* (Oxford: Oxford University Press, 1944), pp. 48–49, one of the lengthiest and most illuminating discussions of demi-Gods and the divinization of mortals in all ancient Greco-Roman literature is to be found in Philo, *Legatio ad Gaium* 78–114. Knox suggests that Philo is using a Stoic source.

So Paul was not telling the Corinthians anything surprising when he said, "There are many so-called Gods in heaven and on the earth." But what was surprising and what was perhaps unexpected was the rest of Paul's statement: "But for us (Christians) there is *one* God, the Father of all things, and *one* Lord, Jesus Christ, *our* Savior." Paul's insistence that there is only *one* God rather than many clearly reveals his Jewish heritage; the Jews had been fighting for this concept for centuries. It was not an idea that Gentile converts to Christianity learned easily.

But other ideas were not as difficult for Gentile converts. For example, when Paul wrote to his Christian converts in the provincial capital of Philippi, "Our citizenship is in Heaven, and from it we await a Savior, the Lord Jesus Christ" (Phil. 3:20; RSV), it was not as if he were using terms (Savior, Lord) of which they had never heard. Even his notion that Christians held citizenship rights in a "heavenly city" was not; an actual utopian experiment called "Uranopolis" (heaven-city) having been constructed nearby some two hundred years earlier by the brother of a local king. Put differently, many of the basic claims of early Christianity may have been *exclusive* in their rejection of other Gods and Lords, but these claims were not *unique* in themselves.

Occasionally, Christian theologians actually commented on the similarity between their beliefs regarding Jesus Christ and rival religious beliefs regarding other Gods. For instance, the Christian philosopher Justin Martyr complained, in an open letter, written around the year A.D. 150 to the Roman Emperor Antoninus Pius, that Christians were being unjustly persecuted *"even though we say the same things* (about Jesus Christ) *that the Greeks* (say about their Gods) . . . we alone are hated because of the name of Christ . . . (and) put to death as offenders."[7] Nor is Justin Martyr reluctant to give abundant evidence to support this startling claim:

> When we say that the Word (*logos*), who is the first-born of God, was born for us without sexual union . . . and that he was crucified and died and after rising again ascended into Heaven, *we introduce nothing new beyond (what you say) regarding those whom you call sons of Zeus.*[8] . . . When we say that Jesus was born of a virgin, you should consider this something in common with Perseus. When we say that he healed the lame, the paralyzed, and those born blind, and raised the dead, we seem to be talking about things like those said to have been done by Asklepios.[9]

To be sure, Justin goes on to insist that these similarities and many

[7]Cyril C. Richardson, *Early Christian Fathers* (Philadelphia: Westminster Press, 1953), p. 257; quoting *Apol.* I. 24.
[8]Ibid., p. 255; *Apol.* I.21; italics added.
[9]Ibid., p. 256; *Apol.* I. 22.

others mentioned later (especially regarding the Christian sacraments) are all due to the malicious conniving of evil demons who had devised all of these surrogates in order to lure unwary souls away from the one true Savior. But even so, the list of parallels Justin provides is surprisingly long.

About one hundred years later, another Christian theologian devotes considerable attention to the same subject. The discussion is in a reply by the Church Father, Origen (c. A.D. 185–c. 254), probably the most learned theologian of his time, to the attack on Christianity by an otherwise unknown Greek philosopher named Celsus (fl. c. A.D. 180). Origen's reply was a lengthy, point-by-point refutation of Celsus' entire position and ranks as a classic of Christian apologetics. The book clearly reveals the fact that both antagonists were very conscious of the similarity between Christian claims about the Savior, Jesus Christ, and the claims of other religions about their Savior Gods. In fact, this very similarity provided Celsus with one of his most caustic criticisms. Repeatedly he demands, "If you Christians believe the stories of Jesus' miracles, if you believe the story of Jesus' miraculous birth, if you believe the story that Jesus was raised from the dead and ascended into Heaven, then how can you refuse to believe precisely the same stories when they are told of the other Savior Gods: Herakles, Asklepios, the Dioscuri, Dionysos, and a dozen others I could name?"[10]

The Greco-Roman world, in general, held conceptions of two different kinds of Savior Gods. One type, including such Gods as Herakles, Asklepios, and Dionysos, were offspring of divine-human unions who had performed outstanding feats of benefaction (*euergesia*) on behalf of the human race, and so they were rewarded with immortality, and worshiped as Saviors.[11] Consider this statement from the first-century B.C. Greek historian, Diodorus Siculus:

> The ancients among men have given to later generations two conceptions (*ennoia*) concerning Gods. They say on the one hand that some are eternal and imperishable such as (Gods named after) the Sun and the Moon and the other stars in Heaven . . . but the others they say were earthly men (*epigeios*) who became Gods, attaining immortal honor and glory because of their benefactions (*euergesia*) toward men, such as Herakles, Dionysos, Aristaios, and other similar to them.[12]

The first-century Roman statesman and philosopher Cicero repeats

[10]Origen's reply is too lengthy to quote here, but we recommend in particular the brilliant passage, III.22–43, where he meets Celsus' attacks head-on; see *Contra Celsum*, trans. and ed. Henry Chadwick (Cambridge: Cambridge University Press, 1965), pp. 140–158.
[11]On this whole subject, see now C. H. Talbert, *What Is a Gospel? The Genre of the Canonical Gospels* (Philadelphia: Fortress Press, 1977).
[12]*Library of History* 6.1; see Talbert, op.cit. p. 27.

this familiar distinction when, in discussing the religious institutions he would have in his ideal city, he declares:

> They shall worship as Gods both those who have always been dwellers in Heaven, and also those whose merits (*merita*) have admitted them to Heaven: Hercules (=Herakles), Liber, Aesculapius (=Asklepios), Castor, Pollus, Quirinius (=Romulus?) . . .[13]

The second general notion of Savior Gods was that great leaders, especially kings, were in fact temporary manifestations or appearances (*epiphaneia*) of the eternal Gods themselves.[14] For example, after nearly a century of bitter, internecine warfare and bloodshed, Caesar's nephew Octavian gained the throne in 44 B.C. and, within a decade or so, managed to bring back into the conduct of Roman public affairs a high degree of order and prosperity. Gratitude poured out toward him from all directions. It was during this period that the famous *Eclogue IV* was written by Virgil, which we have included in our collection.[15] It was also during this period that another court poet, Horace, composed a less well-known poem, which is equally fascinating for our subject. Here it is in part:

> Which of the Gods now shall the people summon
> To prop Rome's reeling sovereignty?
> What prayer shall the twelve Virgins
> Use to reach the ear of Vesta,
> Who grows each day deafer to litanies?
> Whom shall Jupiter appoint
> As instrument of our atonement?
> Come, fore-telling Apollo . . .
> Or thou, (Venus) . . .
> Or thou, (Mars), great parent of our race;
>
> Or else thou, (Mercury) winged boy of gentle Maia.
> Put on the mortal shape of a young Roman;
> Descend and, well contented to be known
> As Caesar's avenger,
> Stay gladly and long with Romulus' people.
> Delay thy homeward, skybound journey.
> . . . (Stay) on earth, enjoy resplendent triumphs.
> Be Prince, be Father—titles to rejoice in!
> And let no Parthian raider ride unscathed
> While Caesar has charge of Rome![16]

Octavian is the incarnation of the God Mercury!

One of the clearest explanations of the incarnation conception of Savior Gods is in an early fourth-century A.D. Christian writing by the Church Father, Eusebius of Caesarea. Like Origen before him, Eusebius was exceptionally well-versed in the manifold varieties of Hellenistic and Roman religious beliefs. The emperor Constantine relied on Eusebius' efforts for a time as he sought to reorganize the Church, following the bloody persecution by Diocletian and Galerius.

During the persecution, a Roman provincial judge named Hierocles had thrown his weight into the fray by publishing a tract unfavorably comparing Jesus Christ, the gospel writers, and Paul with Apollonios of Tyana and Philostratus. Hierocles made it clear that he regarded Jesus of Nazareth as a cheap fake, and the stories published about him as a lot of rubbish put out by a few ignorant foreigners. Apollonios, on the other hand, he regarded as a profound philosopher, in fact, a God, and he believed Philostratus' account of him to be that of a trained, honest historian.

Eusebius' reply, obviously penned sometime after the Edict of Toleration (A.D. 313) when it would have been safe to take on a Roman official such as Hierocles, consisted of an attack not so much upon Hierocles himself as upon his main source, namely, Philostratus' *Life of Apollonios of Tyana*.[17] However, Eusebius interestingly begins by conceding to Hierocles one of his central contentions, namely, that divine Providence does in fact send Saviors from Heaven from time to time, and they temporarily take on a mortal human shape in order to provide some great benefaction for the human race. Indeed, when he needs an authority to fall back on, near the middle of his argument, he does not appeal to Jesus Christ or one of the prophets, but to the Greek philosopher Plato!

Eusebius of Caesarea Against Hierocles (ch. 6)

Do you ask why I say (Apollonios was a charlatan and a liar), and what is my starting point? Listen, and I will tell you.

There are bounds in Nature which embrace the beginnings, middle, and completion of the existence of all things; measures (*metron*) and laws (*thesmos*) for everything by means of which the whole mechanism and construction of the entire universe is being brought to completion. These bounds have been distributed as indestructible laws and indissoluble bonds acting as the guardians everywhere of the wholly-wise will of Providence,

---

[13]*De legibus* II 8.19; cf. *Tusculan Disputations* V 14.32.
[14]See Talbert, op. cit., pp. 53–89.
[15]See below, p. 177ff.
[16]*The Odes of Horace*, Book I, *Ode* 2; trans. James Michie (New York: Washington Square Press, 1965), pp. 7–9.
[17]For the text of this writing, see below p. 205ff.

which regulates all things. No thing may disturb nor any person alter the order of what has been once-for-all everywhere established.

Thus anyone in whom there is a longing to be overly bold and to transgress it is restrained from defying the divine law (*nomos*) by the ordinance (*themis*) of Nature. For this reason, the fish that lives in the water will not be able to transform itself and live against nature on the dry land, nor will the creature born on dry land plunge into the waters and take up living there. Nor will anyone by a great meteoric leap jump up into the air, desiring to live with the eagles, although *they* can, by lowering themselves, in fact walk about on the earth.

. . . In this way then the mortal race of men, possessing soul and body, is circumscribed by supernatural bonds (*theioi horoi*). Nor will anyone who scorns to walk the paths of the earth ever go in the body through the air without instantly paying the price of his folly, nor will he, by lifting up the soul, attain by thought to the unattainable without falling back into the sickness of melancholy. It is more prudent, therefore, to bear one's body about on the earth by means of one's feet, and to sustain one's soul by means of education and philosophy.

But one may indeed also pray for some Helper (*synergos*) from above to come descending from the paths of Heaven, and to manifest a teacher to oneself of the salvation (*sōteria*) there. An excellent illustration of this is the legitimate way a doctor regularly visits the sick or the way a teacher associates himself with the student entering studies, or the way any superior condescends to come from above to those more lowly, but certainly never the opposite.

All the more, therefore, is it legitimate for a supernatural nature (*theia physis*), who is a benefactor (*euergetis*) and a Savior (*sōteira*), and who foreknows the future, to come for communion (*homilia*) with man. There is no reason why this would be prevented by the bounds set by divine Providence either. In fact, it has allowed this, for, as Plato says, it is good and there never springs up in the Good any ill will toward anyone.

But it is hardly only for the welfare of our physical bodies that the Guide of the universe is concerned. Rather, since he *is* good, he is much more concerned for our souls, since he has graciously bestowed upon them the honor of immortality and free will. Naturally, it is to them that the master Designer of the universe, who is a benefactor (*euergetēs*) by nature, presents gifts of grace, since the soul can respond to them. *He will ungrudgingly give rays of the light around himself, as it were, from time to time sending one of the beings from those especially close to him, down to us here below for our salvation and assistance.*

If one of these beings were to become one with some fortunate person, whose mind had been purified and from whom the cloud of mortality had been driven away, that man would be described as a truly supernatural man (*theios*), *one who carried the image of some great God (megas tis theos) in his soul.* Surely so great a person as this would affect the entire human race, shining upon the civilized world more brightly than the sun. He would leave behind as the work wrought by his eternal supernatural nature a monument to be witnessed by future generations . . . (which would) reveal the pattern of his God-indwelling nature *(entheos physis)*.

In this fashion then, human nature may be one with *(koinōnein)* superhuman, but otherwise it is not legitimate to transgress the bounds.[18]

It is intriguing to observe the Christian monotheist Eusebius here envisaging Divine Providence as sending down *multiple* Saviors from time to time as it deems necessary. In any case, Eusebius goes on to argue that Apollonios of Tyana was definitely *not* one of these supernatural men *(theios anēr)*.

In addition to these two major ways of conceiving of Savior Gods in ancient times, there actually was a third category as well. This had to do with manifestations or appearances of divine beings through dreams,[19] visions,[20] and sometimes incognito, as mere human beings.[21] These should all be termed "epiphanies" *(epiphaneia)*, that is, temporary appearances of the God to serve many purposes: to heal, to foretell the future, to warn, to demand some task, to encourage, and so forth.

It has not been our intention to oversimplify what is in fact an extremely complex subject, namely, the ways in which ancient Mediterranean peoples conceived of their Savior Gods. We have given examples of certain major distinctions which the people of that time, including Christians, made with some regularity. Enough examples have been presented here, as well as in the rest of the collection, to demonstrate that Justin Martyr had good reason for saying that Christians did not claim anything about their Savior beyond what the Greeks had said about theirs.

However, it is not our intention to oversimplify in the other direction either, that is, by glossing over or ignoring the manifold ways in which Christianity stood out as a unique and unusual religion in its time. If Christians utilized familiar concepts and terms in order to communicate their faith, they often gave them an exclusive significance. When they worshiped Jesus as their Savior, the effect was a powerful negation: "Neither Caesar, nor Asklepios, nor Herakles, nor Dionysos, nor Ptolemy, nor any other God is the Savior of the world—*Jesus Christ* is!"

The Christians were on fire with a revelation that was so monumental, so elemental that it was incomprehensible as anything less than a new direct action of the God of the universe. He had acted, and was still acting, in Jesus of Nazareth. The Christian message of salvation,

[18]Those interested in reading this writing in complete form can find it at the end of the Loeb edition of Philostratus, *Life of Apollonios of Tyana.*
[19]See, e.g., the dream appearance of Asklepios, pp. 121–25.
[20]See, e.g., the dramatic vision of Isis, pp. 168–70.
[21]As when the Christian missionaries Paul and Barnabas are thought by the people of Lystra to be Hermes and Zeus (Acts 14:11–12), or the castaway picked up by the pirates turns out to be the God Dionysos *(Homeric Hymn 7).*

creatively shaped and proclaimed by the apostles, was a "gospel" which immediately set up a powerful tension over against all other gospels of that time.

So while the Christians took over basic concepts and ideas, they filled them with vibrant new meaning, meaning which often confused and mystified their contemporaries. The same Justin Martyr who was very conscious of the similarities also wrote:

> People think we are insane when we name a crucified man as second in rank to the unchangeable and eternal God, the Creator of all things, *for they do not discern the mystery involved.*[22]

Paul likewise was painfully conscious that his gospel was considered scandalous by his Jewish kinsmen, and utter nonsense by the Greeks who listened to him.[23] In and through all of the familiar concepts and categories being used by them as well as their contemporaries in other religions, the Christians were also saying some new, different, very strange things about the whole divine-human encounter.

And yet the power and vitality of the early Church's portrayals of Jesus Christ echo the depth and intensity of the Hellenistic, Roman, and Jewish religious traditions. Christians would not have adopted dead symbols with which to speak about Jesus! We hope that the many stories, visions, gospels, and accounts collected in this book (and we have hardly scratched the surface) will convey to the reader something of the vast, rich panorama of Savior Gods in the Hellenistic-Roman world.

[22]*Apol.* I.13; italics added.
[23]1 Cor. 1:23.

Part 1

THE CHRISTIAN SAVIOR

The purpose of Part 1 is to provide the reader with a broader perspective on the variety of Christian portrayals of Jesus Christ that had appeared by the year A.D. 300. It is to be expected that some of these selections will contain confusing and possibly even startling ideas regarding Jesus Christ. It is our hope that the reader will compare these documents with the more familiar New Testament Gospels, and thereby arrive at a more vivid impression of the vitality and diversity of the Christian movement during its first three hundred years.

Each selection has been provided with a brief introduction to indicate the generally accepted views regarding date of authorship and place of origin, as well as to explain our reason for including it in this collection.

The Coptic Gospel of Thomas

Introduction: When it was discovered near the town of Nag Hammadi in upper Egypt, this Gospel caused a sensation. It was found in an ancient Coptic monastery's library (of which the Gospel of Philip is a part). Bits of the Coptic Gospel of Thomas had been known in Greek, but the extent and nature of the whole work were virtually unsuspected. Suddenly, the world had a book which called itself a gospel but which was only a collection of sayings; it looked like no other gospel. It had no narratives, no miracles, no passion story.

Moreover, early attempts to show that this Gospel was derived from the first three (synoptic) Gospels were not convincing. There are sayings in the Coptic Gospel of Thomas which do not occur in the New Testament Gospels. And some of the sayings in the Coptic Gospel of Thomas which are also found in Matthew or Luke appear to have been less influenced by later Christian alteration than the same sayings in the synoptic Gospels. This is particularly true of certain parables. Could it be that (1) the Coptic Gospel of Thomas represents a tradition of Jesus sayings which is independent of the New Testament Gospels, and (2) this Gospel has some sayings which are older in form than their parallels in the synoptic Gospels? Many scholars tend to answer yes to both questions.

These are the secret words which the living Jesus spoke, and Didymos Judas Thomas wrote them down.

1. And he said, "He who finds the meaning of these words will not taste death."

2. Jesus said, "Let him who seeks not cease seeking until he finds, and when he finds, he shall be troubled, and when he is troubled, he will marvel, and he will rule over the All."

3. Jesus said, "If the ones who lead you say, 'There is the kingdom, in heaven,' then the birds of heaven shall go before you. If they say to you, 'It is in the sea,' then the fish shall go before you. Rather, the kingdom is within you and outside you. If you know yourselves, then you will be known, and you will know that you are sons of the living Father. But if you do not know yourselves, then you are in poverty and you are poverty."

4. Jesus said, "A man who is old in his days will not hesitate to ask a baby of seven days about the place of life and he will live. For many who are first shall (be) last, and they shall become a single one."

5. Jesus said, "Know what is in front of your face, and what is concealed from you will be revealed to you. For there is nothing concealed which will not be manifest."

6. His disciples asked him, "Do you want us to fast, and how shall we pray, and shall we give alms, and what food regulations shall we keep?" Jesus said, "Do not lie, and do not do what you hate, because all is revealed before Heaven. For nothing is hidden that will not be revealed, and nothing is covered that shall remain without being revealed."

7. Jesus said, "Blessed is the lion which the man eats, and the lion thus becomes man; and cursed is the man whom the lion shall eat, when the lion thus becomes man."

8. And he said, "The man is like a wise fisherman who threw his net into the sea. He drew it up from the sea; it was full of small fish. The fisherman found among them a large, good fish. He threw all the small fish back into the sea; with no trouble he chose the large fish. He who has ears to hear, let him hear."

9. Jesus said, "Behold, the sower went out; he filled his hand; he threw. Some fell on the road. The birds came; they gathered them up. Others fell on the rock and did not send roots into the earth and did not send ears up to heaven. Others fell among thorns. They choked the seed, and the worm ate (the seed). And others fell on good earth, and it raised up good fruit to heaven. It bore sixty per measure and one hundred-twenty per measure."

10. Jesus said, "I have hurled fire on the world, and behold, I guard it until it burns."

11. Jesus said, "This heaven will pass away and your heaven above it will pass away, and the dead are not living and the living shall not die. In the days when you ate what is dead, you made it alive; when you come into the light, what will you do? On the day when you were one, you became two. But when you have become two, what will you do?"

12. The disciples said to Jesus, "We know that you will go away from us; who will become ruler over us?" Jesus said, "Wherever you may be, you will go to James the righteous; heaven and earth came into being for him."

13. Jesus said to his disciples, "Make a comparison and tell me whom I am like." Simon Peter said to him, "You are like a righteous angel." Matthew said to him, "You are like a wise man." Thomas said to him, "Master, my mouth will not be able to say what you are like." Jesus said, "I am not your master. Because you drank, you are drunk from the bubbling spring which I measured out." And he took him; he went

aside. He spoke to him three words. When Thomas returned to his companions, they asked him, "What did Jesus say to you?" Thomas said to them, "If I tell you one of the words which he said to me, you will pick up stones; you will throw them at me. And fire will come from the stones and consume you."

14. Jesus said to them, "If you fast, you will bring sin upon yourselves and, if you pray, you will be condemned and, if you give alms, you will do evil to your spirits. And if you enter any land and wander through the regions, if they receive you, whatever they set before you, eat it. Heal the sick among them. For that which goes into your mouth will not defile you, but that which comes out of your mouth is what will defile you."

15. Jesus said, "When you see him who was not born of woman, throw yourself down on your faces (and) adore him; that one is your Father."

16. Jesus said, "Men might think I have come to throw peace on the world, and they do not know that I have come to throw dissolution on the earth; fire, sword, war. For there shall be five in a house: three shall be against two and two against three, the father against the son and the son against the father, and they shall stand as solitary ones."

17. Jesus said, "I will give you what no eye has seen and what no ear has heard and no hand has touched and what has not come into the heart of man."

18. The disciples said to Jesus, "Tell us how our end will occur." Jesus said, "Have you found the beginning that you search for the end? In the place of the beginning, there the end will be. Blessed is he who will stand at the beginning, and he will know the end, and he will not taste death."

19. Jesus said, "Blessed is he who was before he came into being. If you become my disciples (and) you hear my words, these stones shall serve you. For you have five trees in paradise which are immobile in summer or winter, and they do not shed their leaves. Whoever knows them shall not taste death."

20. The disciples said to Jesus, "Tell us, what is the Kingdom of Heaven like?" He said to them, "It is like a mustard seed, smaller than all seeds. But when it falls on plowed ground, it puts forth a large shrub and becomes a shelter for the birds of heaven."

21. Mary said to Jesus, "Whom are your disciples like?" He said, "They are like little children; they settle themselves in a field that is not theirs. When the owners of the field come, they (the owners) say, 'Give us our field.' They undress before them and release it (the field) to them and give back their field to them. Because of this I say, if the owner of the house knows that the thief is coming, he will watch before he comes and will not let him break into his house of his kingdom and carry away

his goods. But you watch especially for the world; gird your loins with great power lest the robbers find a way to come upon you, because the trouble you expect will happen. Let there be a man of understanding among you. When the fruit ripened, he came quickly, his sickle in his hand (and) he reaped it. He who has ears to hear, let him hear."

22. Jesus saw babies being suckled. He said to his disciples, "These babies who are being suckled are like those who enter the Kingdom." They said to him, "We are children, shall we enter the Kingdom?" Jesus said to them, "When you make the two one, and when you make the inner as the outer and the outer as the inner and the upper as the lower, so that you will make the male and the female into a single one, so that the male will not be male and the female [not] be female, when you make eyes in the place of an eye, and hand in place of a hand, and a foot in the place of a foot, (and) an image in the place of an image, then you shall enter [the Kingdom]."

23. Jesus said, "I shall choose you, one from a thousand, and two from ten thousand, and they shall stand; they are a single one."

24. His disciples said, "Show us the place where you are, for it is necessary for us to seek it." He said to them, "He who has ears to hear, let him hear. There is light within a man of light and he (or it) lights the whole world. When he (or, it) does not shine, there is darkness."

25. Jesus said, "Love your brother as your soul; keep him as the apple of your eye."

26. Jesus said, "The chip that is in your brother's eye you see, but the log in your own eye you do not see. When you take the log out of your eye, then you will see to remove the chip from your brother's eye."

27. "If you do not fast (in respect to) the world, you will not find the Kingdom; if you do not keep the Sabbath a Sabbath, you shall not see the Father."

28. Jesus said, "I stood in the midst of the world, and I appeared to them in the flesh. I found all of them drunk; I did not find any of them thirsting. And my soul was pained for the sons of men because they are blind in their hearts, and they do not see that they came empty into the world; they seek to go out of the world empty. However, they are drunk. When they have shaken off their wine, then they shall repent."

29. Jesus said, "If the flesh exists because of spirit, it is a miracle, but if spirit (exists) because of the body, it is a miracle of miracles. But I marvel at how this great wealth established itself in this poverty."

30. Jesus said, "Where there are three Gods, they are Gods; where there are two or one, I am with him."

31. Jesus said, "A prophet is not acceptable in his own village; a physician does not heal those who know him."

32. Jesus said, "A city being built and fortified upon a high mountain

cannot fall, nor can it be hidden."

33. Jesus said, "What you will hear in your ear and in your [other] ear, preach from your housetops. For no one lights a lamp and puts it under a basket, nor does he put it in a hidden place, but he sets it on a lampstand so everyone who comes in and goes out will see its light."

34. Jesus said, "If a blind man leads a blind man, the two of them fall into a pit."

35. Jesus said, "It is impossible for one to enter the house of the strong man and rob it violently unless he bind his hands; then he can pillage his house."

36. Jesus said, "Do not be anxious from morning to evening and from evening to morning about what you will wear."

37. His disciples said, "On what day will you be revealed to us and on what day shall we see you?" Jesus said, "When you undress without being ashamed, and you take your clothes and put them under your feet as little children and tramp on them, then you shall see the Son of the Living [One], and you shall not fear."

38. Jesus said, "Many times you desired to hear these words which I say to you, and you have no one else from whom to hear them. There will be days when you will seek me, and you will not find me."

39. Jesus said, "The Pharisees and the scribes took the keys of knowledge; they hid them. They did not enter, and they did not allow those to enter who wanted to enter. But you be wise as serpents and as innocent as doves."

40. Jesus said, "A vine was planted without the Father and it has not strengthened; it will be pulled up by its roots (and) it will be destroyed."

41. Jesus said, "He who has something in his hand shall be given more; and he who does not have anything, even the little he has will be taken away from him."

42. Jesus said, "Be wanderers."

43. His disciples said to him, "Who are you that you say these things to us?" "By what I say to you, you do not know who I am, but you have become as the Jews. They love the tree, they hate its fruit; they love the fruit, they hate the tree."

44. Jesus said, "Whoever blasphemes the Father, it will be forgiven him, and whoever blasphemes the Son, it will be forgiven him, but he who blasphemes the Holy Spirit will not be forgiven either on earth or in Heaven."

45. Jesus said, "One does not pick grapes from thorns, nor does one gather figs from thistles; they do not give fruit. F[or a go]od man brings forth good fr[om] his treasure; a b[ad] man brings forth evil from the evil treasure in his heart, and he speaks evil. For out of the abundance of his heart he brings forth evil."

46. Jesus said, "From Adam to John the Baptist, among those born of women no one is greater than John the Baptist, so that his eyes . . . [here the text is uncertain]. Yet I said that whoever among you shall become as a child shall know the Kingdom, and he shall become higher than John."

47. Jesus said, "A man cannot mount two horses; he cannot stretch two bows. A servant cannot serve two masters; either he will honor the one and the other he will scorn . . . No man drinks old wine and right away wants to drink new wine; and one does not put new wine into old wineskins lest they tear; and one does not put old wine into new wineskins lest it spoil. One does not sew an old patch on a new garment, because there will be a tear."

48. Jesus said, "If two make peace between themselves in the same house, they shall say to the mountain, 'Move away,' and it will move."

49. Jesus said, "Blessed are the solitary and the chosen, because you will find the Kingdom; because you come from it, you will again go there."

50. Jesus said, "If they say to you, 'Where did you come from?' say to them, 'We come from the light, where the light came into being through itself. It stood . . . and reveals itself in their image.' If they say to you, '[Who] are you?' say to them, 'We are his sons and we are the chosen of the living Father.' If they ask you, 'What is the sign of your Father who is in you?' say to them, 'It is movement and repose.' "

51. His disciples said to him, "When will be the repose of the dead, and when will the new world come?" He said to them, "What you look for has come, but you do not know it."

52. His disciples said to him, "Twenty-four prophets spoke in Israel and all of them spoke in you." He said to them, "You have left out the Living One who is with you, and you have spoken about the dead."

53. His disciples said to him, "Is circumcision profitable or not?" He said to them, "If it were profitable, their father would beget them circumcized from their mother. But the true circumcision in the Spirit has found complete usefulness."

54. Jesus said, "Blessed are the poor, for yours is the Kingdom of Heaven."

55. Jesus said, "He who does not hate his father and his mother cannot be my disciple, and (he who) does not hate his brothers and his sisters and (does not) carry his cross in my way will not be worthy of me."

56. Jesus said, "He who has known the world has found a corpse, and he who has found a corpse, the world is not worthy of him."

57. Jesus said, "The Kingdom of the Father is like a man who had [good] seed. His enemy came by night, (and) he sowed a weed among the good seed. The man did not let them pull up the weed. He said to

them, 'I fear lest you go to pull up the weed, and you pull up the wheat with it.' For on the day of the harvest the weeds will be apparent; they will pull them up and burn them."

58. Jesus said, "Blessed is the man who has suffered; he has found the Life."

59. Jesus said, "Look upon the Living One as long as you live, lest you die and seek to see him and you cannot see."

60. (They saw) a Samaritan carrying a lamb; he was going to Judea. He said to his disciples, "Why does he carry the lamb?" They said to him, "That he may kill it and eat it." He said to them, "As long as it is alive he will not eat it, but only when he has killed it and it has become a corpse." They said, "Otherwise he cannot do it." He said to them, "You yourselves seek a place for yourselves in repose, lest you become a corpse and be eaten."

61. Jesus said, "Two will be resting on a couch; the one will die, the one will live." Salome said, "Who are you, man? As if from the One you sat on my couch and you ate from my table." Jesus said to her, "I am he who is from him who is the same. The things from my Father have been given to me." (Salome said,) "I am your disciple." (Jesus said to her,) "Therefore, I say, if he is the same, he will be filled with light, but if he is divided, he will be filled with darkness."

62. Jesus said, "I tell my mysteries [to those who are worthy of my] mysteries. What your right (hand) will do, do not let your left (hand) know.

63. Jesus said, "There was a rich man who had many possessions. He said, 'I will use my goods so that I can sow and reap and plant and fill my warehouses with fruit so that I will not be in need of anything.' He truly believed this. And in that night he died. He who has ears, let him hear."

64. Jesus said, "A man had guests and, when he had prepared the banquet, he sent his servant to invite the guests. He went to the first; he said to him, 'My master invites you.' He said, 'Money is owed me by some merchants. They will come to me in the evening; I will go and I will give them orders. Please excuse me from the dinner.' He went to another; he said to him, 'My master invites you.' He said to him, 'I have bought a house and they have asked me (to come out) for a day (to close the deal). I will not have time.' He went to another; he said to him, 'My master invites you.' He said to him, 'My friend is going to marry, and I will prepare a dinner; I will not be able to come. Please excuse me from the dinner.' He went to another; he said to him, 'My master invites you.' He said to him, 'I have bought a farm, I go to collect the rent. I will not be able to come. Please excuse me from the dinner.' The servant returned; he said to his master, 'Those whom you invited asked to be excused from the dinner.' The master said to his servant, 'Go outside to

the streets, bring those whom you find so that they may feast.' Buyers and merchants will not enter the places of my Father."

65. He said, "A good man had a vineyard. He rented it to some farmers so that they would work it, and he would receive its profits from them. He sent his servant so that the farmers would give him the profits of the vineyard. They seized his servant, beat him, and almost killed him. The servant went back; he told his master. His master said, 'Perhaps he did not know them.' He sent another servant. The farmers beat him also. Then the master sent his son. He said, 'Perhaps they will respect my son.' Those farmers seized him, and they killed him, because they knew he was the heir of the vineyard. He who has ears, let him hear."

66. Jesus said, "Show me the stone rejected by those who built. It is the cornerstone."

67. Jesus said, "He who believes (that) the All is wanting in anything lacks all himself.

68. Jesus said, "Blessed are you when they hate you and persecute you, and they will find no place wherever you have been persecuted."

69a. Jesus said, "Blessed are those whom they have persecuted in their hearts; these are they who know the Father in truth."

69b. "Blessed are those who are hungry, so that the belly of him who hungers will be filled."

70. Jesus said, "If you beget what is in you, what you have will save you. If you do not have it in you, what you do not have in you will kill you."

71. Jesus said, "I shall destroy [this] house and no one will be able to build it [again]."

72. [A man] s[aid] to him, "Speak to my brothers, so that they will divide my father's possessions with me." He said to him, "O man, who made me a divider?" He turned to his disciples; he said to them, "I am not a divider, am I?"

73. Jesus said, "The harvest is great, but the workers are few; but beseech the Lord to send workers to the harvest."

74. He said, "Lord, there are many standing around the cistern, but no one (or, nothing) in the cistern."

75. Jesus said, "Many are standing at the door, but the solitary will enter the Bridal Chamber."

76. Jesus said, "The Kingdom of the Father is like a merchant who had goods. Then he found a pearl. This was a prudent merchant. He gave up (i.e., sold) the goods, and he bought the single pearl for himself. You also must seek for the treasure which does not perish, which abides where no moth comes near to eat, nor worm destroys."

77. Jesus said, "I am the light which is above all of them; I am the All. The All came forth from me and the All reached me. Split wood, I am

there; lift up the stone, and you will find me there."

78. Jesus said, "Why did you come to the desert? To see a reed shaken by the wind? To see a [man clo]thed in soft clothes? [Behold, your] kings and your great ones are dressed in soft [clothes] and they are not able to know the truth."

79. A woman in the crowd said to him, "Blessed are the womb which bore you and the breasts which fed you." He said to [her], "Blessed are those who have heard the Word of the Father (and) have kept it in truth. For there will be days when you will say: 'Blessed are the womb which has not conceived and the breasts that have not suckled.'"

80. Jesus said, "He who has known the world has found the body, but he who has found the body, the world is not worthy of him."

81. Jesus said, "He who has become rich, let him become king; and he who has power, let him renounce it."

82. Jesus said, "He who is near me is near the fire, and he who is far from me is far from the Kingdom."

83. Jesus said, "The images are manifest to man, and the light in them is hidden in the image of the light of the Father. He will reveal himself, and his image will be hidden by his light."

84. Jesus said, "When you see your likeness, you rejoice. But when you see your images which came into being before you, (which) do not die nor are manifest, how much you will bear!"

85. Jesus said, "Adam came into existence from a great power and a great wealth, and he was not worthy of you. For, if he had been worthy, he [would] not [have tasted] death."

86. Jesus said, "[The foxes have] h[oles] and the birds have [their] nests, but the Son of Man does not have any place to lay his head and to rest."

87. Jesus said, "The body is wretched which depends on a body, and the soul is wretched which depends on these two."

88. Jesus said, "The angels and the prophets shall come to you, and they shall give you that which is yours. You give them what is in your hands, (and) say to yourselves, 'On which day will they come and receive what is theirs?'"

89. Jesus said, "Why do you wash the outside of the cup? Do you not know that he who made the inside is also he who made the outside?"

90. Jesus said, "Come to me because my yoke is easy and my mastery is gentle, and you will find your repose."

91. They said to him, "Tell us who you are so that we can believe in you." He said to them, "You examine the face of the heavens and the earth, and (yet) you have not known him who is in front of your face, nor do you know how to examine this time."

92. Jesus said, "Search and you will find, but those things which you

asked me in those days, I did not tell you then; now I want to speak them, and you do not ask about them."

93. "Do not give what is holy to the dogs, because they will throw it on the dung heap. Do not throw the pearls to the pigs, lest they make . . ." [text uncertain].

94. Jesus (said), "He who searches, will find . . . it will open to him."

95. Jesus (said), "If you have money, do not lend it at interest, but give (to those) from whom you will not receive it (back again)."

96. Jesus (said), "The Kingdom of the Father is like a woman, she took a bit of leaven, hid it in dough, and made big loaves. He who has ears, let him hear."

97. Jesus said, "The Kingdom of the [Father] is like a woman who was carrying a jar which was full of meal. While she was walking on a distant road, the handle of the jar broke; the meal spilled out behind her onto the road. She did not know; she was not aware of the accident. After she came to her house, she put the jar down, and found it empty."

98. Jesus said, "The Kingdom of the Father is like a man who wanted to kill a powerful man. He drew the sword in his own house; he thrust it into the wall so that he would know if his hand would stick it through. Then he killed the powerful one."

99. The disciples said to him, "Your brothers and your mother are standing outside." He said to them, "Those here who do the will of my Father are my brothers and mother; they will enter the Kingdom of my Father."

100. They showed Jesus a gold coin, and they said to him, "Caesar's men demand taxes from us." He said to them, "Give Caesar's things to Caesar; give God's things to God; and what is mine give to me."

101. "He who does not hate his [father] and his mother in my way will not be able to be my [disciple], and he who does [not] love his father and his mother in my way, will not be able to be my [disciple], for my mother . . . , but [my] true [mother] gave me life."

102. Jesus said, "Woe to the Pharisees; they are like a dog lying in the oxen's food trough, for he does not eat nor let the oxen eat."

103. Jesus said, "Blessed is the man who knows in which part . . . the robbers will come, so that he will rise and gather his . . . and gird up his loins before they come in . . ."

104. They said (to him), "Come, let us pray today, and let us fast." Jesus said, "Why? What sin have I committed, or by what have I been conquered? But after the bridegroom has left the Bridal Chamber, then let them fast and pray."

105. Jesus said, "He who acknowledges the father and the mother will be called the son of a harlot."

106. Jesus said, "When you make the two one, you shall be Sons of

Man, and when you say, 'Mountain, move away,' it will move."

107. Jesus said, "The Kingdom is like a shepherd who had a hundred sheep. One of them, which was the largest, wandered off. He left the ninety-nine; he searched for the one until he found it. After he tired himself, he said to the sheep, 'I love you more than the ninety-nine.'"

108. Jesus said, "He who drinks from my mouth will be as I am, and I will be he, and the things that are hidden will be revealed to him."

109. Jesus said, "The Kingdom is like a man who had a treasure [hidden] in his field, and he did not know it. And [after] he died, he left it to his son. His son did not know; he received the field, and he sold [it]. The one who bought it went plowing; and [he found] the treasure. He began to lend money at interest to whomever he wished."

110. Jesus said, "He who finds the world and becomes rich, let him reject the world."

111. Jesus said, "The heavens and the earth will roll up in your presence, and he who lives by the Living One will not see death . . ." Because did not Jesus say, "He who finds himself, the world is not worthy of him?"

112. Jesus said, "Woe to the flesh which depends on the soul; woe to the soul which depends on the flesh."

113. His disciples said to him, "On what day will the Kingdom come?" (He said,) "It will not come by expectation. They will not say, 'Look here,' or, 'Look there,' but the Kingdom of the Father is spread out on the earth and men do not see it."

114. Simon Peter said to them, "Let Mary leave us, because women are not worthy of the Life." Jesus said, "Look, I shall guide her so that I will make her male, in order that she also may become a living spirit, being like you males. For every woman who makes herself male will enter the Kingdom of Heaven."

The Gospel According to Thomas

The Acts of
the Holy Apostle Thomas

Introduction: The Acts of Thomas is one of five, well-known extracaꞁnonical Acts; each tells of the adventures of an apostle of the church: Andrew, Peter, John, Paul, and Judas Thomas. Didymos Judas Thomas, the hero of the Acts of Thomas, is not well-known to Western Christianity. His real name is Judas ("Judah," in Hebrew); both Didymos and Thomas mean "twin." Judas is the twin of Jesus. His fame was widespread from Egypt to Syria and on to India, where there is an ancient community of Christians which claims Judas Thomas as its founder.

This account of Judas Thomas' adventures was most likely written in the first half of the third century. It makes use, however, of traditions which go back much earlier than that. The origin of the Acts of Thomas is considered by most historians to have been in eastern Syria, probably in the city of Edessa.

Thus the original language of the Acts of Thomas was Syriac, but the extant Syriac text has been "catholicized." That is, it has been altered to be more in line with the Western Church's theology. The Greek versions of the Acts of Thomas thus appear to be translations of a better text than the one now preserved in Syriac manuscripts. There are some exceptions to this rule; the most important is "The Hymn of the Pearl" in chs. 108—113.

The Acts of Thomas is often labeled "gnostic." It fits this label to a great degree. The Acts of Thomas speaks of a mystical, saving knowledge which redeems the faithful from this world; its picture of Jesus is "docetic." That is, the work rejects the concept that human salvation can take place as an historical event, brought about by a savior who is a fully human person. Thus, salvation in the Acts of Thomas involves a sharp denial of the world and its created, physical processes.

Radical world rejection in this work is accompanied by extreme asceticism. Only those who are ascetics can know salvation. This theme is propelled in the Acts of Thomas by plays on the word *koinonia* and its cognates. This family of words means "community," "marriage," and "sexual intercourse." The stories in the document are often built upon plays of meaning which are possible when the same word can refer to the church community (ascetic), a heavenly, transsexual marriage (see chs. 12—15), and the sexual union of male and female (often known as "filthy koinonia").

Thomas' activity is truly an extension of Jesus' in this work. Didymos Judas Thomas is not only Jesus' "twin," the two figures even mingle together and become interchangeable at one point (see ch. 11). Such ideas as these may pose real problems for those familiar only with Western Christian writings, such as those canonized by the Western Churches. For example, what basis in fact might there be for this tradition? Again, by what warrant did the third- and fourth-century Western leadership reject this writing and this unique tradition regarding Jesus' twin brother Judah?

Summary

Act One

1. The apostles are all gathered in Jerusalem: Simon Peter, Andrew, James the son of Zebedee, John his brother, Philip, Bartholomew, Thomas, Matthew, James the son of Alphaeus, Simon the Canaanaean, and Judas the brother of James. They apportion the earth for their missionary activities, each to be an apostle to a separate region. Thomas "who is called Didymos" is assigned to India. He objects because "a weakness of the flesh" prohibits his travel, and, as a Hebrew he cannot preach the gospel to Indians. The Savior appears to him at night and assures Thomas, "My grace is with you." Thomas says, "Send me to some other place you wish, for I am not going to the Indians." 2. Jesus appears to an Indian merchant named Abban and, knowing that Abban has been sent to buy a carpenter slave[1], sells Thomas to Abban. When Jesus leads Thomas to Abban, the merchant asks, "Is this your master?" Thomas says, "Yes, this is my Lord." "I have bought you from him," said Abban. And the apostle stands silent. 3. The next morning, Thomas goes off with Abban. They sail, with a favorable wind, and arrive at Andrapolis. 4. As they leave the ship, they hear the sound of a festival. It is the wedding of the King's daughter. Abban and Thomas go to the wedding. 5. The apostle, to everyone's astonishment, puts on a show of very bad manners by not eating or drinking anything at the banquet. At the guests' questions about his abstinence, he says, "I have come here for something greater than food or drink." The guests at the wedding anoint Thomas with oil. A flute girl, being a Hebrew, recognizes something divine in Thomas and stands near him. 6. One of the cup-bearers slaps Thomas. Thomas curses the cup-bearer, then sings the hymn:

The maiden is the daughter of light,
the royal aura of kings rests and stands upon her,

[1] Judas Thomas, the twin of Jesus, is also a carpenter, of course. He is further a "slave of Christ."

looking upon her is delight,
she is aglow with shining beauty.
Her clothes are like spring flowers,
from them is diffused a scent of sweet fragrance.
The King is established in the crown of her head,
he feeds those who are established under him with his ambrosia.
Truth sits upon her head,
she reveals joy by (the motion) of her feet.
Her mouth is open, it is becoming to her
[Syr. with it she sings loud songs of praise].
Thirty-two sing to her hymns of praise.
Her tongue is like the curtain of the door,
which is flung open to those who are entering.
Her neck is like steps
which the first artisan created.
Her two hands make signs and trace secrets, proclaiming
the dance of the blessed aeons,
her fingers secretly reveal the gates of the city.
Her bedchamber is light,
wafting the fragrance of balsam and all sweet aromatics;
giving out the sweet smell of myrrh and (fragrant) leaves.
Inside are scattered myrtle and all sorts of sweet-smelling blossoms,
the doorways are decorated with reeds.
Her groomsmen surround her, their number is seven;
she has chosen them.
Her bridesmaids are seven;
they dance before her.
There are twelve in number who serve before her;
they are her subjects.
They gaze and look to the bridegroom,
so that they may be enlightened by looking at him,
and they shall be with him forever in that eternal joy,
and they shall be at that marriage at which the princes gather,
and linger over the banquet
of which those who are eternal are worthy.
They shall dress in royal clothes
and shall be garbed in magnificent garments,
and both shall be in joy and exultation,
and they shall glorify the Father of the All,
whose haughty light they received;
they were enlightened by the vision of their Lord,
they received his ambrosial food
which has nothing lacking,

and they drank from his wine
which gives them neither thirst nor desire.
They glorified and praised, with the Living Spirit,
the Father of Truth and the Mother of Wisdom.

Summary

8. Only the flute girl understands the hymn because it is in Hebrew. She adores Thomas; she plays her flute for the guests but keeps looking over at Thomas. The cup-bearer, who slapped Thomas, goes to the well. There he is killed by a lion, and a black dog brings his right hand back to the feast (which fulfills Thomas' curse). 9. This amazes the guests. The King invites Thomas to pray for the bride. The apostle demurs, but is persuaded. 10. Thomas then is led to the Bridal Chamber and he prays over the couple.

11. The King ordered the groomsmen to leave the Bridal Chamber. When all had gone and the doors were closed, the groom lifted the veil of the Bridal Chamber, so that he should bring the bride to himself. He saw the Lord Jesus, in the likeness of Judas Thomas the apostle, speaking to the bride. But Thomas had just blessed them and left them. The groom said: "Did you not leave in front of everyone? How did you get here?" The Lord said to him: "I am not Judas Thomas, I am his brother." And the Lord sat down on the bed and ordered them to sit on chairs, and he began to speak to them.

Summary

12. Jesus begins to preach a sermon to the young couple. He adjures them to refrain from "filthy sexual intercourse" so that they will not beget children who will only force the parents to become thieves in order to support their wants. Furthermore, says Jesus, most children are worthless or demon-possessed, or become lunatics or sick, and so on. Even if the children stay healthy, they will commit innumerable sins. "But if you obey and guard your souls pure to God, you will produce living children, whom hurts do not touch, and you will be carefree, living a life without grief and care . . . waiting to receive that marriage which is incorruptible and true, and you shall be its groomsmen entering that Bridal Chamber which is full of immortality and light."[2] 13. At this, the couple refuses to have sex with each other, they give themselves instead to the Lord, and "abstain from filthy lust." When the King comes in to them in the morning he is surprised to find the couple not shy with each other, but, as the Queen (who has also come in) says to her daughter, "Why are you sitting there that way, child? You are not ashamed but are acting as if you have lived with your husband for a long time!"[3]

---

[2]Notice the way in which the story reflects the wedding hymn of chs. 6–7.
[3]Compare the opposite case, Gen. 3:1–7.

14. The bride answered, "Truly, father, I am much in love, and I pray to my Lord that the love which I have known this night will remain with me, and I seek for the husband whom I knew today. I am no longer veiled, because the mirror (or, veil) of shame has been removed from me. I am no longer ashamed or bashful, for the deed of shame and bashfulness has been taken far from me. And I am not frightened, because the fear did not remain with me. I am in joy and delight because the day of delight was not disturbed, and because I have set aside this man and this marriage which passes away from before my eyes, for I am joined in another marriage. And [I rejoice] because I did not have intercourse with the temporary man whose end is regret and bitterness of soul, but I am yoked with the True Man."

15. (The groom also makes a speech:) "I thank you, Lord, who was preached through the stranger and was found in us; who has put me far from corruption and sown life in me; who has delivered me from this chronic disease which is hard to cure and heal, and has placed me into eternity and wise health; who has shown yourself to me and has revealed to me everything about me which I am; who has redeemed me from the Fall and has led me to the better; who has redeemed me from temporary things and made me worthy of immortal and eternal things; who has humbled yourself to me and my insignificance, so that placing me beside greatness you should unite me with yourself; who did not hold back your own mercy from me who was perishing, but you showed me how to seek myself and to know who I was and who and how I am now, so that I should become again what I was;[4] whom I did not know, but you yourself hunted me out; whom I did not comprehend, but you received me; whom I have experienced and now cannot recall; whose love ferments in me, and I am not able to speak as I ought, but what I am able to say about him is short and very little, and does not come close to his glory. He does not blame me as I am bold to speak to him and say what I do not know; I say this because of love for him."

Summary

16. The King is very unhappy at this. He sends out orders to arrest Thomas. But Thomas has set sail, leaving the flute girl weeping because he did not take her along. When she hears what has taken place, she says, "Now I also have found repose here."

Act Two

17. Thomas and Abban arrive in India and report to King Gundaphorus.

[4]This statement is a very close parallel to a classic gnostic creed found in Clement of Alexandria, *Excerpts from Theodotos*, 78.2. It means that salvation is for man to become as Adam was before his Fall, i.e., nonsexual, or bisexual. Cf. the Gospel of Philip and the Coptic Gospel of Thomas.

The king asks Thomas if he will build a palace for him. Thomas says, "Yes . . . because for this I came to build and to work as a carpenter." 18. The king and Thomas discuss plans for the palace. Thomas will build the palace during the winter, which is not the usual practice. Thomas draws master plans in the dust, with a reed. 19. The money which the king gives Thomas to build the palace is distributed to the poor. The king asks if the palace is built. Thomas says it is, except for the roof. ". . . Let it be roofed," says the king. 20. The king finally finds out how his money has been spent and that the palace has not been built. He calls Thomas for a reckoning. 21. The king asks if the palace is built. Thomas says it is. The king asks to see the palace and is told that he cannot see it in this life, "but when you leave this life you will see it." Thereupon the king orders Thomas thrown into prison and contemplates how best to torture him to death. Meanwhile, the king's brother, Gad, falls ill. Gad blames his illness on Thomas and asks that the apostle be swiftly killed. 22. Gad dies and, in heaven, sees the palace Thomas built for his brother. 23. Gad is released from heaven to tell his brother of the wonderful palace. He does so, 24. and the king sends for Thomas, asking him for instruction in the gospel. 25. The apostle prays joyfully. 26. Gad and Gundaphorus will not let him alone. They finally ask for "the seal"[5] which will make them Christians. 27. The apostle "seals" them. They hear the Lord's voice. The apostle takes oil and pours it on their heads and gives a prayer:

Come, holy name of Christ which is above every name.
Come, power of the Most High and perfect compassion.
Come, highest gift.
Come, compassionate Mother.
Come, fellowship of the male.[6]
Come, you (fem.) who reveal the concealed mysteries.
Come, Mother of the seven houses in order that your repose may be in the eighth house.
Come, Elder of the five members: understanding, thought, wisdom, compassion, reasoning.
Have union[7] with these youths.
Come, Holy Spirit, and cleanse their testicles,[8]
and especially seal them in the name of the Father,
Son, and Holy Spirit.

[5]It is unclear in the Acts of Thomas as to whether "seal" means Baptism or a Chrism (anointing with oil). It may be that originally Chrism was meant and that Baptism has come into the text as a catholicizing tendency.
[6]The "fellowship of the male" needs come comment:
a) It signifies the ascetic nature of the sect which produced the Acts of Thomas.
b) It contains a play on the word *koinonia* which means "community," "marriage," and "sexual intercourse." Therefore, the "community/marriage" of the male is consistently played against "filthy" or sexual marriage (see chs. 13, 14, 82–138).
c) Women who join the sect are transsexual; they become part of the "*koinonia* of the

Summary

When dawn comes they all celebrate a eucharist (Lord's Supper). 28. The apostle preaches an ascetic sermon, 29. he blesses all present, and he fasts. The Lord appears and sends Thomas "two miles down . . . the road." He has a task for the apostle.

Act Three

30. The apostle finds the corpse of a beautiful boy beside the road and discerns evil at work. 31. A great serpent comes out of a hole and admits that he killed the boy. There was a beautiful woman with whom the serpent fell in love. The snake found the young man kissing her and having intercourse (*koinonia*) with her, and killed him. The apostle asks the snake to identify himself. 32. Among other evil deeds, the snake tempted Eve; he caused Cain to kill Abel; he is the Satan. 33. The apostle commands the snake "in the name of Jesus to . . . suck out your poison which you put into this man, and draw it out and receive it from him." The snake is unwilling, but Thomas compels him to do it. The young man becomes healed; the snake swells up, explodes, and dies. 34. The young man expresses his freedom from Satan. 35. Thomas warns him not to take his attraction to Jesus lightly. 36–37. A sermon, by Thomas, based upon the miracle.

Act Four

39. While the apostle was yet standing in the road and talking with the crowd, a donkey's colt came up and stood in front of him. The colt opened his mouth and said: 'Twin Brother (*didymos*) of Christ, apostle of the Most High and brother initiate of the hidden word of Christ, who received his secret sayings,[9] co-worker of the Son of God, who though free became a slave and was sold and led many into freedom; member of a great race which condemned the enemy and redeemed its own; who brings life to many in the country of the Indians—for you came to men who have gone astray, and through your manifestation and your divine words they are now turning toward the One who sent you, the God of truth—climb up and sit on me and rest until you enter the city."

Summary

40. The apostle asks the colt who he is. The colt says that he is a descendant of Balaam's donkey; Jesus rode one of the colt's ancestors into

---

male," cf. The Coptic Gospel of Thomas 114.

[7]Here the verb form of *koinonia* is employed.

[8]*Nephros* (kidney) is often employed as a euphemism for *orchis* (testicle).

[9]Possibly a reference to the preface of the Coptic Gospel of Thomas.

Jerusalem. Thomas is awed at this and refuses to ride. The colt persuades Thomas 41. and, after the ride up to the city, when Thomas dismounts, the colt falls dead. The crowd asks Thomas to raise the colt. Thomas says he could raise the colt "in the name of Jesus," but it is not useful and helpful to do so.

Act Five

42. The apostle is confronted by a "very lovely woman" who says that she has been tormented by "the Adversary" for five years. 43. She says that one day as she was coming from her bath a troubled man, weak with love for her, accosted her. He wanted to have sexual intercourse (*koinonia*) with her. She refused; she never had sexual intercourse even with her betrothed. She asked her maid if she had seen the youth; the maid replied that she had seen an old man. In the night, the demon youth raped her. This violation has been going on for five years. She asks Thomas to exorcise the demon. 44. Thomas, by means of a prayer incantation calls the demon to him. 45. The demon appears and tries to put a counterspell on Thomas, "What have we to do with you, apostle of the Most High?"[10] 46. The demon is unsuccessful and leaves, weeping for love of the woman. He vanishes in smoke and fire. 47–48. Thomas raises a prayer of confession, thanks, and supplication.[11]

50. And he began to say,
   Come, perfect compassion.
   Come, fellowship of the male.
   Come, she who understands the mysteries of the elect.
   Come, she who has companionship in all the contests
      of the noble athlete (or, noble contender).[12]
   Come, silence that reveals the great acts of the whole
      greatness
   Come, she who reveals secret things,
   and makes the forbidden manifest.
   Holy Dove, who begets twin young,
   Come, hidden Mother.
   Come, she who is revealed in her deeds
   and who presents joy and repose to those who are united with her.
   Come and unite with us in this eucharist
   which we celebrate in your name, and in the love feast (*agapē*)
   to which we are gathered at your call."[13]

[10]The whole scene is based on Mark 5:7ff.
[11]There is a possible reference to the Gospel of Thomas 13. Thomas' prayer begins: "O Jesus, who art the hidden Mystery revealed to us, You are He who manifested all mysteries to us, who set me apart by myself from all my companions, also speaking three words in my ears consuming me, nor am I able to say them to others . . ."

Summary

Act Six

51. There is a young man who had committed a sinful act. He comes and takes the eucharist in his mouth; his hands wither so that he is unable to put them to his mouth. The witnesses to this event inform Thomas, and he asks the youth what crime he had committed. The youth replies, "A woman who lives outside the town loved me and I loved her. When I heard your sermon I came forward to receive the seal with the others. But you said, 'Whoever shall unite *(koinonia)* in foul intercourse, especially in adultery, shall not receive life from the God whom I preach.' Since I was very much in love, I asked her, trying to persuade her, that she would become my consort in chastity and pure conduct, which you spoke about. She refused. Because she would not agree, I took a sword and killed her, for I could not stand it if she committed adultery with another." 52. The apostle responds by condemning "insane sexual intercourse." He asks that a bowl of water be brought. He prays over the bowl and tells the young man to wash his hands; the youth does so and is healed. 53. The apostle and the young man go to the inn and find the beautiful girl lying there, dead. 54. Thomas said to the young man, "Go and hold her hand and say to her, 'I, by my hands, killed you with iron, and with my hands, by the faith in Jesus, raise you.'" The youth does so, and the woman is restored to life. 55–57. She tells the apostle that a man in black led her to hell and showed her horrible visions, terrible tortures happening to people who had sexual intercourse and bore children. 58. Thomas assures her of the forgiveness of her sin. 59. All the witnesses to this believe. 60–61. A prayer by Thomas.

Act Seven

62–64. A captain of a certain King Misdaeus comes to Thomas and tells him that the captain's wife and daughter are possessed by demons who are sexually assaulting their women. 65. The captain is told he must believe in Jesus, and then his women will be healed. The captain confesses his faith and says, "Help my little faith."[14] Thomas gathers the crowd around him. 66. A sermon about Jesus' constant care for his own is preached. 67. The apostle blesses all who are gathered there.

Act Eight

68. Thomas travels on with the captain and a wagon driver. 69. It is very hot and the animals pulling their wagon become tired. A herd of wild donkeys is nearby and Thomas tells the wagon driver that if he believes in Jesus he should go to the wild donkeys and ask for four of them to pull the

---

[12]There is a document in the Nag Hammadi codices entitled "The Book of Thomas, the Contender." See the introduction to the Coptic Gospel of Thomas, p. 25.
[13]The Syriac version identifies the object of this call as the Holy Spirit.
[14]Based on Mark 9:24.

wagon. 70. The captain does so, in spite of his fear. The donkeys obey him, all of them, not just four. Thomas rebukes them, asking again for only four. Again all the donkeys want to pull the wagon for the apostle. Thomas rebukes them, and finally the excess number of donkeys moves off. 71. They come to the city where the captain and the driver tell everyone of the miracle and a great crowd gathers. 72. The apostle prays 73. and commands one of the wild donkeys to go to the court of the King to summon all the demons there. 74. The donkey goes, accompanied by a great crowd. He summons the demons. 75. The captain's wife and daughter come forth. The apostle commands the demons to be exorcised "in the name of Jesus." The women fall down as if dead. The demons rebuke Thomas 76. and one asks to be set free. 77. The apostle banishes the demons. The women are still lying as if dead. 78. The wild donkey exhorts the apostle to heal the women and 79. the crowd to believe in Jesus. 80. The apostle replies in a prayer to Jesus, and then 81. restores the women. The wild donkeys go back to their grazing grounds. Thomas watches over them so that they are not harmed.

Act Nine

82. We are introduced to Mygdonia, wife of Charisius, a close relative of the King. She comes, from curiosity, to see this wonderworker, Thomas. Mygdonia arrives in a sedan chair, borne by her slaves, but the crowds are so great around Thomas that she must send for more servants to beat aside the throng so that she can see Thomas. Thereupon, the apostle rebukes them. 83. To bear their burdens they must refrain from adultery, murder, theft, and other vices, especially "from horrid intercourse and the couch of uncleanness."[15] 85–86. Thomas continues his speech, and exhortation to "holiness." 87. The crowd is very excited over his sermon. Mygdonia throws herself at the apostle's feet and begs that "I may become God's dwelling place, and rejoice in the prayer and the hope and his faith, and that I too may receive the seal, and become a holy temple and he should dwell in me." 88. The apostle adjures Mygdonia to give up her wealth, fame, pomp of adornment, and to renounce sex, "the fellowship of childbearing." He bids her to "go in peace." She is afraid she will not see Thomas again, but he assures her that Jesus will be with her. She goes home. 89. Charisius, her husband, comes to the dinner table and sees that his wife is not present. At his inquiry, the servants tell him that Mygdonia is ill in her bedchamber. He hurries to her and asks what is wrong. She says she is ill. 90. Charisius brings dinner to the room, but she still refuses to eat; he dines alone. She also refuses to sleep with him. 91. When Charisius wakes, he describes a strange dream to her. He says that he and his friend the King were at table and an eagle came and bore off two partridges to its nest. The eagle came back and took a dove and a pigeon. The King shot an arrow at the eagle, but it passed harmlessly through the bird. Mygdonia says, "Your dream is good, for you eat partridges daily, but the eagle has

---

[15]According to the Syriac text.

not tasted partridge till now." 92. Charisius gets up, and accidentally puts his left sandal on his right foot. He takes this for another bad omen. 93. Mygdonia hurries to Thomas. 94. She confesses to the apostle that she has accepted Thomas' words. Thomas delivers a sermon urging her to an ascetic life.

95. Charisius comes to breakfast and misses his wife. She has, he is told, gone to the "stranger" who is a doctor of souls. She returns and goes to bed alone. Again she will not come to dinner. 96. Charisius remonstrates with her, warning her that Thomas is a magician. 97. Mygdonia is silent; when Charisius leaves she prays for strength to overcome her husband's "shamelessness." 98. Her husband returns to her after dinner and wants to have sexual intercourse. She rejects him for "My Lord Jesus, who is with me and rests in me, is greater than you." She runs, naked, away from him and goes to sleep with her nurse. 99. Charisius is very upset. He expresses his woe in a long speech in which he bemoans the loss of his wife. 100. Charisius continues his complaint. He has lived with his wife less than a year and an "evil eye" has snatched her away. Charisius vows vengeance upon Thomas. He asks King Misdaeus to give him "the stranger's head." He also wants satisfaction in the matter of Siphor, the captain, who brought Thomas to the city and who is sheltering the apostle. Charisius describes Thomas as one who "teaches a new teaching, saying this, that no one is able to live unless he gives away all his goods and becomes a renouncer like he is; and he works fast to make many consorts (koinonos) for himself." 101. Day dawns and Charisius goes to King Misdaeus and reports what has happened. 102. Misdaeus promises action. He sends messengers to Thomas (Mygdonia is again there, listening to the apostle's sermon) and they rebuke Thomas through the captain, Siphor. The apostle tells Siphor not to worry. 103. Thomas asks Mygdonia what caused this uproar. She tells him it is because she will not sleep with her husband. Thomas encourages her to continue her good works. 104. Meanwhile, the captain reports back to the king and tells him how Thomas has helped him by healing his wife and daughter. 105. The king sends men to bring Thomas to him, but the crowds frighten them and they return without Thomas. Charisius vows he will fetch Thomas himself. 106. He accosts Thomas, arrests him, and brings him to King Misdaeus. To the king's questions, the apostle stands mute. They give Thomas one hundred twenty-eight lashes and lock him up. The King and Charisius consider, meanwhile, how they will kill him. 107. The apostle goes to prison rejoicing that he can suffer for his Lord. 108. Thomas, in prison, sings the famous Hymn of the Pearl.[16]

> When I was a small child (lit. "a speechless infant")
> in the realms of my father
> I reposed in wealth and among delicacies.
> My parents provisioned me

[16]Syriac text in brackets has been taken from the translation by G. Bornkamm and E. Hennecke–W. Schneemelcher, eds. *New Testament Apocrypha,* Vol. 2 (Philadelphia: Westminster, 1965.).

and sent me from the East, our home;
from the riches of the treasury
they made up a load, both great and yet light,
so that I was able to bear it alone.
[Gold from Beth 'Ellaye and silver from great Gazak]
and chalcedony stones from India [and opals from
Kushan.]
They girdled me with steel, [which crushes iron.
And they took off me the splendid robe
which in their love they had wrought for me,
and the purple toga
which was woven to the measure of my stature],
and they made an agreement with me,
engraving it in my heart, so I would not forget.
They said to me, "If you go down into Egypt
and carry off from there the one pearl
[which is in the midst of the sea,
in the abode of the loud-breathing serpent,
you shall put on again your splendid robe
and your toga, which lies over it],
and with your brother you shall become
herald [heir] in our kingdom."

109. I left the East upon the difficult and
dangerous way, with two couriers,
for I was very inexperienced to do this.
I went over the borders of Mesene,
the gathering place of the East's merchants;
I came to the country of Babylon
[and entered within the walls of Sarbug].
When I came into Egypt, the couriers with me left me.
I went immediately to the serpent
and [nearby his abode I stayed,
until he should slumber and sleep],
so that I could take my pearl away from him.
As I was alone, [I was a stranger
to my hosts who were my companions].
But there I saw one of my fellow countrymen
from the East, a free man, a youth gracious and favored,
a son of the mighty.
He came and joined me,
and I made him my bosom companion,
my friend, to whom I communicated.
I warned him to watch the Egyptians

and their unclean companionship[17]
But I put on clothes like theirs
[that they might not suspect] that I had
come from without to take the pearl,
and the Egyptians would wake the serpent against me.
But for some reason I do not know, they learned
that I was not their countryman.
They treated me with guile and I ate their food.
I forgot that I was the son of a king,
and I served their king,
[and I forgot the pearl
for which my parents had sent me].
And from the heaviness of their food,
I fell into a deep sleep.

110. While I suffered all this,
my parents were aware of it and suffered for me.
A proclamation was announced in our kingdom
that all should come to our gate.
And then the kings of Parthia and those
in office and the rulers of the East
[made a resolve] concerning me [that I
should not be left] in Egypt.
[They wrote to me a letter,
and every noble set his name to it.
(When it arrived)
I awoke and stood up from my sleep],
I took it and I kissed it and read it.
It had been written
concerning what was engraved in my heart.
I remembered immediately that I am
the son of kings, and [my noble birth asserted itself].
I remembered the pearl for which I was sent into Egypt.
I began to cast a spell on the fearful serpent.
I subdued him by naming my father's name.
[And the name of our next in rank,
and of my mother, the Queen of the East.]
And I snatched the pearl,
and I turned to go to my father's house.
I stripped off their dirty robe
and left it in their country.
I directed myself to the way
to the light of my homeland, the East.

[17]The text seems incorrect. It probably should read, "He warned me, etc."

[And my letter, my awakener,
I found before me on the way.]
It, by voice, had awakened me
as I was sleeping, and it led me to the light.
[Written on Chinese tissue with red ochre,
gleaming before me with its aspect
and with its voice and its guidance
encouraging me to haste],
"From your father, King of Kings, and
your mother, the Queen of the East,
and your brother [our other son],
to our son in Egypt, peace.
Arise and wake from sleep,
and hear the words of [our letter],
and remember you are a son of kings.
Become sane again concerning your yoke of slavery!
Remember your robe with the golden hem!
Remember the pearl for which you were sent to Egypt!
[Remember your splendid robe,
and think of your glorious toga,
that you may put them on and deck yourself therewith.],

112. I did not remember my splendor [its dignity,
for I had left it in my childhood in my father's house].
Suddenly I saw my garment;
it became like me as in a reflection,
and I saw all myself upon it,
and I knew, and I saw myself through it;
because we were divided apart,
and then, again, we were one form.
It was not otherwise
concerning the treasurers
who brought me the garment;
I saw them as two,
but both a single form;
there was one symbol of the king
impressed on them both.
They had treasure and riches in their hands,
they gave me honor;
and my splendid robe
was decorated in gold and gleaming colors
[with gold and beryls,
chalcedonies and opals,
and sardonyxes of varied color.

This also was made ready in its grandeur;
and with stones of adamant
were all its seams fastened].
And the image of the King of Kings
was all over it.
And sapphire stones
in its magnificence were sewn to it with harmony.

113. And I saw that throughout it
were moving the motions of knowledge.
And it was ready to become speech.
I heard its homily,
[which it whispered at its descent]:
"I am his, the most manly of all men,
on account of whom [they reared me
before my father].
And I perceived myself his manhood.
And all the kingly motions
rested on me; its motions increasing."
It hurried forward from the hands of [its
bringers, that I might take it],
and my desire quickened me to hasten
to greet and receive it.
Reaching out I (took it);
I was decorated with (its) colors,
and I put on my royal toga completely.
I put it on and went
into [the gate of greeting and homage].
I bowed my head and worshiped
the glory of the Father who had sent it to me,
because I had done his commandments,
and he also had done what he promised.
I joined [at the gate of his satraps . . .
with his great ones].
He rejoiced over me and he received me
with him in the kingdoms.
All his subjects hymned with beautiful voices.
He promised me that
I indeed would go with him into the gate of kings,
in order that with my gifts and my pearl
we would appear before the King.[18]

[18]This hymn is taken by many scholars to be a classic example of the "redeemed redeemer" of gnostic theology. For more on this hymn, see H. Jonas, *The Gnostic Religion* (Boston: Beacon Press, 1963), pp. 112–129.

Summary

114. We again join Charisius who goes home thinking that he has solved his problem. He finds Mygdonia in mourning. He rebukes her, reminding her of his conjugal rights. 115. Mygdonia does not listen. Charisius renews his attack. 116. He reminds Mygdonia of how much he loves her. 117. She replies, "The one whom I love is better than you and your wealth . . . Your beauty will vanish . . . Jesus alone abides eternally. Jesus himself will liberate me from the shameful things I did with you." Charisius offers to free Thomas if his wife will love him again. 118. He falls asleep, and Mygdonia sneaks out to meet Thomas.

Act Ten

119. Thomas reassures Mygdonia that Jesus will not desert her. (Thomas has miraculously escaped from prison.) 120. Mygdonia asks for "the seal" of Jesus. They go and wake Mygdonia's nurse and she fetches water and bread for a eucharist. 121. Oil is poured out and Mygdonia is baptized in a nearby spring. 122. Thomas returns to prison (again with a miracle). 123. Charisius goes in to his wife, finds her praying and again begs her to return to him.

124. Charisius continues, "Recall the day on which you first met me. Tell me straight, was I more beautiful to you then, or Jesus at this time?" And Mygdonia said, "That time demanded its things; this time requires its own. That time was of the beginning; this is of the end. That was the time of a passing life; this is the time of eternal life. That was the time of passing pleasure; this is of one that endures forever. That was the time of day and night; this is one of day without night. You have seen that marriage which passes away; but this marriage remains forever. That joining [koinonia] was of corruption; but this is of life eternal. Those wedding attendants were transitory men and women; but these now remain to the end. [Syr. That marriage was founded on earth, where there is a ceaseless pressure; but this on the fiery bridge, upon which grace is sprinkled.] That Bridal Chamber is taken down again; this remains forever. That bed is covered with blankets; but this with love and faith. You are a passing and decaying bridegroom, but Jesus is a true bridegroom, remaining immortal forever. That bridal gift was money and robes that grow old, but this is living words which never pass away."[19]

Summary

125. Charisius goes and tells the king all that happened. The king wants to kill Thomas, but Charisius wants to frighten the apostle so that Thomas will

19. Cf. the bride's speech in ch. 12.

tell Mygdonia to return to her husband. Thomas is brought before the king. 126. They argue about what he is preaching and the effects it is having. 127. Misdaeus sets Thomas free and tells him to repair Charisius' marriage. Thomas refuses. 128. Charisius pleads with the apostle to give Mygdonia back to him. Thomas again refuses. 129. They return to Charisius' house where Mygdonia expresses her new happiness. 130. Thomas tests Mygdonia by telling her to go to Charisius. She passes the test by refusing. Charisius threatens to tie up his wife to keep her from Thomas. 131. Thomas leaves and goes to captain Siphor's house.

132. Thomas began to speak about baptism: "This baptism is forgiveness of sins. It begets anew a light which shines all around; it begets anew the new man, mixes spirit and man, makes new the soul. It resurrects the new man three times and is the fellow (*koinonos*) of the forgiveness of sins. Glory be to you, unspeakable one who is united (*koinonein*) with us in baptism! Glory be to you the invisible power in baptism. Glory be to you, renewal through whom those who are baptized are renewed, those who join with your state.' And when he said this, he poured oil on their heads and said, 'Glory to you, love of compassion. Glory to you, name of the Christ. Glory to you, the power built in Christ.' And he ordered a bowl to be brought, and he baptized them in the name of the Father and the Son and the Holy Spirit."[20]

133. When they were baptized and had put on their clothes, he placed bread on the table, blessed it, and said, "This is the bread of life; those who eat of it remain incorruptible. Bread which fills the hungry souls with its blessing, you are the one deemed worthy to receive a gift, so that you may be for us forgiveness of sins, and, so that those who eat you become immortal. We utter over you the name of the Mother, of the unutterable mystery of the hidden archons and powers. We utter your name, Jesus." And he said, "Let the blessed power come, and let the bread be empowered, in order that all souls which partake may be saved from sins." He broke it and gave it to Siphor, his wife, and his daughter.[21]

Summary

Act Eleven

134–138. In this act, Tertia, the wife of Misdaeus, the king, becomes a member of Thomas' group. She, of course, begins to withhold her favors from her husband. Misdaeus says that Thomas has bewitched Tertia and in a rage has Thomas seized.

20. The introduction of the sacrament of Baptism into this section may be the work of a catholicizing editor.
[21]Note: no mention of cup, wine, or water. See chs. 120–121 in which the eucharist is also an "ascetic" one.

Act Twelve

139–149. Vazan, the son of Misdaeus, is converted.

Act Thirteen

150–158. Vazan receives baptism. His wife is miraculously healed. There is a eucharist.[22] In ch. 153, the apostle utters this striking prayer: "Glory to you, many-guised Jesus. To you be glory who shows yourself in the form of our poor humanity."

The Martyrdom of the Holy Apostle Judas Thomas

159. Thomas goes to prison. Tertia, Mygdonia, and Marcia go with him to be imprisoned. Thomas tells them he will "no longer speak to them while still in his body." He is to be taken up to Jesus. 160. The apostle states that he is not Christ, but is his slave. He tells the women to wait in Christ and to stand fast in the faith. 161. He enters the house and prays that the doors be as they were. The doors shut and seal themselves. The women are left grieving. 162. Thomas finds the guards upset because the apostle goes out and comes into the prison at will. They go to Misdaeus and entreat him to let Thomas, "that magician," go or move him to another prison. They shut the doors, go to sleep, and, when they awaken, the doors are open. The king goes to inspect the seals on the door; the seals are intact. The king accuses the guards of lying, but they protest that they are telling the truth. 163. Thomas is brought before the king. In the dialogue which follows "Misdaeus asked him: 'Who is your master? And what is his name? And of what country?' Thomas said, 'My Lord is my master and yours, the Lord of heaven and earth.' Misdaeus said, 'What is his name?' And Judas (Thomas) said, 'You are not able to hear his true name at this time. But I say to you the name given to him for a time is Jesus the Christ." Misdaeus points out that he has not been precipitous in ordering Judas Thomas to be killed, but that this is the last straw. 164. The king considers how to kill the apostle, for Misdaeus is afraid of the crowds. The king and some soldiers decide to take Judas Thomas outside the city. Misdaeus commands four soldiers to kill Judas Thomas and he returns to the city. 165. The crowd wants to rescue Thomas, but he is led away. Thomas comments, in prayer, that as he was made from four elements he will be killed by four soldiers. 166. Thomas preaches to the soldiers. 167. He asks Vazan to persuade the soldiers to let him go aside and pray. Vazan does so. Thomas confesses that his work is done. He was a slave; now he is to be set free. "I say these things not as a doubter, but that those who need to hear may hear." 168. Thomas tells the soldiers to fulfill their instructions, and they proceed to kill him with their spears. All the brethren grieve. They wrap Thomas in fine cloths and put him in an ancient royal tomb. 169. Siphor and Vazan are reluctant to go home. During their vigil, Thomas appears to

[22]Remember, the eagle took two partridges, a pigeon, and a dove.

them and tells them that he has gone to heaven. Meanwhile, Misdaeus and Charisius attempt to lead their wives astray but with no success. Thomas appears to Tertia and Mygdonia and gives them encouragement. The two husbands give up. All the brethren assemble under the new leadership of Siphor and Vazan, whom Judas Thomas had appointed as elder and deacon. 170. One of Misdaeus' sons becomes demon-possessed. The King decides that he will go to the apostle's tomb, get one of Thomas' bones and use it to heal his son.

Thomas appeared (to the king) and said, "If you did not have faith in the living, will you, indeed, believe in the dead? But do not be afraid. Jesus, the Christ, acts humanely toward you because of his great goodness." But Misdaeus did not find the bones, for one of the brethren had taken them away, and carried them to the West. So he took dust from the place where the bones of the apostle had lain; he attached it to his son and said, "Jesus, I believe in you, now that he (i.e., Satan) who always confuses men so that they cannot look to your rational light, has left me." And when his son became healthy by this deed, Misdaeus joined the rest of the brethren, submitting himself to Siphor (now an elder in the new congregation). And Misdaeus asked all the brethren to pray for him so that he should have mercy from our Lord Jesus Christ. 171. The acts of Judas Thomas the apostle are hereby completed, which he did in the land of the Indians, fulfilling the command of the One who sent him; to Whom be glory forever. Amen.

Jesus After the Resurrection

Introduction: This Gospel is actually a collection of works, running to some 384 pages in the Coptic edition. The title comes only from a small section of one of the works and was added at a date later than the book's composition. The various parts of the collection should be assigned different dates: the third century A.D. appears to be a period encompassing the whole collection.

The manuscript of the Pistis Sophia is long; therefore, we can only present here a few excerpts. The form of the work is a series of discourses and speeches in which Jesus, after his resurrection, reveals sacred and saving knowledge to his disciples. There is a great variety of material, such as the recitation of myth, liturgies, prayers, exegeses of the Old Testament, and more. Therefore, this sampling is not representative of the whole.

Pistis Sophia presents a Jesus whose acts and teachings take place after the resurrection, not before. Jesus before the resurrection is of no interest to the document.

Pistis Sophia, Books 1.1; 2.1–8; 4.142–143

Book One

1. It so happened, however, that after Jesus had risen from the dead, he remained there eleven years, speaking with his disciples, and he taught them only up to the places (*topoi*) of the first laws and up to the places of the first mystery, that within the veil, which is inside the first law, which is the twenty-fourth mystery outside, and below those which are found in the second space of the first mystery, which is before all mysteries—the Father in the form of a dove.

And Jesus said to his disciples, "I have come here from that first mystery, which is the last mystery, the twenty-fourth." The disciples did not know and understand that mystery, that there was something inside that mystery. Rather they thought that that mystery was the Head of the All and the head of all being. And they thought it was the perfection of all perfections, because Jesus had said to them regarding that mystery, that it surrounds the first law and the five impressions and the great light, and the five defenders, and the whole treasure of light.

There is more that the disciples do not understand. The disciples are sitting

55

on the Mount of Olives, rejoicing in the knowledge that Jesus has given them in the eleven preceding years. As the text has indicated, they are only now going to receive the most important knowledge.

Book Two

1. It so happened now that the disciples were sitting together on the Mount of Olives. They were talking about these things which were told them and rejoicing with a great joy; they were very happy and said to one another, "We are blessed, we beyond all men on earth; because the Savior has revealed these things to us; and we have received the fullness (*pleroma*) and the whole perfection." They said these things to each other while Jesus sat a bit away from them.

2. It happened, then, on the fifteenth of the month of Tybi, which is the day of the full moon. On that day, as the sun had risen from its resting place, there came after it a great light—power, shining exceedingly bright. There was no measure to the surrounding light. For this light came from the light of lights, and it came from the last mystery, which is the twenty-fourth mystery of the inside and the outside, which is in the orders of the two spaces of the first mystery. That light-power came over Jesus and totally surrounded him. He was seated away from his disciples, and he was shining with a great light. And there was no measure of the light which was on him.

> The disciples can only see the light and they are struck with awe and confusion at this epiphany. Jesus then ascends, shining, into heaven, leaving the disciples to gaze after him.

3. . . . It happened then, when Jesus had ascended to heaven, after the third hour, all the (evil) powers of heaven were in confusion, and they were shaken against each other, they and all their aeons and their places (*topoi*) and their orders, and the whole earth shook and all that lived in it.

> At this cosmic cataclysm, the whole creation is in chaos; the disciples are also frightened. They are afraid that the Savior will destroy the whole world; they weep.

4. As they said this and wept together, the heavens opened at the ninth hour, and they saw Jesus descending.

> Jesus is even more shining than when he ascended. The disciples cannot stand the light and ask Jesus to lessen it. He does so and Jesus begins the new and greatest revelation.

6. . . . "Rejoice and be jubilant from this hour, because I have gone to the places from which I came . . .

7. It came to pass, as the sun rose in the East, that then through the first mystery which existed from the beginning, for which the All is created, out of which I have now come, not in the time before my crucifixion, but now, it happened that through the order of this mystery, this garment of light was sent to me . . ."

Jesus now expounds on the manner of his first coming to earth.

8. And Jesus went on in the speech, "It happened after this, I looked down from there out of the order of the first mystery to the world of mankind, and I found Mary, who is called my mother in respect to the body made of matter. I spoke to her in the form of Gabriel. When she had given herself to me in exaltation, I thrust into her the first power which I had taken from Barbelo, that is, the body which I had borne into the heights. Instead of the soul, I thrust into her the power which I had taken from the great Sabaoth, the good, who is in the place of the right . . ."

These excerpts are from the beginning of Pistis Sophia. In the course of this Gospel Jesus enters into conversation with Mary Magdalene and with several of the disciples. He explains many mysteries and tells the story of the heavenly being, Pistis Sophia, who "falls" and then "repents." Much of what ensues is exegesis of Old Testament texts, particularly the Psalms.

Our last excerpt is from the fourth section of the collection, a separate gospel. In the climax of this Gospel, there are some rituals presented. The incantations are not translatable; they are meant to be mystic, foreign sounds (such as "abracadabra"). We have written them phonetically.

Book Four

142. Jesus said to them, "Bring me fire and vine branches." They brought them to him. He laid out the offering and placed on it two wine jugs, one on the right and the other on the left of the offering. He placed the offering before them. He placed a goblet of water before the wine jug on the left. And he set bread, according to the number of the disciples, in the middle between the wine goblets and he placed a goblet of water behind the bread. Jesus stood before the offering; he placed the disciples behind him, all garbed in linen garments. In their hands was the number of the names of the father of the light-treasure. He cried out, saying, "Hear me, Father, father of all fatherhood, unlimited light. *Eeaoh, eeaoh, eeaoh, aohee, oheea, pseenother, thernopseen, nopseether, nephthomaoth, marachachtha, marmachachtha, ee-ay-ahnah,*

menaman, amanayee too ooranoo, eesrahee ohmayn, ahmayn soobaheebahee, apahahp, hahmayn, hahmayn, derahahrahee hahpahoo, ahmayn, ahmayn, boobiahmeen, meeahee, ameyn, amayn, etc. . . ."
(The incantations and prayers continue. Be cautious when repeating these.) Then Jesus spoke to them, "This is the method and this is the mystery which you shall celebrate for men who will believe in you . . . but hide this mystery and do not give it to all men, only to him who does all things which I have said to you in my commandments. This, therefore, is the true mystery of baptism for those whose sins are forgiven and whose misdeeds are blotted out. This is the baptism of the first offerings, which leads forth to the true place and to the place of light."

143. Then the disciples said to him, "Rabbi, reveal to us the mystery of the light of your Father, since we heard you say, 'There is a baptism of fire, and a baptism of the Holy Spirit of light, and there is a spiritual anointing (*chrism*) which leads the souls to the light-treasure.' Speak to us now of their mystery, so that we may inherit the Kingdom of God."

Jesus said to them, "These mysteries about which you ask, there is no mystery higher, which will lead your soul to the light of lights, to the places of truth and the good, to the place of the holy of all holies, to the place in which there is neither female nor male, nor form in that place, but a continuing, indescribable light."

The Gospel of Philip

Introduction: The Gospel of Philip, virtually unknown until 1946, was discovered in the same collection as the Gospel of Thomas. Certain gnostic Christians in Egypt and Syria considered these two gospels, along with the Secret Sayings of the Savior, recorded by Matthias, to be three especially sacred writings, containing nothing less than the secret wisdom that Jesus entrusted to Philip, Thomas, and Matthias, as one gnostic source relates:

> When Jesus had finished speaking these words, Philip arose quickly, letting fall to earth the book he was holding, for it was he who wrote down all that Jesus said and all that he did. Philip stepped forward and said, "My Lord, is it to me alone that you have entrusted the care of this word, so that I am to write all that we shall say and all that we shall do?" . . . Jesus answered, "Listen, blessed Philip, so that I may tell you. It is to you, as well as to Thomas and to Matthias that I, by the authority of the First Mystery, have entrusted the writing of all that I shall say and that I shall do, as well as all that you shall see . . . (Pistis Sophia 42).

The Gospel of Philip contains allusions to the Gospels and Letters of the New Testament. This indicates that these gnostic Christians knew and used these writings, although they considered them to be only the ordinary, common tradition accessible to all Christians, including those who were only "infants" in terms of their spiritual development. But the gnostics valued the Gospels of Philip, Thomas, and Matthias as the gospels of an *esoteric* tradition, which could be communicated only to those who were spiritually "mature." For to be "mature" meant to be "initiated" into gnostic tradition (the same Greek word, *teleios,* can be translated either way).

The Gospel of Philip is neither a narrative gospel, like those included in the New Testament, nor a collection of sayings, like the Gospel of Thomas. Instead it contains a series of short meditations on mystical subjects. The present form of this manuscript comes from a fourth-century Coptic text, although apparently it is related to a second-century Greek "Gospel of Philip," from which only a fragment remains (Epiphanius, *Pan.* 26.13.2–3). Commentators disagree on the question of whether the present manuscript preserves the original form of that earlier Gospel; it may have been abridged or amplified.

In one sense, it is paradoxical that the gnostics wrote gospels at all. The Valentinian gnostics, from whom the Gospel of Philip comes, claimed that truth could not be communicated in writing, but only in "living speech" to those who were ready to receive it (Irenaeus, *Against Heresies* 3.1–3). This may explain why this Gospel is written in strange, symbolic language: it was meant to be read only by initiates, and to remain unintelligible to the casual, "uninitiated" reader.

The theme of this gospel message is the relation between the "immature"—the "uninitiated" Christians—and the "mature," or "initiated," *gnostic* Christians. The opening section (1—6) characterizes these two distinct groups: the "immature" are represented as Hebrews, slaves, the dead, by contrast with the "mature" who are Gentiles, sons, the living.

Paradoxically, these two groups, as different as light and darkness, life and death, right and left, are actually "brothers to one another" (10). What has separated them (so that they now seem like opposites) is that the "immature" have been misled and deceived by the words and the names used in Christian teachings. For example, a person may hear the name "God" without knowing the reality the name expresses: to him, the name conveys only an image of God (11). One cannot learn truth without using names (12), but such names (i.e. Father, Son, Holy Spirit) often have been used to deceive people into worshiping those that are not gods (13, 14, 50). Logion 85 describes this situation with irony: "God created man, and man created God. So it is in the world. Men make gods and they worship their creation. It would be appropriate for the gods to worship them!"

Immature Christians, deceived by mere words, speak "in error" about two basic Christian doctrines—the virgin birth and the resurrection. They say of the virgin birth that "Mary conceived by the Holy Spirit" (17). They say of the resurrection that "the Lord died first and then rose" (21). But such persons "do not know what they are saying" (17).

Gnostic Christians interpret each of these doctrines symbolically (67). They say of the virgin birth that Mary symbolizes Wisdom (*sophia*), the true Mother from whom Christ comes; and his father is the "Father in Heaven" (17). This is a "mystery: the Father of all united with the Virgin who came down" (82). The writer goes on to explain that the resurrection does not mean that dead bodies are to revive: rather, to receive the *logos* and *spirit* of Christ is to be "resurrected" (63), i.e., "raised from the deadness of (worldly) existence." He adds that in one way it is valid to speak of rising "in the flesh"—in the sense that all we are and all we do is done "in the flesh" (23).

The reason that there are two such different views of Jesus is explained in saying 25: "Jesus did not reveal himself as he really was, but he revealed himself as people would be able to see him." To the great he appeared as great; to the small as small. To some he appeared as *Christ*, to others only as *Jesus* (19, 20). In every case he adapted his revelation to the capacity of his audience.

There are, then, basically two types of Christians. Some only see Jesus in the same way that they see the sun, or anything else, as something outside themselves (44). But those who are "mature" *become what they see:* "you saw the Spirit, and you became Spirit; you saw the Christ and became Christ; you saw the Father, and you shall become the Father" (44). They are no longer simply "believers" like the rest; they themselves are being transformed, and becoming divine!

Furthermore, these two types of Christians understand Baptism in different ways. To the "immature," Baptism means that they receive the *names* of the Father, Son, and Spirit (67). From that time on, "they call themselves Christians" (59). Yet so far they have only the *name*, but not the reality (59). The "mature" actually receive the Father, Son, and Spirit: not their names only, but their actual indwelling *presence*. Such a person is "no longer (merely) a Christian, but a *Christ!*" (67, 95).

The Eucharist, too, has a different meaning for each. The "immature" see it only in terms of an animal sacrifice (14, 50); they offer the bread and wine as the "body and blood" of Jesus, sacrificed as a lamb slain for "the sins of the world" (27, cf. John 1:29; Matt. 26:28). From a gnostic point of view, this conception is utterly repulsive; it turns God into "a man eater" (50)—and those who participate in the meal, by inference, are cannibals! The gnostics, however, receive the bread and wine as symbols of the *logos* and *spirit* of Christ (23, 100). They recognize that to receive it in this way is to receive *and to become* the "wholly perfect man" (100, 106, 108). For them, the Eucharist signifies not an animal sacrifice, but a *royal wedding feast* (cf. Matt. 22:11) which celebrates their union with the Spirit (27).

Yet the symbol of marriage has another dimension: it also signifies the final reunion of the *immature* Christians with the *gnostics*! Although for the present they form two separate groups, in the future they shall be rejoined into one. According to sayings 73 and 78, this is the secret symbolic meaning of the story of Adam and Eve. As Eve was separated from Adam, so the naïve believers have been separated from the gnostics; yet these two shall be rejoined as a man and woman are joined in marriage. This is the "mystery of marriage" which is celebrated in the sacrament that the gnostics call the "Bridal Chamber" (82, 103).

Is the Bridal Chamber a secret gnostic sacrament unknown to other Christians? Some scholars think that it is a gnostic version of the "sacred marriage" enacted in ancient fertility religions as well as in certain of the mystery cults contemporary with early Christianity. Did the gnostics enact ritual intercourse in their "Bridal Chamber"? Some ancient sources suggest that they did, although one phrase in the Gospel of Philip suggests that the gnostic sacrament culminated with a kiss, symbolizing spiritual conception (31, 55).

Yet the conclusion of the Gospel of Philip suggests another interpretation: that the "mystery of marriage" is the gnostic term for the *secret meaning of the Eucharist* that all Christians celebrate in common. For this "mystery," according to saying 125f, is "hidden" but not "in darkness": it is "hidden in a clear and perfect day." In one sense, it is perfectly open, being celebrated daily in the church, in plain view of all Christians; but it is hidden in the sense that only initiates recognize it as a *marriage feast* and perceive its true meaning. It symbolizes not only the union that "mature" gnostics enjoy with the divine; but it also signifies that the "immature" will eventually also attain *gnosis,* and be joined in union ("in marriage") with the "mature." This means that eventually *all* shall be joined with the divine, and become divine!

For this purpose the gnostics, although they are "free," must be willing to serve and to help the "slaves" (87, 110, 114). They do this out of love (110), being careful not to hurt or offend anyone (118). The gnostic teacher must learn to recognize what each person needs, and offer to each the appropriate "nourishment" (119).

The immature, the slaves, will finally become free (125). But the one already initiated into gnosis already has "received the light" (127). For such a person, "the world has become the *aion*"—that is, his present existence already has been transformed into the fullness of the divine presence (127).

For the author of the Gospel of Philip there are, then, *two* Christian traditions: one is the public, *exoteric* tradition (which includes the Gospels and Letters of the New Testament); the other is this secret, *esoteric* tradition that was originally given by Jesus only to a few of the disciples and is now communicated only in private to those who are "spiritually mature." The gnostics' claim to have access to secret, esoteric Christian tradition proved intolerable to many Christians in the second century: it came to be branded as "heresy" and "false teaching." Its teachers, accused of being satanically inspired, were given the choice of either repudiating their claims or leaving the church (see, e.g., Irenaeus, *Against Heresies* 5.26).

This introduction and the notes offered below are of the most elementary sort: the serious student is referred to the commentaries of R. M. Wilson and J. E. Menard, as well as to articles mentioned in the notes.

1. A Hebrew man makes a Hebrew, and he is called a proselyte. But a proselyte does not make a proselyte . . . there are those who are as they are . . . and they make others . . . it is enough for them that they exist.
2. The slave seeks only to be free. However, he does not seek after his lord's properties. The son, however, is not only a son but writes himself into the inheritance of the father. 3. Those who inherit the dead are dead and inherit the dead. Those who inherit living things are alive, and they inherit the living and the dead. Those who are dead inherit nothing. For how will the one who is dead inherit? If the dead one inherits the living he will not die, but the dead one will live more.
4. A Gentile does not die. He has not lived, so he cannot die. He lives who has believed the truth; and he is in danger that he will die, for he is alive. Now that Christ has come 5. the world is created, the cities are bedecked, the dead are carried out. 6. When we were Hebrews, we were orphans. We had only our mother. But when we became Christians, we gained a father and mother.
7. Those who sow in winter reap in summer. The winter is the world; the summer is the other aeon. Let us sow in the world so that we may reap in the summer. On account of this it is seemly for us not to pray in the winter. That which comes out of the winter is the summer. But if someone reaps in the winter, he really will not be reaping, but he will be tearing things out, 8. since this will not produce . . . not only will it [not] produce . . . but on the Sabbath [his field] is unfruitful.
9. Christ came to ransom some, but others he saved, others he redeemed. Those who were strangers he ransomed and made them his, and he set them apart. These he made as securities in his will. Not only when he appeared did he lay aside his life as he wished, but at the establishment of the world he laid aside his life. He came to take it when he wished to, because it had been set aside as a pledge. It came under the control of robbers, and it was held prisoner. But he saved it, and he ransomed the good ones and the evil ones who were in the world.

The last lines of v. 9 refer to the conception that those who are "from above" have been captured by "the robbers," the powers (archons) that rule this lower world (see Paul's phrase in Rom. 8:38; also Eph. 6:12; John 12:31). According to saying 13, these "rulers" wanted to deceive man, who had an affinity with the "truly good ones"—the divine powers—in order to enslave him to themselves. Compare the conception in *Poimandres*, which describes how a portion of the higher realm of Light became mixed in the lower realm of Darkness, Evil, and Matter.

10. Light and darkness, life and death, the right and the left are each other's brothers. They cannot separate from one another. Therefore,

the good are not good nor are the evil evil, nor is life life, nor death death. On account of this, each one will dissolve into its beginning origin (*archē*). But those who are exalted above the world cannot dissolve; they are eternal.

11. The names which are given to the worldly things contain a great occasion for error. For they twist our consideration from the right meaning to the wrong meaning. For whoever hears (the word) "God," does not know the right meaning but the wrong meaning. It is the same way with (such words as) "the Father" and "the Son" and "the Holy Spirit" and "the life" and "the light" and "the resurrection" and "the Church" and all the other names. Folk do not know the right meaning; rather they know the wrong meaning [unless] they have come to know the right meaning . . . they are in the world . . . in the aeon they would never be used as names in the world, nor would they list them under worldly things. They have an end in the aeon.

12. There is only one name which one does not speak out in the world, the name which the Father gave to the Son. It is above everything. It is the name of the Father. For the Son will not become the Father, if he does not put on the name of the Father. Those who have this name truly know it, but they do not speak it. Those who do not have it do not know it.

But the truth engendered names in the world for us, because it is impossible to know it (the truth) without names. The truth is a single thing and is many things. It is this way for our sake, in order to teach us this one thing in love through its many-ness. 13. The archons wanted to deceive man because they saw that he was kindred to the truly good ones. They took the name of the good ones and gave it to those that are not good, so that by names they could deceive him and bind them to the ones that are not good. If they do them a favor, they are taken away from those who are not good and given their place among those that are good. They knew these things. For they (the archons) wished to take the free man and enslave him forever.

14. There are powers which . . . man; they do not wish him . . . Therefore, they will become . . . For, if the man . . . sacrifices become . . . and they offered up animals to the powers . . . these are the ones to whom they make offerings . . . They offered them up, to be sure, still living. When, however, they were offered, they died. The Man was offered up dead to God, and he lived.

15. Before the Christ came there was no bread in the world. So also in paradise, the place where Adam was, there were many trees as food for the animals, but there was no wheat for human food. Man ate as the animals. But when the Christ, the perfect man came, he brought bread from heaven so that man could eat in a human way. 16. The archons

believed that what they did was by their own power and will. However, the Holy Spirit secretly worked all through them as he willed. The truth is sown in every place; she (the truth) was from the beginning, and many see her as she is sown. But only a few see her being gathered in.

This passage sets forth an idea fundamental in gnostic thought: that the cosmic rulers (*archons*), although they think they are free to act on their own, are actually being used as the instruments of the higher powers: see Irenaeus, *Against Heresies* 1.5.1–6.

17. Some say Mary was impregnated by the Holy Spirit. They err. They do not know what they say. When did a woman become pregnant by a woman? Mary is the virgin whom no power corrupted. She is a great anathema[1] to the Hebrews, who are the apostles and apostolic men. This virgin whom no power defiled . . . the powers defiled them (or, themselves). The Lord (would) not have said, "My [Father, who is in] Heaven," if he had not had another Father. But he would have simply said: ["My Father."][2]

In later Jewish tradition, the spirit was understood to be female, as the Hebrew word (*ru'ah*) for spirit is feminine. Here this is used to argue against the popular Christian view of the virgin birth.

18. The Lord said to the disciples . . . "Enter the Father's house, but do not take anything in the Father's house, nor remove anything."
19. "Jesus" is a secret name; "Christ" is a revealed name. For this reason, "Jesus" does not exist in any (other) language, but his name is always "Jesus", as they say. "Christ" is also his name; in Syriac, it is "Messiah," but, in Greek, it is "Christ." Actually, everyone has it according to his own language. "The Nazarene" is the one who reveals secret things. 20. The Christ has everything in himself: man, angel, mystery, and the Father.
21. They err who say, "The Lord first died and then he arose." First he arose, and then he died. If someone does not first achieve the resurrection, will he not die? So truly as God lives, that one would . . . [text uncertain].
22. No one will hide an extremely valuable thing in something of equal value. However, people often put things worth countless thousands into a thing worth a penny. It is this way with the soul. It is a precious thing which came into a worthless body.
23. Some fear that they will arise naked. Therefore, they wish to arise

---

[1]So Isenberg; Wilson, Till suggests "oath" (*Eid*).
[2]Conjecture suggested by Till; Isenberg.

in the flesh, and they do not know that those who carry the flesh are naked.

> In this passage one can see an ancient dispute concerning the resurrection. The question was, "In what form does a person rise from the dead?" Some gnostics argued that both the body and the soul are "taken off" like garments and left behind while the spirit rises to divine life. This author cites Paul's discussion in 1 Cor. 15:50 and Jesus' saying in John 6:53 to show that whoever "leaves off" his own "flesh and blood" is not "naked," because he is "clothed" with the "flesh and blood" of Christ, which symbolize the *logos* and *spirit*. For discussion, see A. H. C. Van Eijk, "The Gospel of Philip," *Vigilae Christianae* 25 (1971), 94f.

They who . . . who disrobe themselves are not naked. Flesh [and blood can] not inherit the Kingdom [of God]. What is this which will not inherit? That which is on us. But what is this which will inherit? That which is of Jesus and of his blood. Therefore he said: "The one who does not eat my flesh and drink my blood does not have life in him." What is it? His flesh is the Logos, and his blood is the Holy Spirit. Whoever has received these has food and drink and clothing. I blame those who say it will not rise. Then they are both to blame. You say, "The flesh will not rise." But tell me what will rise, so that we may praise you. You say, "The spirit in the flesh and this light in the flesh." This is also a Logos (or, saying) which is fleshly. Whatever you say, you do not say anything outside the flesh. It is necessary to rise in this flesh; everything is in it. 24. In this world those who put on clothes are worth more than the clothes. In the Kingdom of Heaven the clothes are worth more than those who have put them on.

Through water and fire, which purify the whole place, 25. those things which are revealed are revealed by those which are manifest, those which are secret by those which are secret. Some are hidden through those which are manifest. There is water in water; there is fire in an anointing (*chrisma*).

26. Jesus secretly stole them all. For he showed himself not to be as he really was, but he appeared in a way that they could see him. To those . . . he appeared. [He appeared] to the great as great. [He appeared] to the small as small. [He appeared] to the angels as an angel and to men as a man. Because of this, his Logos hid from everyone. Some, to be sure, saw him, and they thought that they saw themselves. But, when he appeared in glory to the disciples on the mountain he was not small. He became great; however, he made the disciples great, so that they were able to see him as he was, great.

He said on that day in the thanksgiving (*eucharistia*), "You who have united with the perfect, the light, the Holy Spirit, have united the angels also with us, with the images." 27. Do not scorn the Lamb. For without it one cannot see the King. No one who is naked will be able to find his way to the King.

28. The heavenly Man has many more children than the earthly man. If the children of Adam are more numerous, and still die, how much more the children of the Perfect One who do not die but are always begotten.

These phrases "heavenly Man" and "earthly man" are taken from Paul's discussion of resurrection, 2 Cor. 15:47f. But a very peculiar twist is added at the end when the text turns toward the subject of "begetting sons." Although the text is partly destroyed, it is clear that "spiritual conception" is being described, and that it somehow parallels the original conception of the Logos, the Word (=Christ), which came forth out of the mouth of God.

29. The father makes a child, and the child cannot make a child. For he who is begotten cannot beget; the child creates brothers, not children. 30. Everyone who is born in the world is born by natural means and the others through [the Spirit]. [Those] born through him . . . to the man . . . from the promise . . . above 31. . . . from the mouth . . . [if] the Logos came from there, he would [be nourished³] . . . from the mouth and become perfect. The perfect become pregnant through a kiss and give birth. Because of this we also kiss each other and are made pregnant by the grace among us.

Is this "holy kiss" the sacramental act of the "Bridal Chamber"? Irenaeus, a contemporary opponent of the gnostics, says that the same gnostics acted out repeated sexual unions in the "Bridal Chamber": see his account, *Against Heresies* 1.13 and 1.21.3 (*ANF* 1.334f.). For discussion, see Grant, "The Mystery of Marriage in the Gospel of Philip," in *After the New Testament* (Philadelphia: Fortress, 1967), pp. 183–94; E. Segelberg, "The Coptic-Gnostic Gospel According to Philip," *Numen* 7 (1960) 189–200.

32. There were three who always walked with the Lord: Mary, his mother and her sister and Magdalene, whom they call his lover. A Mary is his sister and his mother and his lover.

Just as Christ came to remove the separation of female from male, which was the cause of death (see v. 71), so also he was at all times "united" with his female alter ego in the successive states of his activity: as Christ was with the Holy Spirit in Heaven, then as Savior with Sophia, then with Mary his mother—in conception, and as Jesus with Mary Magdalene; see Irenaeus, *Against Heresies* 1.1.7; 1.3.3. (*ANF* 1.319, 325).

³The meaning of the Coptic is uncertain. Till, Wilson, and Isenberg suggest "nourish."

33. "The Father" and "the Son" are single names. The "Holy Spirit" is a double name. They are everywhere. They are above; they are below; they are in the secret; they are in the revealed. The Holy Spirit is in the revealed; it is below; it is in the secret; it is above.

34. The saints are ministered to by the evil powers, for the powers are blind because of the Holy Spirit. Therefore, they will believe that they serve a man when they work for the saints. Because of this, one day a disciple sought from the Lord something from the world. He said to him, "Ask your mother, and she will give you from a stranger's (things)."

35. The apostles said to the disciples, "Let our whole offering become salt." They named [Sophia] "salt." Without it no offering is acceptable.

36. But Sophia is barren, [without] child. Because of this, they call her . . . salt. The place where they . . . in their manner, the Holy Spirit . . . her children are numerous.

37. What the father has belongs to the son also, and as long as the son is little he is not entrusted with what is his. When he becomes a man his father hands over to him everything.

38. Those who have gone astray, whom the Spirit engenders, they also go astray because of the Spirit. Because of this, through the same breath (*pneuma*) the fire burns and is extinguished.

39. Echamoth is one thing and Echmoth is another. Echamoth is simply Sophia (i.e., "wisdom"). Echmoth, however, is the Sophia of death, which is the Sophia of death (dittography), which is she who knows death, whom one calls "the little Sophia" (i.e., "the little wisdom").

40. There are animals which are tamed by man such as the calf and the donkey and others such as these. There are others not tamed; they live to themselves in the desert. Man plows the field with the animals which are domesticated. Thus from the field he feeds himself and the animals, whether they are tamed or wild. It is this way with the perfect Man. Through powers which are tamed, he plows and readies everything to come into being. For an account of this, the whole place (i.e., "this world") stands, the good as well as the evil, the right and the left. The Holy Spirit shepherds everyone and reigns over all powers which are subordinate (i.e., tame) and those not subordinate, (i.e., wild) and those who are to themselves . . . [text is mutilated here].

41. . . . he who has been moulded . . . you would find his sons high-born creations. But if he was not moulded but was begotten, you would find that his seed was well begotten. But he was moulded, and he begot. What kind of lofty birth is that? 42. First came adultery and, afterwards, murder. He was begotten in adultery, for he was the child of the serpent. Therefore he became a man killer like his father, and he killed his brother. Every copulation between those different from one

another is adultery.

43. God is a dyer. As the good dyes, which are called "true", perish with the things which are dyed in them, thus it is with those whom God has dyed. Since his dyes are unfading, they are immortal through his dye herbs. God baptizes (or "dips") whom he baptizes (or, "dips") in water.

44. No one can see anything of created things unless he becomes as they. It is not thus with the man who is in the world. He sees the sun and is not a sun, and he sees the heaven and the earth and all other things, and he is not these—it is this way with the truth. But you (singular) saw something of that place and you became these: you saw the Spirit and became Spirit; you saw the Christ and became Christ; you saw [the Father, you] shall become Father. On account of this . . . you surely see everything and [see] not yourself. But you see yourself [in that place]. What you see you shall [become] . . .

45. Faith receives; love gives [no one can receive] without faith. No one will be able to give without love. Because of this, so that we indeed can receive, we have faith. But it is so, in order that we can give truly, [that we love], since if someone gives without love, he gains nothing from what he has given. 46. He who has not received the Lord is still a Hebrew.

47. The apostles who were before us named [him] thus, "Jesus the Nazoraian, the Messiah," which is to say, "Jesus, the Nazoraian, the Christ." The last name is "Christ"; the first is "Jesus." The one in the middle is "Nazoraian." "Messiah" has two meanings: "Christ" and also "the measured" (ed. note: the Coptic *shēu* [measure] is punned with "Messiah.") "Jesus" means in Hebrew "the salvation." "Nazara" means "the truth." Thus, "The Nazarene" means "the truth". Christ has been measured. The Nazarene and Jesus are they who have been measured.

48. When the pearl is thrown down in the muck it does not become despised, nor, if it is anointed with balsam, will it become more valuable. But it always has its value to its owner. It is the same way with the children of God. Wherever they may be, they still have value to the Father.

49. If you say, "I am a Jew," no one will be moved. If you say, "I am a Roman," no one will be troubled. If you say, "I am a Greek, a barbarian, a slave, a freeman," no one will be bothered. If you [say], "I am a Christian" . . . will tremble. May it be . . . this way . . . The one . . . cannot endure . . . name.

50. God is a man eater. On account of this the Man [was killed] for him. Before they killed the Man, they killed animals, for those were not Gods for whom they killed.

51. Glass and pottery vessels are both made with fire. But if glass

vessels are broken they are made again, for they are created with a breath (*pneuma*). But if pottery vessels are broken, they are destroyed, for they are created without a breath.

52. An ass which turns a millstone in a circle went one hundred miles. When he was turned loose he found he was still at the same place. There are men who make many trips and get nowhere. When evening came upon them, they saw no city or town, no creation or nature, no power or angel. The poor fellows labored in vain.

53. The Eucharist is Jesus. For they call him in Syriac *pharisatha*, which is, "the one who is spread out." For Jesus came and he crucified the world.

54. The Lord went into the dye shop of Levi. He took seventy-two colors and threw them into the kettle. He took them all out white, and he said, "Thus the Son of man came, a dyer."

> It was popularly believed that there were seventy-two nations in the inhabited lands of the earth. This same idea lies behind the story of Jesus sending out seventy-two more disciples, after he had already sent out the Twelve, in Luke 10:1–20.

55. Wisdom (*sophia*), whom they call barren, is the mother of the angels, and the consort of Christ is Mary Magdalene. The [Lord loved Mary] more than all the disciples, and he kissed her on the [mouth many times]. The other [women/disciples saw] . . . him.

> This is another reference to the male/female union of Jesus-Christ and Sophia-Mary. Note the "holy kiss" performed by them as an example to Christians.

They said to him, "Why do you [love her] more than all of us?" The Savior answered and said to them, "Why do not I love you as I do her?"

56. If a blind man and one who can see are in the dark, there is no difference between them. When the light comes, then the one who sees will see the light, and the one who is blind will stay in the darkness.

57. The Lord said, "Blessed is the one who exists before he came into being. For he who exists was and will be."

> The elect are in actuality splinters of the light which became trapped in the realm of darkness; the individual soul, once "awakened," finally "knows itself," i.e., whence it came and whither it is going; cf. Gospel of Thomas 49, 50; Acts of Thomas 15.

58. The greatness of man is not revealed, but it is hidden. Because of this he is lord of the animals which are stronger than he and are great

according to that which is clear as well as hidden. And this mastery gives to them their stability. But if a man leaves them alone, they kill one another (and) bite one another. And they ate one another because they could find no food. But they have now found food because man has worked the ground.

59. If anyone goes down into the water and comes up having received nothing and says, "I am a Christian," he has borrowed the name at interest. But if he receives the Holy Spirit, he has taken the name as a gift. If someone has received a gift, it is not taken back. But he who has borrowed something at interest has to meet the payment. 60. It is this way . . . if anyone should be in a mystery.

The mystery of marriage is great. For . . . the world . . . for the constitution (*systasis*) [of the world is the m]an, but the constitution [of the man] is marriage. Understand [the union] for it has [great] power. Its image is in [a defilement of the body].

61. Among the unclean spirits there are males and females. The male [spirits] cohabit with the souls which dwell in a female form. But the females are those which are mixed with the ones in a male form, through one who is foolish. And no one can escape them, because they detain him if he does not receive a male or female power (namely the bridegroom and the bride). But one receives (these) from the imaged (*eikonikos*) Bridal Chamber. When the ignorant women see a male who is alone, they leap on him and play with him and defile him. It is the same way with ignorant men. If they see a beautiful woman sitting alone, they persuade her and force her, wishing to defile her. If, however, they see a man with his wife living with one another, the female cannot go in to the man, nor can the male go in to the woman. Thus it is, if the image and the angel are joined with one another; neither can any dare to go in to the man or the woman.

He who comes out of the world cannot be held any more, because he was in the world. It is clear that he is raised above desire . . . fear. He is lord over . . . he is more precious than envy. If . . . comes, they seize him and strangle . . . and how will [this one] be able to escape . . . how will he be able . . . often some . . . we are faithful . . . demons. For if they had the Holy Spirit, an unclean spirit could not cling to them.

This passage suggests that an actual husband/wife union may have been a prerequisite for participation in the "Bridal Chamber" sacrament. Alternatively, the passage may have a symbolic meaning: the "man" symbolizes the "mature," gnostic Christian, and the "woman" the "immature" believer (cf. Gospel of Thomas 113). Read this way, the passage shows that although each must struggle with temptations included by demonic forces when alone, the two become invulnerable and strong when they are joined together.

62. Do not be afraid of the flesh nor love it. If you fear it, then it will be your master. If you love it, it will swallow and strangle you.

63. Either one is in this world, or in the resurrection, or in the places in the middle. God forbid that I be found in them. In this world there is good and evil. Its good is not good, and its evil is not evil. But there is evil after this world, true evil, which they call "the middle." It is death. As long as we are in this world, it is fitting to us to acquire the resurrection, so that when we peel off the flesh we will be found in repose, not making our way in "the middle." For many wander astray off the path. For it is good to come out of the world before one sins.

> Gnostic writers often describe this world as "the middle place"—midway between lifeless matter and the divine spirit. Ordinary existence in this world is "death" compared to spiritual awareness. Whoever is raised from ordinary existence into spiritual awareness is "raised from death to life": to experience this is to be "resurrected"!

64. A few neither want [to sin] nor are able [to sin]. Others, if they want [to sin] gain nothing even if they do not do so . . . for wanting makes them sinful. Even if some do not want [to sin] righteousness will be hidden from them both (those who want not, and those who do not).

65. An apostolic man [in a vision[4]] saw some who . . . their house on fire. They . . . air [?] in . . . fire, they lay . . . the fire . . . and he said to them . . . able to be saved . . . they willed. They received . . . as punishment, which they call . . . darkness.

66. Out of water and fire the s[oul] and the Spirit were created; it is out of water and fire and light (that) the son of the Bridal Chamber was created. The fire is the Chrism; the light is the fire. I do not speak of the fire which is formless, but of the other, whose form is white, which is shining and beautiful and gives beauty.

67. The truth did not come naked into the world, but came in types and images. One will not receive the truth in any other way. There is a being-born-again, and an image of being-born-again. It is truly necessary that they become born again through the image. What else is the resurrection? It is necessary that the image arise through the image. The Bridal Chamber and the image necessarily enters into the truth through the image; this is the recapitulation (*apokatastasis*). It is necessary not only that those who have it received the name of the Father and the Son and the Holy Spirit, but that they took it themselves. If someone does not take it himself, the name also will be taken away from him. But one receives them in the anointing (*chrisma*) of the power of [the cross] . . . the apostles call it "the right" and "the left." For this reason one is no

[4]So Isenberg. Till suggests "in Asia."

longer a Christian, but a Christ.

68. The Lord [did?] all in a Mystery, a Baptism, an Anointing, a Eucharist, a Salvation, and a Bridal Chamber . . .

This verse is significant, for it lists what seem to be six sacraments, perhaps in ascending order of importance for salvation. See also below v. 76.

69. [Text is mutilated for 9 lines] . . . who is called "the one below," and he who possesses the hidden is over him. For it is right that they should say "the inside and the outside with what is outside the outside." Because of this the Lord called destruction the outer darkness; there is nothing outside it. He said, "My Father, who is in secret." He said, "Go into your chamber, close the door, (and) pray to your Father who is in secret," who is he who is inside them all. He who is inside them all is the fullness (*pleroma*). After it there is nothing inside of it. It is the One of whom they say, "That which is over them."

70. Before Christ, some came forth; where they came from they can no longer enter, and they entered where they can no longer come out. When Christ came, those who went in he brought out; those who came out he brought in.

71. When Eve was in Adam there was no death. When she was separated from him, then there was death. If she goes in again and he takes her, there will be no death.

This verse refers to a specific interpretation of Gen. 1:27, "God created man (Adam) in his own image, in the image of God he created him; male and female he created them." This was understood to mean: male-female he created *each one*, i.e., that Adam was originally androgynous (explaining how God could take Eve out of Adam's side), and furthermore that God himself was male/female, since he made Adam a male-female in *his own image*. Redemption, i.e. the defeat of death, will occur when the whole process is reversed. See below v. 78.

72. "My God, my God, why, Lord, did you forsake me?" He said these words on the cross, for he separated at that place . . . whoever was begotten by [the Holy Spirit] through God . . . [Text broken] (A translation based on Till's reconstruction reads: "The [Lord rose] from the dead. [He became as he was], but [his body had become] perfect. [He had] flesh, but this [flesh was] true flesh. [Our flesh] is not true, but it is [a flesh] of the image of the true.")

73. The Bridal Chamber is not for animals, nor is it for slaves nor for women who are defiled, but it is for free men and virgins.

74. We are born again through the Holy Spirit, but we are born through

Christ. In both we are anointed through the Spirit. When we were born we were united.

75. Without light no one can see himself in water or in a mirror. Furthermore, you will not be able to see in light without water or a mirror. On account of this it is right to baptize in both the light and the water. The light is the anointing (*chrisma*).

76. There were three houses for offering places in Jerusalem. One was open to the West; they called it "the holy." Another was open to the South; they called it "the holy of the holy." The third was open to the East; they called it "the holy of the holies." It was the place into which only the High Priest came. Baptism is the holy house . . . (*chrisma*) the holy of the holy. The holy of the holies is the Bridal Chamber. Baptism contains the resurrection (and the) salvation, salvation which hastens to enter the Bridal Chamber. But the Bridal Chamber is in that which is greater than . . . you will not find . . . those who pray . . . Jerusalem . . . Jerusalem . . . Jerusalem, those who wait . . . which one calls . . . [h]oly of the holy ones . . . veil . . . Bridal Chamber except the image . . . above . . . its veil was torn from the top to the bottom. For it was right for some from below to go up.

> An allegory of their sacraments based on the Temple in Jerusalem. Unfortunately the text breaks off at this point, but it does reveal the superior importance and rank of the sacrament of the Bridal Chamber.

77. The powers cannot see those who put on the perfect light, and they cannot hold them. But one will put on this light in the mystery, in the joining.

> Referring to the powers, i.e., in the Midst, who try to restrain the souls of men and women ascending towards the heavens after death. The "light" put on in the Bridal Chamber is of course the "light" toward which they shall rise. See above v. 63.

78. If the woman had not separated from the man, she would not die with the man. His separation became the beginning (*archē*) of death. Christ came, so that he would remove the separation, which was from the first. He again joined the two, and to those who died from the separation he gave life and joined them. 79. But the woman joins with her husband in the Bridal Chamber. Those who have joined in the Bridal Chamber will no longer be separated. On account of this, Eve separated from Adam, because she was not joined with him in the Bridal Chamber.

80. The soul of Adam came from a breath. Which is a joining . . . which was given to him in his mother . . . his soul they gave him

a . . . her place, when he . . . words higher than the powers. They envied him . . .

> The text becomes too broken to translate further. The "separation" here is the division of Adam-Eve into two different physical bodies, with differing sexes. These people took Gen. 1—3 very seriously and could read quite clearly that the separation into Adam and Eve preceded lust, which preceded banishment and death. So they proposed to reverse the whole process, or, better, they gratefully accepted the reversal brought by Christ.

81. . . . Again, he was begotten. Again he was begotten as a child (son). Again he was anointed. Again he was redeemed. Again he redeemed.

82. Is it all right to speak a mystery? The Father of all joined himself with the virgin who came down, and a fire[?][5] was burned for him that day. He appeared in the great Bridal Chamber. Therefore, his body came into being that day. He came out of the Bridal Chamber as one who came into being from the bridegroom and the bride. Thus, Jesus established all through these. And it is fitting for each of the disciples to enter his repose.

83. Adam came into being from two virgins: from the Spirit and from the virgin earth. Therefore, the Christ was born from a virgin so that he could bring order to the stumbling which occurred in the beginning.

84. There are two trees in paradise. The one engenders a[nimals]; the other engenders men. Adam [ate] from the tree which brought forth animals; [he be]came a beast and he begot beasts. Because of this they worship . . . of Adam. The tree . . . fruit is . . . engenders men . . . the man . . . God created the m[an . . . ma]n created God. 85. It is like this in the world: men create Gods and they worship those whom they have created. It would be proper if the Gods worshiped men.

86. Truly the works of man are created by his power. Because of this we call them strengths. His works are his children; they are created from a repose. Therefore, his strength dwells in his works, but the repose is revealed in the children. And you will find this applies to the image. And this is the image-man, who does his works by his strength, but produces his children from a repose.

87. In this world the slaves serve the free. In the Kingdom of Heaven, those who are free will serve the slaves. The children of the Bridal Chamber will serve the children of the marriage. The children of the Bridal Chamber have a name . . . the repose . . . them. They do not need . . . [text broken].

88. [Text broken.]   89. [Text broken] . . . Thus we should fulfill all righteousness.

[5]If one reads kōht for kōt.

90. Those who say they will die first and rise again are in error. If they do not first receive the resurrection while they live, when they die they will receive nothing.

In typical gnostic fashion, the resurrection is considered to be a present event, happening now; cf. Gospel of Thomas 51; Gospel of John 5:24; 2 Tim. 2:18. See note on v. 63.

So also they speak about Baptism, saying that Baptism is a great thing, because if people receive it they will live.
91. The apostle Philip said, "Joseph the carpenter planted a garden because he needed the wood for his craft. He made the cross from the trees which he planted. And his seed hung on what he had planted. His seed was Jesus, and the planting was the cross."

The idea that Joseph made the cross for his own son is a typically late, legendary addition to the "biographical" details of Jesus' life. In the section which follows, there is more discussion of the two trees, one which killed Adam ("the law"), i.e., the tree of knowledge of good and evil, and one which gives life ("the tree of knowledge" [gnosis]). Cf. the Gospel of Truth 18.23f.

92. But the tree of life is in the middle of Paradise and so is the olive tree from which the Chrism is made for the resurrection.
93. This world is an eater of corpses. Everything eaten in it dies. The truth is an eater of life. B[ecause of th]is no one who is nurtured by [the truth] will die. Jesus came out from the place and brought foods out from there. He gave [life] to those who wished, (so that) they do not die.
94. God [made a] Paradise. Man [. . . Para]dise . . . [text broken][6] . . . This is the place where I will eat all things, since the tree of knowledge (gnosis) is there. That one killed Adam, but the tree of knowledge made man live. The law was the tree. It has the power to give the knowledge of good and evil; it neither made him cease evil, nor did it cause him to do good, but it created death for those who ate. For when he said, "eat this; do not eat that," he created the beginning of death.
95. The Anointing (chrisma) is greater than baptism. For from anointing (chrisma) we are called "Christians," not from baptism. And they call Christ (so) because of his anointing. For the Father anointed the Son, and the Son anointed the apostles, and the apostles anointed us.

[6]It is conjectured that the broken text describes man living in Eden. He is told what and what not to eat (as in Gen. 2:15–17). Then, the man is speaking as the text resumes. See Isenberg.

He who has been anointed has all; he has the resurrection, the light, the cross, the Holy Spirit. The Father gave him these things in the Bridal Chamber; he accepted. 96. The Father was in the [Son], and the Son in the Father.

97. The Lord spoke well when he said, "Some went into the Kingdom of Heaven laughing and came out . . . a Christian . . . and when . . . [went down] into the water, he came [out (laughing)] . . . a joke, but . . . scorns it. But, the [one who des]pises these . . . the Kingdom [of Heaven]. If he scorns it . . . a joke . . . [come] out laughing. 98. So it is also with the bread and the cup and the oil, even if there is something higher than these.

99. The world came into being through an error. For he who created it intended to create it imperishable and immortal. He failed to attain his hope. For the world is not imperishable and neither is he who created the world. For there is no imperishability of things, but there is of sons. And no thing can attain imperishability if it does not become a son. But if someone cannot receive, how much more will he not be able to give?

> A very important passage indicating the gnostic belief that *creation as such* was evil. The power here referred to is clearly a rebellious, malevolent, and demonic God. It apparently means the Creator God of the Jews, i.e., the God of Genesis 1—3, who created the world in the vain attempt to create it "imperishable." But since he could only create "things," and had no power to generate "sons," his creation remained perishable.

100. The Cup of Prayer holds wine and it holds water. It serves as a type of the blood for which they give thanks. And it is full of the Holy Spirit and belongs to the completely perfect Man. When we drink this, we will take to ourselves the perfect Man.

101. The living water is a body. It is right that we clothe ourselves with the living Man. Therefore, when he comes to go down to the water, he disrobes in order that he may put this one on.

102. A horse begets a horse; a man begets a man; a God begets a God. It is thus with the bridegroom and the bride. Their [children] were [begotten] in the [Bridal Chamber]. There is no Jew who [was born] from Gr[eeks] . . . and we . . . from the Jews . . . Christians . . . These are called . . . the chosen people of the . . . and the True Men and the Son of Man and the Seed of the Son of Man. This is called, in the world, the true people.

> This is a discussion of the three main sacraments: the Eucharist, a Greek word meaning "thanksgiving," Baptism, and the Bridal Chamber. *Living* water simply means "running" water. All lead toward the creation of a divine being, immortal, clothed in light.

103. Those in this place are where the children of the Bridal Chamber are.

The union in this world is of man and woman, a conjunction of the power and weakness. In the aeon the form of the union is different, though we name them by these names. There are other names. They are higher than all those that are named, and they are stronger than the strong. For in a place of violence there are those who are great in violence. There is no difference, both are a single one. This is the one who cannot rise above the understanding of the flesh.

105. Those who have the All, is it not required that they all know themselves? Indeed, if some do not know themselves, they will not enjoy what they have. However, those who have learned themselves will enjoy what they have.

106. They will not only be unable to seize the perfect Man, they will not be able to see him. For if they see him they will seize him. In no other way will anyone be able to have for himself this grace, except he puts on the perfect Light and becomes perfect himself. Everyone [who has p]ut this on will enter [the Kingdom]. This is the perfect . . . that we become . . . we leave [the world] . . . One who has received the All . . . of these places will not be able . . . that place but will [enter the mid]dle as imperfect. 107. Jesus alone knows the end (*telos*) of his man.

108. The holy man is all holy, including his body. For, if he holds the bread, will he make it holy? Or the cup, or anything else which he holds, will he make it pure? And how is it he will not make the body pure?

109. Jesus made perfect the water of baptism; in his way he poured out death. Therefore, we go down into the water but not into death, in order that we be not poured out into the spirit of the world. When that [spirit] blows, it brings winter. The Holy Spirit, when it blows, brings summer.

> The gnostics said that the Baptism administered in the Christian church was only the "Baptism of John the Baptist" which cleanses mankind from sin and death (*Against Heresies* 1.21.1). But they claimed to have received also the "Anointing" (v. 95) which conveys the Holy Spirit. Those who receive it become gnostics (v. 95); indeed, they become "Christ" (v. 67).

110. He who has the knowledge (*gnosis*) of the truth is free. But the free man does not sin. For he who sins is the slave of sin. The Mother is truth; knowledge is the Father. Those who do not believe sinning is relevant to them are called free by the world. The knowledge of the truth puffs up the heart, that is what "it makes them free" means, and they arrogate themselves over the whole place (the world). Love (*agapē*), however, builds up. Actually, he who has become free through

knowledge is a slave because of his love for those who cannot yet achieve the freedom of knowledge. But knowledge makes them fit to become free. Love [calls] nothing its own, . . . it does not [say, "This is mine"] or, "That is mine," but ["all things] are yours." 111. Love . . . it is wine and perfume. It is a delight to all who anoint themselves with it. Those who stand nearby while the anointed are present are also delighted. If those who are anointed with ointment go away, those not anointed but only standing near them continue still in their own stink. The Samaritan gave nothing to the wounded man except wine and oil. That is nothing other than the ointment. It healed the wounds, for love covers a great many sins.

112. The children a woman bears are like the man who loves her. If he is her husband, they are like her husband. If he is an adulterer, they are like the adulterer. Often, when a woman has sexual intercourse with her husband because she must, and her heart is with the adulterer with whom she usually has intercourse, the child she will birth is like the adulterer. Do not love the world, you who are with the Son of God, but love the Lord in order that those whom you bring forth will not be like the world but like the Lord.

113. Man mixes with man; horse mixes with horse; ass mixes with ass. Those of a race mix with the same race. Therefore the Spirit also mixes with the Spirit, and the Logos has union with the Logos, [and the light] has union [with the light. If you] are human, [a human will] love you. If you become [Spirit], it is the Spirit who will unite with you. If you become Logos, the Logos will mix with you. If [you] become light, the light will have union with you. If you become one of those above, those above will rest in you. If you become horse or ass or calf or dog or sheep or any other animal outside and below, neither the Man nor the Spirit nor the Logos nor the light nor those above nor those inside, will be able to love you. They will not be able to find rest in you, and you will have no part in them.

114. He who is an unwilling slave will be able to be free. He who has become a freeman by the grace of his lord and has sold himself into slavery will no more be able to be a freeman.

115. Farming in the world is (done) through four elements. A crop is gathered into the barn because of water and earth and wind and light. God's farming is also through four: through faith (*pistis*) and hope (*elpis*) and love (*agapē*) and knowledge (*gnōsis*). Our earth is faith; in it we take root. The water is hope; through it [we are nourished]. The wind is love; through it we grow. The light, however, is knowledge; through it we [ripen]. 116. Grace is . . . earthly, it is . . . the highest Heaven.

Blessed is he who . . . their souls. This is Jesus, the Christ. He tricked the whole place (i.e., the world) and did not burden anyone. This is why this kind of person is blessed; he is a perfect man. For this is the Logos. 117. Tell us about it, as it is difficult to set someone straight. How can we accomplish this great deed? How are we to 118. give repose to everyone? First of all, it is not right to afflict anyone, either someone great or small, unbeliever or believer. Then [one must] give repose [only] to those who repose in what is good. There are some for whom it is profitable to give repose to him who lives affluently. He who does good cannot give repose to such people, for he does not do so willingly. But he does not afflict them [either]; for he does not oppress them. Yet he who does good sometimes afflicts people, only not because he wants to, but because their own wickedness causes them to be grieved. He who has the nature [of the perfect man], rejoices in the good. Some however are grieved badly by this.

119. The master of a house had everything: child, slave, cattle, dog, pig, corn, barley, chaff, grass . . . meat, acorn. He was wise and he knew the food for each. He set bread and [meat] before the children. To the slaves he gave castor [oil and] meal; to the cattle [he gave barley] chaff and grass; [to the] dogs he threw bones; [to the pigs] he threw acorns; and . . . bread. It is like this with the disciple of God. If he is wise he understands discipleship. The bodily forms will not deceive him, but he will look to the condition of the soul of each person and speak to him. There are many animals in the world who have the form of humans. If he recognizes them, he will give acorns to the pigs, but he will give barley and chaff and grass to the cattle. He will give bones to the dogs. He will give first [lessons] to the slaves; he will give the full [course] to the sons.

120. There is the Son of Man and the son of the Son of Man. The Lord is the Son of Man, and the son of the Son of Man is he who is created through the Son of Man. The Son of Man received from God the power to create. He is able to beget. 121. He who has received the ability to create is a creature. He who has received the power to beget is an offspring. He who creates cannot beget. He who begets can create. But they say, "He who creates, begets." But his offspring is really a creature. Therefore his offspring are not children but [creatures]. He works in the open and he is visible. He who begets [secretly] and . . . image. He who cre[ates creates] in the open. He who begets [begets] a child in secret. 122. No [one can] know on which d[ay the man] and the woman couple with one another except they alone. For worldly marriage is a mystery for those who have taken a wife. If the marriage of pollution is secretive, how much more is the unpolluted marriage a true mystery. It is not fleshly, but it is pure. It does not belong to lust but to the will. It does not belong to the darkness or the night but belongs to

the day and the light. If a marriage is done openly it has become fornication. And the bride becomes a whore not only when she receives the seed of another man but indeed if she leaves her bedchamber and is seen. She may show herself only to her father and mother and the friend of the bridegroom and the children of the bridegroom. These may go into the Bridal Chamber each day. The others may desire only to hear her voice and to enjoy the ointment; let them be fed with what falls from the table, like the dogs. Bridegrooms and brides belong to the Bridal Chamber. No one can see the bridegroom or the bride unless one becomes one.

123. When Abraham . . . he should see what he was going to see, [he circumciz]ed the flesh of uncircumcision. He taught us that it is right to destroy the flesh.

. . . this world so long as their . . . and they stand and live . . . they die according to . . . of the revealed man . . . the guts of the man are hidden, he is alive. If the guts come out of him and are exposed, the man will die. It is the same with a tree: as long as its root is hidden it sprouts and grows. If its root is exposed, the tree withers. It is thus with every birth in the world, not only with the revealed but with the hidden. As long as the root of evil is hidden, it is strong. If, however, it is recognized, it is destroyed. If it is revealed, it perishes. Therefore the Logos (or, saying) says, "The axe is already laid at the root of the tree." It will not just cut it off. What one cuts off sprouts again. But the axe digs down to the bottom until it digs up the root. Jesus pulled out the root of the whole place, but others only did it partially. Let each of us dig down to the root of evil in himself and pull it out of his heart from the root. It will be pulled out if we recognize it. But if we do not know it, it makes its root fast in us and brings forth its fruit in our hearts. It is our lord, and we are its slaves. It captures us so that we do what we do [not wish] and what we wish, we do [not] do. It is powerful because we have not recognized it. As long as it is, it works. Ignorance . . . is mother of . . . ignorance . . . those who come from [ignorance] were not, are not, nor shall be . . . they will be perfect when the whole truth is revealed. For the truth is like ignorance: when it is hidden it rests in itself, when it is revealed and recognized, it is praised, because it is stronger than ignorance and error. It gives freedom. The Logos [or, the saying] said, "If you know the truth, the truth will make you free." Ignorance is a slave. Knowledge (*gnōsis*) is freedom. If we know the truth, we shall find the fruits of the truth inside us. If we are united with it, it will bring our fullness (*plērōma*).

124. We now have the revealed things of creation. We say, "The strong are worthy. But the hidden things are weak and worthless." It is this way with the revealed things of the truth; they are weak and worthless,

but the hidden things are strong and considered worthwhile. However, the mysteries of the truth are revealed as types and images. But the Bridal Chamber is hidden. It is the holy in the holy.

125. The veil at first covered up how God administered the creation. But when the veil is torn, and the things within are revealed, it will leave this house deserted; rather, it will be [destroyed]. But the whole divinity will not flee out of these places back into the holies of holies. For it will not be able to mix with the [unmixed light] and the faultless fullness (*plērōma*) but it will [be] under the wings of the Cross [and under] its arms. This ark will [be for them] an escape when the deluge of water floods over them. If some are of the tribe of the priesthood, they will be able to enter behind the veil with the High Priest. Because of this the veil was not torn only on top, because then it would have been open only to those above. Nor was it torn only at the bottom, since it would have been revealed only to those below. Rather, it was torn from the top to the bottom. Those above opened to us below, so that we will go into the secret of the truth. This truly is worthwhile because it is strong. But we shall go in there through worthless and weak types. They are really weak in respect to the perfect glory. There is a glory which is greater than glory. There is a power greater than power. Therefore, this has opened to us the perfect and the secret of truth. And the holies of the holies were revealed, and the Bridal Chamber invited us in.

As long as it is hidden, wickedness is really brought to nothing, but it is still not removed from the midst of the seed of the Holy Spirit. They are slaves of evil. When it is revealed, then the perfect light will pour over everyone, all those in it will receive the [anointing]. Then the slaves will become free, and the prisoners will be redeemed. 126. [Every] plant my Father in Heaven does not plant [will be] rooted out. Those who are alienated will be united. They will be filled. Everyone who [will go in] to the Bridal Chamber will [light the light]. For [it shines] as in the marriages which [are seen, although they] are in the night. The fire [burns] in the night, then it is extinguished. But the mysteries of this marriage are fulfilled in the day and the light. That day and its light do not set. 127. If anyone becomes a child of the Bridal Chamber, he will receive the light. If anyone does not receive it while he is in these places (i.e., this world), he will not be able to receive it in the other place. The one who has received light cannot be seen nor can he be held. And no one can torment him, even while he lives in the world. And further, when he goes out of the world, already he has received the truth in images. The world has become the aeon, for the aeon has become for him the fullness (*plērōma*). It is thus; it is revealed only to him. It is not hidden in the darkness and the night, but it is hidden in a perfect day and a holy light. _____

The Gospel of Peter

Introduction: This Gospel is known to have been in circulation around A.D. 175 in Syria, and could be based on traditions going back into the first century. This translation is based on the only extant Greek fragment still preserved and it was discovered in 1886 in the grave of a Christian monk near Akhmim, in Upper Egypt. It is clearly a part of a larger document, perhaps originally resembling one of the canonical Gospels, from which it seems to have drawn many phrases and scenes, intermixing new (or older) material with what has been taken over. Besides the remarkable resurrection scene, which is unique in presently known gospel literature, this Gospel is significant in the way it reflects the rising tide of militant anti-Semitism in the second-century Church, as evidenced by the way in which the gospel writer systematically altered his narrative (assuming he relied on the canonical Gospels) to intensify the Jewish elders' fierce desire to exterminate Jesus, while at the same time altering Pilate's role to one of innocent helplessness. It may also be that the author of the Gospel of Peter had traditions independent of the canonical Gospels which underlie the work as we have it. The uniqueness of the resurrection scene would be evidence for this supposition. The tendency for increasing anti-Semitism in the Church is nonetheless present here.

---

1. . . . None of the Jews washed his hands, neither did Herod nor any of his judges. As they did not wish to wash, Pilate got up. 2. And then Herod the king ordered the Lord to be taken away. He said to them, "What I ordered you to do to him, do it."
3. Joseph, who was a friend of Pilate and of the Lord, stood there and, seeing that they were about to crucify him, came to Pilate and requested the body of the Lord for burial. 4. Pilate sent to Herod and requested his body. 5. Herod said, "Brother Pilate, if someone had not asked for him, we would have buried him, for the Sabbath dawns. It is written in the Law: the sun is not to set on one who has been killed." And he delivered him to the people on the day before Adzumos (Unleavened Bread), their feast.
6. They took the Lord and they ran, roughed him up, and said, "Let us drag the Son of God (to judgment); we have him in our power." 7. They garbed him in purple and seated him upon the judgment seat and

said, "Judge justly, king of Israel!" 8. And one of them brought a crown of thorns and put it on the Lord's head. 9. Others standing there spit in his face; others slapped his cheeks; some stuck him with a reed, and whipped him, saying, "By this honor, we honor the Son of God!" 10. And they brought two criminals, and they crucified the Lord between them. He was silent as if he had no pain. 11. When they had set up the cross, they inscribed on it, "This is the King of Israel." 12. And when they had taken away his clothes, in front of him they divided them and cast lots for them. 13. But one of the criminals reviled them and said, "We suffer thus because of the evil we did; this man is the Savior of men, what wrong did he do you?" 14. So they were angry with the thief and gave orders that the criminal's legs should not be broken; thus, he died in torment.

15. It was noon, and darkness gripped all Judea. (The Jews) were worried and anguished lest the sun had already set, since he (Jesus) still lived. It is written for them that the sun is not to set on one who has been killed. 16. One of them said, "Give him gall mixed with vinegar to drink." They mixed it and gave it to him to drink. 17. Indeed, they fulfilled everything, and they brought their sins to full fruition on their own heads. 18. Many went around with lamps; they thought it was night. They fell. 19. And the Lord cried out, "My power, power, you have left me!" He said this and was taken up. 20. That same hour the veil of the Jerusalem Temple was split in two.

21. Then they pulled the spikes out of the Lord's hands, and they placed him on the ground. There was an earthquake which shook the whole earth, and there was great fear. 22. Then the sun shone again and they realized it was the ninth hour. 23. The Jews rejoiced, and they gave his body to Joseph in order that he should bury it, because he had seen what good things he (Jesus) did. 24. He took the Lord, washed him, wrapped him in linen, and placed him in his own tomb, called the Garden of Joseph.

25. Then the Jews, the elders, and the priests, knowing what evil they did to themselves, began to beat their breasts and say, "Woe, on account of our sins; the judgment and the end of Jerusalem are at hand." 26. I with my companions was aggrieved. We trembled and were wounded to the heart; we were hiding, for we were sought by them as criminals, as if we wished to burn down the Temple. 27. Because of all these things, we fasted and sat mourning and crying night and day until the Sabbath.

28. The scribes, Pharisees, and elders gathered together and, hearing that all the people murmured and beat their breasts, said, "If such great miracles have happened at his death, behold how righteous he is!" 29. The elders were afraid, and they came begging to Pilate and said,

"Give us soldiers in order that they may guard his tomb for three days, so that his disciples will not come and steal him for then the people will assume that he is risen from the dead and they will harm us." 31. Pilate gave them Petronius, the centurion, along with soldiers to guard the tomb; and the elders and scribes came with them to the tomb. 32. They with the centurion and the soldiers—since they were all there together—rolled a huge stone and placed it over the door of the tomb. 33. They sealed it with seven seals, erected a tent there, and stood guard.

34. The morning of the Sabbath dawned; a crowd came from Jerusalem and its surroundings in order that they might see the tomb sealed up. 35. In the night before the dawn of the Lord's day, while the soldiers guarded two by two, there was a great noise in heaven, 36. and they saw the heavens open and two men, having great splendor, come down from there and draw near the tomb. 37. The stone which had been placed at the door rolled away by itself and moved to the side. The tomb was opened and the two youths went in.

38. When the soldiers saw this, they awakened the centurion and the elders, for they were there on guard. 39. As they recounted what they had seen, again they saw three men coming out of the tomb; two supported one of them and a cross followed them. 40. The heads of the two reached to heaven, but the one whom they bore with their hands reached beyond the heavens. 41. And they heard a voice speaking from the heavens, "Have you preached to those who are sleeping?" 42. And, obediently, (a voice) was heard from the cross, "Yes."

43. Therefore, they decided among themselves to go and reveal these things to Pilate. 44. While they were deciding, again the heavens were seen to open, and a certain man descended and went into the tomb. 45. When they saw these things, those with the centurion went quickly by night to Pilate, abandoning the tomb they guarded. They explained everything which they had seen; they were greatly upset and said, "Truly he was a Son of God." 46. Pilate answered, "I am pure in regard to the blood of the Son of God; this was your decision." 47. Then they all approached and begged him to order the centurion and the soldiers to say nothing of what they had seen. 48. "For it would be better for us," they said, "to bear the guilt of a great sin before God than to fall into the hands of the Jewish people and to be stoned." 49. Pilate, therefore, ordered the centurion and the soldiers to say nothing.

50. At the dawn of the Lord's day, Mary Magdalene, a disciple of the Lord, afraid because of the Jews since they were inflamed by wrath, had not done at the tomb what custom demanded that women should do for those who had died and whom they loved. 51. [Thus she] brought with

her some friends and came to the tomb where he was buried. 52. They were afraid lest the Jews should see them, and they said, "Because we were not able to weep and beat our breasts on the day he was crucified, let us now do these things at his tomb. 53. But who will roll away for us the stone placed before the door of the tomb, so that, when we go in, we can sit beside him and do what ought to be done? 54. For the stone is huge, and we are afraid lest someone should see us. Even if we are not able to enter, at least we can place beside the door that which we bring in his memory; let us weep and beat our breasts until we return to our house."

55. They came and found the tomb opened and, approaching, they bent down to look in. There they saw a youth seated in the middle of the tomb; he was handsome and wore a shining robe. He said to them, 56. "Why did you come? Whom do you seek? Not him who was crucified? He is risen and has gone. If you do not believe, bend over and see the place where he was laid, because he is not there. For he is risen and has gone to the place from which he was sent." 57. Then the women were frightened and fled.

58. It was the last day of Adzumos, and many returned to their homes; the feast was over. 59. We, the twelve disciples of the Lord, wept and were grief-stricken. Each, grieving at what had happened, returned to his own house. 60. But I, Simon Peter, and Andrew, my brother, took our nets and went to the sea; and with us was Levi, the son of Alphaeus, whom the Lord . . . [text breaks off at this point].

A Letter from Pilate to Claudius and The Trial of Pilate in Rome

Introduction: The letter appears in several places in the late literature of the early Church and in medieval texts. We have used the text in The Acts of Peter and Paul 40–42. Although the letter is late, as early as Tertullian (late second-century) there is mention of a dispatch from Pilate to Tiberius (Tertullian, *Apol.* 5:21) which is of such character that Tertullian regards Pilate as a converted Christian. The letter of which Tertullian spoke may be akin to the following letter.

The subsequent account of the arrest, trial, and death of Pilate is from *The Paradosis* (handing over) *of Pilate.* Both the letter and *The Paradosis* are considered by some to be earlier than the Acts of Pilate which may have its roots in such literature.

We have included this comparatively late literature to illustrate the tendency to whitewash Pilate and the Romans and to lay more and more blame for the death of Jesus upon the Jews.

A Letter from Pilate to Claudius

40. Pontius Pilate to Claudius, greeting.[1]

Something recently occurred which I myself uncovered. For the Jews through envy have taken vengeance upon themselves and their posterity with a fearful judgment.

Their fathers of course had received a promise that God would send them his Holy One from Heaven, one who correctly would be called their king; this Holy One, God had promised to send to earth through a virgin. He came to Judea when I was governor.

41. They (the Jews) saw him give sight to the blind, cleanse lepers, heal paralytics, exorcise demons, raise the dead, command the winds, walk upon a rough sea, and do many other miracles. And all the Jewish folk said him to be the very Son of God.

Therefore, the High Priests, moved by envy, seized him and delivered him to me. Piling lie upon lie, they said he was a sorcerer and that he had broken their law.

42. I believed this, ordered him whipped, and handed him over to their

[1] The letter of course should have been addressed to Tiberius.

will. And they crucified him. When he was buried, they placed a guard over him. But while my soldiers were standing guard over him, on the third day, he arose. The wickedness of the Jews had flared up to such an extent that they gave money to my soldiers, saying, "Report that his disciples stole his body."

But although they took the bribe, they could not remain silent about what had happened. They testified to the resurrection and that they had taken money from the Jews.

Because of this, I have reported these matters to you, lest someone else lie about this and you should be inclined to believe the Jews' lies.

The Trial of Pilate in Rome

1. When the reports (from Pilate) reached Rome and were read to Caesar, he and the many standing near were astonished that on account of the lawlessness of Pilate, darkness and an earthquake occurred over all the known world. Caesar, full of anger, ordered soldiers sent to take Pilate prisoner.

2. When Pilate had been brought to Rome, Caesar, hearing that Pilate had arrived, sat in the Temple of the Gods, with the whole Senate, the Army, and his officials, and he ordered Pilate to stand before him. And Caesar said to him, "What have you dared to do, you doubly impious man, when you had seen such great signs concerning that man? By your daring to do such an evil deed you have destroyed the whole world."

3. But Pilate said, "Great King, I am innocent of these things. The rashness and guilt belong to the multitude of the Jews." And Caesar said, "Who are they?" Pilate said, "Herod, Alexander, Philip, Annas, Caiaphas, and the whole crowd of Jews." Caesar said, "Why did you bend to their will?" And Pilate said, "Their nation is seditious and unruly; they do not submit to your authority." And Caesar said, "When they delivered him to you, you should have kept him in strict security and sent (word) to me, and you should not have been persuaded by them to crucify this righteous man who did such beneficent signs, as you indicated in your report. For from these signs it is clear that Jesus was the Christ, the King of the Jews."

4. When Caesar had said this and had named the name of Christ, the whole company of the (statues of the) Gods tumbled down, and they became as dust, right where Caesar sat with the Senate. The crowd that stood there with Caesar all trembled at the speaking of the word and the fall of their Gods; and all, gripped by fear, went each to his own house, astonished at the occurrence. Caesar ordered Pilate guarded closely, so that he might learn the truth about Jesus.

5. The next day Caesar sat in the Capitolium with the whole Senate,

wanting to question Pilate again. And Caesar said, "Tell the truth, doubly impious man, because of your impious deed, which you did against Jesus, even here the action of your evil work was demonstrated by the (statues of the) Gods being overthrown. Speak then. Who is the one who was crucified, that his name should even destroy all the Gods?" Pilate said, "The charges brought against him are really true, for I myself was persuaded by his works that he is greater than all the Gods we worship." And Caesar said, "Why did you charge him with recklessness and wickedness if you knew him, or did you want to harm my kingdom?" Pilate said, "I acted because of the lawlessness and wickedness and atheism of the Jews."

6. Caesar was full of anger and took counsel with all the Senate and his officials. He then ordered a decree to be written against the Jews: "To Licianus, chief governor of the East, greeting. I know about the recent lawless and reckless crime which was committed by those Jews living in Jerusalem and the nearby towns, that they misled Pilate to crucify a man, Jesus, who was called God. It was because of their crime that the world was darkened and dragged to destruction. I order through this decree, therefore, that at once a large company of soldiers be dispatched there to take them captive. Obey and move against them. Scatter them into the Diaspora, among all nations, and enslave them. Exile them from Judea; make their nation the least of all, so that it cannot be seen by anyone, for they are full of evil."

7. When this decree arrived in the Eastern lands, Licianus obeyed and carried out the terrible decree by the destruction of the whole Jewish nation. Those who were left in Judea he delivered into slavery in the Diaspora. When Caesar learned that these things had been done against the Jews in Eastern lands by Licianus, he was pleased.

8. And again Caesar interrogated Pilate, and he ordered an officer named Albius to behead Pilate, saying, "As this man raised his hand against the righteous man called Christ, he shall likewise fall and not find salvation."

9. When Pilate had gone up to the place of execution, he prayed silently, saying, "Lord, do not destroy me with the wicked Hebrews, because I raised my hand against you because of the nation of the lawless Jews; they plotted revolution against me. You know that I acted from ignorance. Do not destroy me on account of this sin, but acquit me, Lord, and your servant Procla who stands with me in this hour of my death, whom you caused to prophesy that you must be nailed to a cross. Do not condemn her because of my sin, but forgive us and number us among your righteous ones."

10. And behold, when Pilate had finished the prayer, a voice came from Heaven and said, "All the generations and families of the Gentiles will

bless you, because all things spoken about me by the prophets were fulfilled by you. And you yourself, as my witness, shall appear at my Second Coming, when I am about to judge the twelve tribes of Israel and those who do not confess my name." And the prefect cut off Pilate's head, and behold, an angel of the Lord took it up. His wife, Procla, saw the angel come and take his head, and she was filled with joy, and she immediately gave up the spirit and was buried with her husband.

Jesus' Medical Correspondence
with King Abgar

Introduction: Around the year A.D. 300, the Christian historian Eusebius described the evangelization of Eastern Syria, telling of Abgar, a former king of the region around Edessa. Abgar became ill, and, having heard of Jesus' remarkable healing powers, sent a letter to him requesting him to come to Edessa to heal him. Eusebius then quotes Jesus' letter in reply. Of the authenticity of these letters, Eusebius was quite convinced, saying, "We have written evidence of these (epistles) from the archives of Edessa, then the capital city."

Eusebius *Ecclesiastical History* 1.13.1–10

Abgar's Letter

Abgar Ouchama, the Toparch, to Jesus, the good Savior who has appeared in the area of Jerusalem, greeting. I have heard all about you and about your healings which you do without medicines and plants. According to the report, you make the blind see, the lame walk; you cleanse those with leprosy, you exorcise unclean spirits and demons, you heal those tormented by chronic disease, and you raise the dead.

I heard these things concerning you and I decided you are one of two things: either you are God and you came down from Heaven to do these things, or you do them because you are a son of God. I, therefore, write to you and beg you to take the trouble to come to me and to heal the suffering I have. I also heard that the Jews are spreading evil rumors about you and wish to hurt you. My city is small and pious, and there is room for both of us.

Jesus' Reply

Jesus to Abgar: You are blessed; you believe in me; and you have not seen me. It is written concerning me, "Those who have seen me will not believe in me," and "Those who have not seen me will believe and will be saved." Regarding what you wrote to me, that is, to come to you, I have to complete everything I was sent to do and, after this fulfillment, to be taken up to him who sent me. After I have been taken up, I will send to you one of my disciples to heal your suffering and to provide life for you and those with you.

The Infancy Gospel of Thomas

Introduction: One of the earliest (A.D. 125) writings devoted to "filling the gap" left by some of the other gospels, namely, what happened to Jesus before his twelfth year, this Gospel became very popular, and was translated into numerous languages. It is a classic example of the influence of the Hellenistic "divine man" concept on a Christian description of Jesus Christ.

---

1. I, Thomas the Israelite, announce and make known to all you brethren from the Gentiles the childhood and great deeds of our Lord Jesus Christ, which he did when he was born in our country. This is the beginning.

2.1. When this child Jesus was five years old, he was playing at the ford of a stream. He made pools of the rushing water and made it immediately pure; he ordered this by word alone. 2. He made soft clay and modeled twelve sparrows from it. It was the Sabbath when he did this. There were many other children playing with him. 3. A certain Jew saw what Jesus did while playing on the Sabbath; he immediately went and announced to his father Joseph, "See, your child is at the stream, and has taken clay and modeled twelve birds; he has profaned the Sabbath." 4. Joseph came to the place, and seeing what Jesus did he cried out, "Why do you do on the Sabbath what it is not lawful to do?" Jesus clapped his hands and cried to the sparrows, "Be gone." And the sparrows flew off chirping. 5. The Jews saw this and were amazed. They went away and described to their leaders what they had seen Jesus do.

3.1. The son of Annas the scribe was standing there with Joseph. He took a branch of a willow and scattered the water which Jesus had arranged. 2. Jesus saw what he did and became angry and said to him, "You unrighteous, impious ignoramus, what did the pools and the water do to harm you? Behold, you shall also wither as a tree, and you shall not bear leaves nor roots nor fruit." 3. And immediately that child was all withered. Jesus left and went to the house of Joseph. The parents of the withered one bore him away, bemoaning his lost youth. They led him to Joseph and reproached him, "What kind of child do you have who does such things?"

4.1. Once again he was going through the village, and a child who was running banged into his shoulder. Jesus was angered and said to him,

"You shall go no further on your way." And immediately the child fell down dead. Some people saw this happen and said, "From whence was this child begotten, for his every word is an act accomplished?" 2. The parents of the dead boy went to Joseph and blamed him: "Because you have such a boy, you cannot live with us in the village; your alternative is to teach him to bless and not to curse, for he is killing our children."
5.1. Joseph took the child aside privately and warned him, saying, "Why do you do such things? These people are suffering and they hate us and are persecuting us!" Jesus said, "I know that these are not your words, but on account of you I will be silent. However, they shall bear their punishment. [1] Immediately, those who accused him were blinded. 2. Those who saw were very frightened and puzzled, and they said about him, "Every word he speaks, whether good or evil, happens and is a miracle." When he saw what Jesus had done, Joseph arose and took hold of Jesus' ear and pulled it hard. 3. The child was angry and said to him, "It is fitting for you to seek and not find. You have acted very stupidly. Do you not know I am yours? Do not vex me."
6.1. A man named Zaccheus, a teacher, was standing there and he heard, in part, Jesus saying these things to his father. He was greatly astonished that he said such things, since he was just a child. 2. And after a few days he approached Joseph and said to him, "You have a smart child, and he has a mind. Come, hand him over to me so that he may learn writing. I will give him all understanding with the letters, and teach him to greet all the elders and to honor them as grandfathers and fathers and to love his peers." 3. He told him all the letters from the Alpha to the Omega plainly, with much discussion. But Jesus looked at Zaccheus the teacher, and said to him, "You do not know the Alpha according to nature, how do you teach others the Beta? You hypocrite! First, if you know it, teach the Alpha, then we shall believe you about the Beta." Then he began to question the teacher about the first letter and he could not answer him. 4. Many heard as the child said to Zaccheus, "Listen, teacher, to the order of the first element, and pay attention to this, how it has lines, and a central mark which goes through the two lines you see, (they) converge, go up, again come to head, become the same three times, subordinate, and hypostatic, isometric . . . [The text is unreliable.] You now have the lines of Alpha."
7.1. When the teacher, Zaccheus, heard so many such allegories of the first letter spoken by the child, he was puzzled about such expoundings and his teaching. He said to those present, "Woe is me, I am wretched and puzzled; I have shamed myself trying to handle this child. 2. I beg you, brother Joseph, take him away. I cannot bear the severity of his

---

[1] An interesting Syriac variant: "If these children had been born in wedlock they would not be cursed."

glance. I cannot understand his speech at all. This child is not earthborn; he is able to tame even fire. Perhaps he was begotten before the world's creation. What belly bore him, what womb nurtured him, I do not know. Woe is me, friend, he completely confuses me.[2] I cannot followhis understanding. I have fooled myself; I am thrice wretched. I worked anxiously to have a disciple, and I found myself with a teacher. 3. I consider my shame, friends; I am an old man and have been conquered by a child; for at this hour I cannot look into his gaze. When they all say that I have been conquered by a little child, what can I say? What can I discuss about the lines of the first element he spoke to me? I do not know, O friends, for I do not know its beginning and end. Therefore, I beg you, brother Joseph, take him into your house. He is something great: a God, an angel, or what I should say I do not know."

8.1. While the Jews were comforting Zaccheus, the child gave a great laugh, saying, "Now let what is yours bear fruit, and the blind in heart see. I am from above in order that I may curse them and call them into the things which are above, because he who sent me on your account ordered it." 2. And as the child ceased talking, immediately all those who had fallen under his curse were saved (or, healed). And after that no one dared to anger him, lest he should curse him, and he should be crippled.

9.1. After some days Jesus was playing upstairs in a certain house, and one of the children playing with him fell from the house and died. And when the other children saw this they ran away, and Jesus remained alone. 2. The parents of the dead child came and accused Jesus of throwing him down. Jesus replied, "I did not throw him down." But still they accused him. 3. Then Jesus leaped down from the roof and stood by the body of the child and cried out in a great voice, saying "Zenon!"—that was his name—"rise up and tell me, did I throw you down?" He immediately rose up and said: "No, Lord, you did not throw me down, but you raised me." Those who saw this were astonished. The parents of the child glorified God because of this sign that happened, and they worshiped Jesus.

10.1. After a few days a young man was splitting wood in the vicinity; the axe fell and split the bottom of his foot, and he was bleeding to death. 2. There was an outcry and people gathered. The child Jesus ran there. He pushed through the crowd, and seized the injured foot of the youth; immediately he was healed. He said to the youth, "Now get up, split your wood, and remember me." The crowd, seeing what had happened, worshiped the child, saying, "Truly, the Spirit of God lives in this child!"

---

[2]Tischendorf conjectures the *stupefacit me* as the translation for an unclear verb here.

11.1. When he was six, his mother sent him to draw water and to bring it into the house, giving him a pitcher. But in the crowd, he had a collision; the water jug was broken. 2. Jesus spread out the garment he had on, filled it with water, and bore it to his mother. When his mother saw the miracle she kissed him, and she kept to herself the mysteries which she saw him do.

12.1. Again, during planting time the child went with his father to sow seed in their field. While they planted, his father sowed, and the child Jesus planted one grain of wheat. 2. When he had reaped and threshed it, it yielded one hundred measures, and he called all the poor of the village to the threshing floor and gave them the grain. Joseph took the remainder of the grain. He was eight when he did this sign.

13.1. His father was a carpenter and at that time made ploughs and yokes. He received an order from a certain rich man to make a bed for him. One beam came out shorter than the other, and he did not know what to do. The child Jesus said to Joseph his father, "Lay the two pieces of wood alongside each other, and make them even at one end." 2. Joseph did as the child told him. Jesus stood at the other end and grasped the shorter beam; he stretched it and made it equal with the other. His father Joseph saw and was astonished, and embracing the child he kissed him and said, "I am blessed because God has given this child to me."

14.1. When Joseph saw the mind and age of the child, that he was growing up, he again wished him not to be ignorant of letters. And he took him and gave him to another teacher. But the teacher said to Joseph, "First I will teach him Greek, and then Hebrew." For the teacher knew the child's learning and feared him. Nevertheless he wrote the alphabet and taught him for many hours, but Jesus did not answer him. 2. Then Jesus said to him, "If you really are a teacher, and you know the letters well, tell me the power of Alpha and I will tell you that of Beta." The teacher was angered and hit Jesus on the head. The child was hurt and cursed him. Immediately the teacher fainted, falling to the ground upon his face. 3. The child returned to the house of Joseph. But Joseph was grief-stricken and gave this order to his mother: "Do not let him go outside the door, because anyone who angers him dies."

15.1. After some time there was another teacher, a good friend of Joseph. He said to him, "Bring the child to me at school, maybe by flattery I can teach him letters." Joseph said, "If you dare, brother, take him with you." He took him with fear and much anxiety, but the child went with pleasure. 2. Jesus went boldly into the school and found a book lying on the lectern, and taking it, did not read the letters in it, but opened his mouth and spoke by the Holy Spirit and taught the Law to those standing nearby. A great crowd gathered and stood listening to him. They were astonished at the beauty of his teaching and the eloquence of his words, that being a babe he could say such things. 3. Joseph heard and was frightened. He ran into the school, wondering whether this teacher was also without skill, but the teacher said to Joseph, "Know, brother, that I took the child as a disciple, but he is full of much grace and wisdom, and I beg you brother, take him into your house." 4. When the child heard this, immediately he smiled at him and said, "Since you spoke correctly and witnessed correctly, on account of you the one who was stricken shall be healed." And immediately the other teacher was healed. Joseph took the child and returned home.

16.1. Joseph sent his son James to gather wood and to bring it into the house. The child Jesus followed him. While James was gathering the sticks, a snake bit James's hand. 2. As he lay dying, Jesus came near and breathed on the bite. Immediately James ceased suffering, the snake burst, and James was healed.

17.1. After this, in the neighborhood of Joseph a certain child took sick and died. His mother wept bitterly. Jesus, hearing the great mourning and clamor, ran quickly and found the child dead. He touched his breast and said, "I say to you, child, do not die, but live and be with your mother!" And immediately the child looked up and laughed. Jesus said to the woman, "Pick him up and give him milk, and remember me." 2. The crowd standing around saw and was amazed, and they said, "Truly this child is a God or an angel of God, because his every word becomes a finished deed." And Jesus left there and played with the other children.

18.1. After some time a house was being built and there was a great clamor. Jesus arose and went there. Seeing a man lying dead he took his hand and said, "I say to you, man, arise, to your work!" And immediately he arose and worshiped him. 2. Seeing this, the crowd was astonished and said, "This is a heavenly child, for he saved many souls from death, and can save them all his life."

19.1. When he was twelve his parents, according to custom, went to Jerusalem to the Passover with their traveling companions. After the Passover they returned to their house. While they were going home, the child Jesus went back to Jerusalem. His parents thought that he was in the caravan. 2. After a day's travel, they sought him among their kinfolk and when they did not find him they were troubled. They returned again to the city to seek him. After three days they found him in the Temple, seated in the midst of the teachers, listening and questioning them. They all were attentive and amazed at how he, being a child, could argue with the elders and teachers of the people, solving the chief problems of the Law and the parables of the prophets. 3. His mother, Mary, came up and said to him, "How can you have done this to us, child? Behold, we have looked everywhere for you, grieving." And Jesus said to them, "Why did you look for me? Do you not know that I must be in my Father's house?" 4. The scribes and Pharisees said, "Are you the mother of this child?" She said, "I am." They said to her, "You are blessed among women, because God has blessed the fruit of your womb. We have never before seen or heard such glory or such excellence and wisdom." 5. Jesus arose and followed his mother and was obedient to his parents. But his mother kept (in her heart) all that had happened. Jesus grew in wisdom and stature and grace. Glory be to him forever and ever. Amen.

The Gospel of Pseudo-Matthew

Introduction: This Gospel was written perhaps as late as the eighth or ninth century, although some would place it much earlier.

The first section of the Gospel (chs. 1–17) is based upon the Gospel of James; the third portion (chs. 25–41) relies upon the Infancy Gospel of Thomas.

We have included part of the middle section of Pseudo-Matthew because it demonstrates the tendency to ascribe to Jesus the aura of the "divine man" miracle worker, and it also demonstrates the use of prophecy-fulfillment as a narrative device. This device is used in the canonical Gospel of Matthew, hence the popular title Pseudo-Matthew for this work. Pseudo-Matthew's actual title is "The Book About the Origin of the Blessed Mary and the Childhood of the Savior." The age and identity of the source(s) of chs. 18–24 are not known.

Selections

10. . . . Joseph was in Capernaum-by-the-Sea, on the job; he was a carpenter. He stayed there for nine months. When he returned home he found Mary pregnant. Totally gripped by anguish, he trembled and cried out, "Lord God, accept my spirit, because it is better for me to die than to live." The virgins with Mary said to him, "What are you saying, Lord Joseph? We know ourselves that no man has touched her; we know ourselves that, in her, innocence and virginity were preserved unspoiled. For she has been guarded by God; she always persists with us in prayer. Daily an angel of the Lord speaks with her; daily she accepts food from the hand of an angel. How is it possible that there should be any sin in her? For if you want us to voice our suspicion to you, this pregnancy was caused by none other than God's angel." Joseph, however, said, "Would you try to have me believe that an angel of the Lord impregnated her? It is indeed possible that someone dressed up as an angel of the Lord and tricked her." As he said this, he wept and said, "With what aspect am I to go to God's Temple? With what pretext am I to visit the priests of God? What am I to do?" After he said this he made plans to hide her and set her aside.

11. When he planned to arise in the night and flee, so that he could live in hiding; behold, in that very night, an angel of the Lord appeared to him in a dream and said, "Joseph, son of David, do not fear to accept Mary as your wife, because that which is in her womb is from the Holy

98

Spirit. She will bear a son who will be called Jesus; he will save his people from their sins." Joseph arose from his sleep, gave thanks to his God, and told his vision to Mary and the virgins with her. And after having been reassured by Mary, he said, "I have sinned because I was suspicious of you."

12. It so happened that after this a rumor went out that Mary was pregnant. Joseph was seized by the Temple's agents and led to the High Priest who, together with the priests, began to reproach him, saying, "How have you been cheated of such a wedding and a virgin whom the angels of God nourished as a dove in the Temple, who wished never to see any man, who had excellent learning in the law of God? If you yourself had not violated her, she today would remain a virgin." Joseph, however, took an oath, swearing that he had never touched her. Abiathar, the High Priest, said to him, "As God lives, therefore I will have you drink water of the Lord's testing, and at once he will demonstrate your sin."

All the multitude of Israel gathered together, so many that it was impossible to count them, and Mary was led to the Lord's Temple. Indeed, priests and neighbors and her parents cried out and said to Mary, "Confess your sin to the priests, you who were as a dove in the Temple of God and who accepted nourishment from the hand of an angel." Joseph also was called to the altar and given the water of the Lord's testing—which, if a man at fault should drink and then circle the altar seven times, God will cause (his sin) to show in the man's face. When therefore a cheerful Joseph drank and circled the altar, no sign of sin was revealed in him. Then all the priests and ministers and people sanctified him, saying, "Blessed are you because no guilt was discovered in you." Then they called Mary and said to her, "Now what excuse can you have? Or what sign will he manifest in you beyond that which your pregnancy reveals in your womb? This alone will we require from you that—because Joseph is clear in respect to you—you should confess who it is who deceived you. It is better indeed that your confession betray you than that the wrath of God give a sign in your face and expose you in the midst of the people."

Then Mary, standing firm and intrepid, said, "If there is in me any pollution or sin, or if there was in me any concupiscence or lewdness, may the Lord expose me in view of all the people, so that I may be an example for the correction of all." And she went to the altar of God confidently, drank the water of testing, went around the altar seven times, and no fault was found in her.

And while all the people marveled and stammered, seeing that she was pregnant and yet no sign of guilt appeared in her face, they began to be agitated and to murmur among themselves as crowds do. Some said a blessing, others through bad conscience accused her. Then, seeing the suspicions of the people, that they had not been purged by her integrity, with everybody listening, Mary spoke in a clear voice, "As God lives, Adonai of hosts, in whose view I stand, I have never known a man; I have never even considered to know a man, because from my infancy through my lifetime I have been of this mind. And this offering I made to God from my infancy so that I should continue in integrity with him who created me, to live in him alone with whom I confide, and, as long as I should live, to remain with him alone without stain."

Then they all kissed her, asking that she give forgiveness for their nasty suspicions. And all the people and the priests and all the virgins, with exultation and praise, led her to her house, shouting and saying, "Blessed be the name of the Lord, who has revealed your sanctity to all the masses of Israel."

13. (The birth of Jesus. The story appears to be based on the Gospel of James, and it features Salome's gynecological inspection of Mary. This chapter also recapitulates the Lukan birth narrative.)

14. On the third day after the Lord's birth, Mary went out of the cave; she went into the stable and placed the child in a manger, and an ox and a donkey worshiped him. Then that which was spoken through Isaiah the prophet was fulfilled: "The ox knows his owner and the donkey his lord's manger."[1] These animals, with him between them, unceasingly worshiped him. Thus that which was spoken through the prophet Habbakuk was fulfilled: "You will be known between the two animals."[2] Joseph and Mary stayed there with the child three days.

15–17. (They go to Bethlehem. Jesus is circumcised. The presentation at the Temple [see Luke 2]. The coming of the Magi. The massacre of the Jewish children.)

18. When they came to a certain cave and wanted to rest in it, Mary got down from the pack mule, and, sitting down, held Jesus in her lap. There were three boys traveling with Joseph and a girl with Mary. And behold, suddenly, many dragons came out of the cave. When the boys saw them in front of them they shouted with great fear. Then Jesus got down from his mother's lap, and stood on his feet before the dragons. They, however, worshiped him, and, while they worshiped, they backed away. Then what was said through the prophet David was fulfilled: "You dragons of the earth, praise the Lord, you dragons and all creatures of the abyss (or, all abysses)."[3] Then the infant Jesus walked before them and ordered them not to harm any man. But Mary and Joseph were very afraid lest the child should be harmed by the dragons.

[1] Isaiah 1:3.
[2] Habbakuk 3:2, LXX.
[3] Psalm 148:7.

Jesus said to them, "Do not be afraid, nor consider me a child; I always have been a perfect man and am so now; it is necessary that all the wild beasts of the forest be tame before me."

19. Similarly, lions and leopards worshiped him and accompanied them in the desert. Wherever Mary and Joseph went, they preceded them; showing the way and inclining their heads, they worshiped Jesus. However, the first time that Mary saw the lions and other types of wild beasts around her, she was very frightened. The child Jesus, with cheerful face, looked back and said, "Do not be afraid, mother, they did not rush here to hurt you but they rush to obey you." When he said this, he cut off the fear in her heart. The lions traveled with them and with the oxen and donkeys and the pack animals which carried their necessities, and they hurt none of them while they remained. They were tame among the sheep and rams which they brought with them from Judea and had with them. They traveled among wolves and they were not frightened; there was no harm to the one from the other. Then that which was said by the prophet was fulfilled: "Wolves shall be pastured with lambs, the lion and the ox shall eat fodder together."[4] There were two oxen and the wagon, in which they carried their necessities, which the lions guided on their journey.

20. It so happened, that on the third day after their departure, that Mary was fatigued by the excessive heat of the sun in the desert and, seeing a palm tree, said to Joseph, "I want to rest a bit under its shadow." Joseph quickly led her to the palm and let her get down from the animal. While Mary sat, she looked at the top of the palm and saw it full of fruit. She said to Joseph, "I wish, if it is possible, that I have some fruit from this palm." Joseph said to her, "I am astonished that you say this, when you see how high this palm is, that you think to eat from the fruit of the palm. I think more of the lack of water, which already fails us in the water bags; we now have nothing by which we can refresh ourselves and the animals."

Then the infant Jesus, who was resting with smiling face at his mother's bosom, said to the palm, "Bend down, tree, and refresh my mother with your fruit." And immediately, at this voice, the palm bent down its head to the feet of Mary, and they gathered fruit from it by which all were refreshed. After they had gathered all its fruit, it remained bent down, waiting so that it should raise up at the command of him who had commanded it to bend. Then Jesus said to it, "Raise up, palm, and be strong, and be a companion of my trees which are in my Father's Paradise. Open a water course beneath your roots which is hidden in the earth, and from it let flow waters to satisfy us." And the

[4]Isaiah 11:6f.

palm raised itself at once, and fountains of water, very clear and cold and sweet, began to pour out through the roots. When they saw the fountains of water they rejoiced with great rejoicing, and they and the beasts of burden were all satisfied, and they gave thanks to God.

21. The next day they went on from there. At the time they began the journey, Jesus turned to the palm and said, "I give you this privilege, palm, that one of your branches be carried by my angels and planted in my Father's Paradise. I confer upon you this blessing, that all who win in any contest, it shall be said to them, 'You have attained the palm of victory.' " When he said this, behold an angel of the Lord appeared and stood above the palm tree. He took one of its branches and flew to Heaven with the branch in his hand. When they saw this they fell on their faces and were just as if they were dead. Jesus spoke to them, saying, "Why has fear gripped your hearts? Do you not know that this palm, which I have had carried into Paradise, will be ready for all the saints in the place of delight, just as it was ready for you in this desert place." They were all filled with joy and arose.

22. While they traveled on, Joseph said to him, "Lord, the excessive heat is cooking us; if it pleases you, let us go by the sea, so that we can travel, resting in the coastal towns." Jesus said to him, "Fear not, Joseph, I will shorten your journey, so that what you were going to travel across in the space of thirty days, you will finish in one day." While this was being said, behold, they began to see the mountains and cities of Egypt.

Rejoicing and exulting they came to the region of Hermopolis, and went into one of the Egyptian cities called Sotinen. Since they knew no one in it from whom they could ask for hospitality, they went into the temple which was called the "Capitolium of Egypt." There had been placed in this temple three hundred and sixty-five idols, to which, on appointed days, divine honor was given in sacrilegious ceremonies.

23. It happened that, when the most blessed Mary, with her child, had entered the temple, all the idols were thrown to the ground, so that all lay flat, convulsed and with their faces shattered. Thus they revealed openly that they were nothing. Then that which was said by the prophet Isaiah was fulfilled: "Behold, the Lord shall come on a swift cloud and enter Egypt, and all (the idols) made by Egyptians shall be moved from his face."[5]

24. When this had been announced to Afrodosius, the governor of the city, he came to the temple with his whole army. When the priests of the temple saw that Afrodosius hastened to the temple with his whole army, they supposed to see his revenge on those because of whom the idols were overthrown. He entered the temple, and when he saw that all the

[5]Isaiah 19:1.

idols lay prostrate on their faces, he went to Mary and worshiped the child whom she carried at her bosom, and while he worshiped him, he said to his whole army and his friends, "If he were not the God of our Gods, our Gods would certainly not have fallen before him on their faces, nor would they lie prostrate in his presence. They thus silently confess he is their Lord. If we all do not do with prudence what we see our Gods do, we shall possibly incur his indignation and all come into destruction, just as happened to Pharoah, king of the Egyptians, who did not believe in such marvels and was drowned in the sea with his whole army. Then all the people of that city believed in the Lord God through Jesus Christ."

25. After a little time the angel said to Joseph, "Return to the land of Judah; they who sought the life of the boy are dead."

The Birth of Jesus

Introduction: This Gospel is a medieval document which exists in two manuscripts. Most of this Gospel is based upon Pseudo-Matthew and the Gospel of James. However, there are passages which are unique to this Gospel, which appear to use a source that is probably from the Church's early years, and which have a birth narrative unknown elsewhere. M.R. James, who first published the Arundel and Hereford manuscripts of the Gospel, claims that the birth narrative may be from the second century. We have selected passages from the Arundel manuscript—it is more primitive than the Hereford version—which rely upon the unknown source.

A Latin Infancy Gospel

Selections from the Arundel Manuscript

68. . . . Behold a girl came with a chair which was customarily used to help women giving birth. She stopped. When they saw her they were amazed, and Joseph said to her, "Child, where are you going with that chair?" The girl responded, "My mistress sent me to this place because a youth came to her with great haste and said, 'Come quickly to help with an unusual birth; a girl will give birth for the first time.' When she heard this, my mistress sent me on before her; look, she herself is following."

Joseph looked back and saw her coming; he went to meet her and they greeted each other. The midwife said to Joseph, "Sir, where are you going?" He replied, "I seek a Hebrew midwife." The woman said to him, "Are you from Israel?" Joseph said, "I am from Israel." The woman said to him, "Who is the young woman who will give birth in this cave?" Joseph replied, "Mary, who was promised to me, who was raised in the Lord's Temple." The midwife said to him, "She is not your wife?" And Joseph said, "She was promised to me, but was made pregnant by the Holy Spirit." The midwife said to him, "What you say, is it true?" Joseph said to her, "Come and see."

69. They entered the cave. Joseph said to the midwife, "Come, see Mary." When she wished to enter to the interior of the cave, she was afraid, because a great light shone resplendent in the cave, the light did not wane in the day nor through the night as long as Mary stayed there . . .

104

Joseph said, "Mary. Behold, I have brought to you a midwife, Zachel, who stands outside in front of the cave, who because of the brightness not only dares not enter the cave, but even cannot." When she heard this, Mary smiled. Joseph said to her, "Do not smile, but take care; she comes to examine you in case you need medicine." He ordered the midwife to enter to [Mary] and she stood before her. For hours Mary permitted herself to be watched, then the midwife cried with a loud voice and said, "Lord, great God, have mercy, because never has this been heard, nor seen, nor even dreamed of, until now, that the breasts should be full of milk and a male child, after birth, should make his mother known to be a virgin. There was no offering of blood in the birth, no pain occurred in the parturition. A virgin conceived, a virgin has given birth and after she gave birth, she remained a virgin."

70. (The midwife is asked to relate what she had seen to Symeon, Joseph's son. See Matt. 13:55; Mark 6:3. The following is, therefore, a flashback.)

71. "When I entered to the maiden, I found her face looking upward; she was inclined toward Heaven and speaking to herself. I truly believe that she prayed to and blessed the Most High. When I had come to her, I said to her, 'Daughter, tell me, do you not feel some pain, or is not some part of your body gripped with pain?' She, however, as if she heard nothing, remained immobile like solid rock, intent on Heaven.

72. "In that hour, everything ceased. There was total silence and fear. For even the winds stopped, they made no breeze; there was no motion of tree leaves; no sound of water was heard. The streams did not flow; there was no motion of the sea. All things produced in the water were quiet; there was no human voice sounding; there was a great silence. For the pole (or, people) itself ceased its rapid course from that hour [Latin uncertain here]. Time almost stopped its measure. All, overwhelmed with great fear, kept silent; we were expecting the advent of the most high God, the end of the world.

73. "As the time drew near, the power of God showed itself openly. The maiden stood looking intently into Heaven; she became as a grapevine (or, she became snow-white). For now the end of good things was at hand. When the light had come forth, (Mary) worshiped him to whom she saw she had given birth. The child himself, like the sun, shone bright, beautiful, and was most delightful to see, because he alone appeared as peace, soothing the whole world. In that hour, when he was born, the voice of many invisible beings in one voice proclaimed "Amen." And the light, when it was born, multiplied, and it obscured the light of the sun itself by its shining rays. The cave was filled by the bright light together with a most sweet odor. The light was born just as the dew descends from heaven to the earth. For its odor is fragrant

beyond all the sweet smell of ointments.

74. "I, however, stood stupefied and amazed. Awe grasped me. I was gazing intently at the fantastically bright light which had been born. The light, however, after a while, shrank, imitated the shape of an infant, then immediately became outwardly an infant in the usual manner of born infants. I became bold and leaned over and touched him. I lifted him in my hands with great awe, and I was terrified because he had no weight like other babies who are born. I looked at him closely; there was no blemish on him, but he was in his body totally shining, just as the dew of the most high God. He was light to carry, splendid to see. For a while I was amazed at him because he did not cry as newborn children are supposed to. While I held him, looking into his face, he laughed at me with a most joyful laugh, and, opening his eyes, he looked intently at me. Suddenly a great light came forth from his eyes like a great flash of lightning."

———————————————

The Gospel of James

Introduction: The Gospel of James (*Protevangelium Jacobi*) has been one of the most influential of all the Christian gospels. Scholars have long agreed that at least the major portion of it was written in the second century. It is one of the earliest expositions of the idea of the virgin birth, and contains also the story of the birth of Mary and the circumstances of her betrothal to Joseph. In addition, there has come from the Gospel of James a great deal of the imagery which Christian artists have used in portraying the birth of Jesus.

Protevangelium Jacobi

1.1. According to the histories of the twelve tribes of Israel, Joachim was a very wealthy man. He brought his offerings twofold to the Lord, saying to himself, 2. "This from my abundance will be for all the people, and this which I owe as a sin offering will be for the Lord God as a propitiation for me."
3. Now the great day of the Lord drew near, and the children of Israel brought their offerings. Reuben stood up against Joachim, saying, 4. "It is not permissible for you to bring your offerings first, for you did not produce offspring in Israel."
5. Joachim was greatly distressed, and he went to the book of the twelve tribes of Israel, saying to himself, 6. "I will look at the records of the twelve tribes of Israel to determine whether I alone did not produce offspring in Israel." 7. He searched, and he found that all the righteous had raised up offspring in Israel. 8. Further, he remembered the patriarch Abraham, that near his last day the Lord God gave to him a son, Isaac.
9. Joachim was very sorrowful; he did not appear to his wife, but betook himself into the desert and pitched his tent there. 10. Then he fasted for forty days and forty nights, saying to himself, "I will not return, either for food or drink, until the Lord my God considers me. Prayer will be my food and drink."
2.1. Now his wife Anna sang two dirges and beat her breast in a twofold lament, saying, "I will mourn my widowhood, and I will mourn my barrenness."
2. The great day of the Lord drew near and Euthine, her maid, said to her, "How long will you humble your soul? Behold, the great day of the Lord has come, and it is not proper for you to mourn. 3. Rather, take

this headband which the mistress of work gave to me; it is not permissible for me to wear it, because I am your servant-girl and it has a mark of royalty." 4. Then Anna said, "Get away from me! I have not done these things; the Lord God has humbled me greatly. 5. Perhaps someone gave this to you deceitfully, and now you have come to make me a partner in your sin." Euthine, her maid, said, 6. "What am I to you, since you do not listen to my voice? The Lord God closed your womb in order not to grant you fruit in Israel."

7. Anna was very grieved, and she took off her mourning garments and cleansed her head and put on her bridal garments.

8. About the ninth hour she went down into her garden to walk and she saw a laurel tree and sat down beneath it; and she entreated the Lord, saying, 9. "O God of my fathers, bless me and hear my prayer, even as you blessed the womb of Sarah and gave to her a son, Isaac."

3.1. Anna looked up toward heaven and saw a nest of sparrows in the laurel tree; and she sang a dirge to herself, saying, 2. "Woe is me! Who gave me birth? What sort of womb brought me forth? For I was born a curse among the children of Israel. I was made a reproach, and they derided me and banished me out of the Temple of the Lord my God.

3. "Woe is me! To what am I likened? I am not likened to the birds of heaven, for even the birds of heaven are fruitful before you, O Lord.

4. "Woe is me! To what am I likened? I am not likened to the wild beasts of the earth, for even the wild beasts of the earth are fruitful before you, O Lord.

5. "Woe is me! To what am I likened? I am not likened to the voiceless creatures, for even the voiceless creatures are fruitful before you, O Lord.

6. "Woe is me! To what am I likened? I am not likened to these waters, for even these waters are fruitful before you, O Lord.

7. "Woe is me! To what am I likened? I am not likened to this earth, for even the earth brings forth her fruit in its season and blesses you, O Lord."

4.1. And behold, an angel of the Lord appeared, saying, "Anna, Anna, the Lord God heard your prayer, and you will conceive and give birth, and your offspring shall be spoken of in the whole inhabited world." 2. Anna said, "As the Lord my God lives, if I give birth, whether male or female, I will present it as a gift to the Lord my God, and it shall be a ministering servant to him all the days of its life." 3. And behold, two angels came, saying to her, "Behold, your husband Joachim is coming with his flocks."

4. Now an angel of the Lord had come down to Joachim, saying, "Joachim, Joachim, the Lord God heard your prayer. 5. Go down

from here; for behold, your wife Anna is pregnant." Joachim went down, and he summoned his shepherds, saying, "Bring here to me ten female lambs, spotless and without blemish, and the ten lambs shall be for the Lord my God; 6. and bring to me twelve choice calves, and the twelve calves shall be for the priests and the council of elders; and a hundred year-old he goats, and the hundred he goats shall be for all the people."

7. And behold, Joachim came with his flocks, and Anna stood at the door and saw Joachim coming with his flocks. Anna ran and threw her arms around his neck, saying, 8. "Now I know that the Lord God has blessed me very greatly, for behold, the widow is no longer a widow, and she who was barren has conceived!" 9. Then Joachim remained in his house for the first day.

5.1. On the next day he brought his offerings, saying to himself, "If the Lord God has had mercy on me, the golden plate of the priest's headdress will make it apparent to me." 2. Joachim brought his offerings, and he observed the priest's golden plate intently as he went up to the altar of the Lord; and he did not see sin in himself. 3. Joachim said, "Now I know that the Lord God has had mercy on me and forgiven me all my sins." 4. Then he went down from the Temple of the Lord, justified, and came into his house.

5. Now her time was fulfilled, and in the ninth month Anna gave birth. She said to the midwife, "What have I borne? 6. The midwife said, "A girl." Then Anna said, "My soul is exalted this day;" and she laid herself down.

7. When the required days were completed, Anna cleansed herself of the impurity of childbirth, and gave her breast to the child. She called her name Mary.

6.1. Day by day the child grew strong. When she was six months old her mother stood her on the ground to see if she could stand. Walking seven steps, she came to her mother's bosom. 2. Her mother caught her up, saying, "As the Lord my God lives, you shall not walk on this earth until I bring you into the Temple of the Lord." 3. Then she made a sanctuary in her bedroom, and prohibited everything common and unclean from passing through it; and she summoned the undefiled daughters of the Hebrews, and they served her.

4. Now the child came to be a year old, and Joachim gave a great feast; he invited the High Priests, the priests, the scribes, the elders of the council, and all the people cf Israel. 5. Joachim brought the child to the priests and they blessed her saying, "O God of our fathers, bless this child, and give to her a name famous forever in all generations." All the people responded, "So let it be. Amen." 6. Then he brought her to the

High Priests and they blessed her, saying, "O God of the high places, look upon this child, and bless her with the highest blessing which has no successor."

7. Her mother picked her up and brought her into the sanctuary of her bedroom, and gave her breast to the child. 8. Then Anna sang a hymn to the Lord God, saying, "I will sing a sacred song to the Lord my God, because he considered me and took away from me the reproach of my enemies; 9. and the Lord my God gave me a fruit of his righteousness, one yet manifold before him. Who will report to the sons of Reuben that Anna gives suck?"

10. She laid the child to rest in the bedroom, in her sanctuary, and she went out and served them at the feast. 11. When the meal was finished, they went down rejoicing and they glorified the God of Israel.

7.1. Months passed. The child became two years old, and Joachim said, 2. "Let us take her up into the Temple of the Lord, in order that we may fulfill the pledge which we have made; lest the Lord send to us for it and our gift be unacceptable." 3. Anna said, "Let us await the third year, lest the child long for her father and mother." And Joachim said, "So let it be."

4. When the child was three years old, Joachim said, "Let us call the undefiled daughters of the Hebrews, and let each one take a torch, and let them be burning, 5. in order that the child not turn back and her heart be misled out of the Temple of the Lord." Thus they did, until they had gone up into the Temple.

6. The priest received her, and kissing her he blessed her and said, "The Lord God has magnified your name in all generations; in you, at the end of days, will the Lord God manifest his deliverance to the children of Israel." 7. He set her on the third step of the altar, and the Lord God gave grace to her; and she danced with her feet, and all the house of Israel loved her.

8.1. Her parents returned, marveling and giving praise and glorifying the Lord God that the child did not turn back.

2. Now Mary was in the Temple of the Lord like a dove being fed, and she received food from the hand of an angel.

3. When she was twelve years old there took place a conference of the priests, saying, "Behold, Mary has become twelve years old in the Temple of the Lord our God. 4. What, therefore, shall we do with her, lest she defile the sanctuary of the Lord?" 5. The High Priests said to Zacharias, "You stand at the altar of the Lord. Enter and pray concerning her; and whatever the Lord God may reveal to you, this let us do."

6. The priest entered the Holy of Holies, taking the vestment with the twelve bells, and he prayed concerning her. 7. And behold, an angel of

the Lord appeared, saying, "Zacharias, Zacharias, go out and call together the widowers of the people, and let each of them bring a rod; and to whomever the Lord God shows a sign, to this one shall she be wife." 8. The heralds therefore went forth through the whole Jewish countryside and sounded the trumpet of the Lord, and all came running. **9.**1. Now Joseph, casting down his adze, came himself into their meeting. When they all were gathered together, they came to the priest, taking the rods. 2. He, having received the rods of all of them, went into the Temple and prayed. When he finished the prayer he took the rods and came out and returned them; and there was no sign on them. 3. Joseph received the last rod, and behold, a dove came forth from the rod and settled on Joseph's head. 4. Then the priest said, "Joseph, Joseph, you have been designated by lot to receive the virgin of the Lord as your ward."

5. Joseph refused, saying, "I have sons, and I am an old man, but she is a young maiden—lest I be a laughing stock to the children of Israel." 6. The priest said, "Joseph, fear the Lord your God! Remember what God did to Dathan and Abiram and Korah, how the earth was split in two and they were all swallowed up on account of their disputing. 7. And now, Joseph, beware lest these things be also in your house."

8. Joseph frightened, received her as his ward; and Joseph said to her, "Mary, I have received you from the Temple of the Lord. 9. Now I am leaving you behind in my house, and I am going away to build houses; later I will return to you. The Lord will guard you."

10.1. There took place a council of the priests, saying, "Let us make a veil for the Temple of the Lord." 2. The priest said, "Call the undefiled virgins from the tribe of David." 3. The attendants went out and sought [them], and they found seven. 4. Then the priest remembered the child Mary, that she was of the tribe of David and was pure before God; and the attendants went forth and brought her.

5. They brought them into the Temple of the Lord, and the priest said, "Assign by lot for me here someone who will spin the gold thread and the white and the linen and the silk and the hyacinth-blue and the scarlet and the genuine purple." 6. The genuine purple and the scarlet were assigned by lot to Mary, and taking them she went into her house. 7. Now at that time Zacharias was dumb, and Samuel replaced him until the time when Zacharias spoke. 8. Mary, taking the scarlet, spun it.

11.1. She took her pitcher and went out to fill it full of water; and behold, there came a voice saying, "Hail, highly favored one! The Lord is with you; you are blessed among women." 2. Mary looked about, to the right and to the left, to see whence this voice might be coming to her. 3. Filled with trembling she went into her house; and putting down the pitcher, she took the purple and sat down on a chair and drew out the purple thread.

4. Behold, an angel of the Lord stood before her, saying, "Do not fear, Mary, for you have found favor before the Lord of all, and you will conceive by his Word." 5. Mary, having heard this, considered to herself, saying, "Shall I conceive by the Lord, the living God? As all women do, shall I give birth?" 6. And behold, the angel appeared, saying to her, "Not thus, Mary, for the power of God will overshadow you; therefore also that holy thing which is born shall be called Son of the Most High. 7. You shall call his name Jesus, for he shall save the people from their sins." Then Mary said, "Behold the servant-girl of the Lord is before him. 8. Let it be to me according to your word."

12.1. She worked the purple and the scarlet and brought them to the priest; and the priest blessed her and said, "Mary, the Lord God has blessed your name, and you will be blessed among all the families of the earth."

2. Mary, full of joy, went to her kinswoman Elisabeth and knocked on the door. Elisabeth, hearing (her), put down the scarlet and ran to the door and opened it to her; 3. and she blessed her and said, "How is it that the mother of the Lord should come to me? For behold, that which is in me leapt and blessed you." 4. But Mary forgot the mysteries of which the angel Gabriel spoke; and she looked up toward heaven and said, "Who am I that, behold, all the families of the earth bless me?" 5. She remained three months with Elisabeth. Day by day her womb became larger; Mary, becoming fearful, came to her house and hid herself from the children of Israel. 6. Now she was sixteen[1] years old when these strange events happened to her.

13.1 It came to be the sixth month for her, and behold, Joseph came from his buildings; and he came into his house and found her pregnant. 2. He struck his face and threw himself to the ground on the sackcloth and wept bitterly, saying, 3. "With what sort of countenance shall I look to the Lord God? What shall I pray concerning this maiden? For I received her a virgin from the Temple of the Lord God, and I did not guard her. 4. Who is he who has deceived me? Who did this evil thing in my house and defiled her? 5. Is not the story of Adam summed up in me? For just as Adam was in the hour of his giving glory to God and the serpent came and found Eve alone and deceived her, thus it has also come about for me."

6. Joseph arose from the sackcloth and called Mary and said to her, "Having been cared for by God, why did you do this, forgetting the Lord your God? 7. Why have you humbled your soul, you who were

[1]The manuscripts give Mary's age variously from twelve to seventeen years. The oldest, as well as the largest number, of the manuscripts have sixteen.

nurtured in the Holy of Holies and who received food from the hand of an angel?"

8. She wept bitterly, saying, "I am pure, and I do not know a man." Joseph said to her, "Whence then is this which is in your womb?" 9. She said, "As the Lord my God lives, I do not know whence it came to me."

14.1. Then Joseph feared greatly and stopped talking with her, considering what he would do with her. 2. Joseph said, "If I should hide her sin, I will be found disputing with the law of the Lord; 3. if I show her to the children of Israel, I am afraid lest that which is in her is angelic and I shall be found delivering innocent blood to the judgment of death. 4. What therefore shall I do with her? Shall I put her away secretly from me?"

5. Night came upon him; behold an angel of the Lord appeared to him in a dream, saying, "Do not fear this child, for that which is in her is from the Holy Spirit. 6. She will bear a son, and you shall call his name Jesus, for he will save his people from their sins." 7. Then Joseph arose from his sleep and glorified the God of Israel who had given to him this favor; he guarded the child.

15.1. Now Annas, the scribe, came to Joseph and said to him, "Joseph, why have you not appeared in our assembly?" Joseph said to him, "Because I was weary from my journey, and I rested the first day."

2. Annas turned and saw Mary pregnant; and he came running to the priest and said to him, "Joseph, to whom you have borne witness, has acted very lawlessly." 3. The priest said, "What is this?" Annas answered, "The virgin whom Joseph received from the Temple of the Lord he has defiled; 4. he married her secretly and did not reveal it to the children of Israel." 5. The priest said to him, "Joseph did these things?" Annas responded, "Send attendants, and you will find the virgin pregnant."

6. The attendants went forth and found her as he said; and they brought her into the sanctuary, and she stood at the tribunal. 7. The priest said to her, "Mary, why did you do this? Why did you humble your soul, forgetting the Lord your God? 8. You who were nurtured in the Holy of Holies, and received food from the hand of an angel, and heard their hymns, and danced before the Lord—why did you do this?" 9. But Joseph said, "As the Lord God lives, I am pure regarding her." 10. Then the priest said, "Do not bear false witness, but tell the truth. You married her secretly and did not reveal it to the children of Israel; 11. you did not incline your head beneath the Mighty Hand so that your seed might be blessed." And Joseph was silent.

16.1. The priest then said, "Give back the virgin whom you received from the Temple of the Lord." Joseph began to weep. 2. The priest went on, "I will give you to drink the water of the Lord's testing, and it will make your sins manifest in your eyes."[2]   3. Taking it, the priest gave Joseph to drink and sent him into the desert; and he came back whole. He also gave the child to drink and sent her into the desert; 4. She also returned whole. 5. And all the people wondered, since their sin did not appear in them.

6. The priest said, "If the Lord God did not make your sin manifest, neither will I judge you"; and he released them. 7. Then Joseph took Mary and went into his house, rejoicing and glorifying the God of Israel.

17.1. Now there came an order from Augustus the emperor for all who were in Bethlehem of Judea to be enrolled. 2. Joseph said, "I will enroll my sons, but this child—what shall I do with her? How shall I enroll her? As my wife? I am ashamed to do so. As my daughter? 3. The children of Israel know that she is not my daughter. This day of the Lord he will do as he wishes."

4. He saddled his donkey and set her upon it; his son led, and Samuel followed. 5. They drew near to Bethlehem—they were three miles distant—and Joseph turned and saw Mary looking gloomy, and he said, "Probably that which is in her is distressing her." 6. Once again Joseph turned and saw her laughing, and he said, 7. "Mary, how is it that I see your face at one moment laughing and at another time gloomy?" She said to Joseph, 8. "It is because I see two peoples with my eyes, the one weeping and mourning, the other rejoicing and glad."

9. They were in the midst of the journey, and Mary said to him, "Joseph, take me down from the donkey, for that which is in me is ready to be born." 10. He took her down from the donkey and said to her, "Where shall I take you to shelter your shame? For the place is desolate."

18.1. He found there a cave, and he brought her in and placed his sons beside her. Then he went out to seek a Hebrew midwife in the country of Bethlehem.

2. [Now I, Joseph, was walking about, and I looked up and saw the heaven standing still, and I observed the air in amazement, and the birds of heaven at rest. 3. Then I looked down at the earth, and I saw a vessel lying there, and workmen reclining, and their hands were in the vessel. 4. Those who were chewing did not chew, and those who were lifting did not lift up, and those who were carrying to their mouths did not carry, but all faces were looking upward. 5. I saw sheep standing still, and the shepherd raised his hand to strike them, and his hand remained up. 6. I observed the streaming river; and I saw the mouths of the kids at the water, but they were not drinking. 7. Then suddenly all things were driven in their course.]

[2]See Numbers 5:11–31.

19.1. Finding a midwife, he brought her. They came down from the mountain, and Joseph said to the midwife, 2. "Mary is the one who was betrothed to me, but she, having been brought up in the Temple of the Lord, has conceived by the Holy Spirit." And she went with him. 3. They stood in the place of the cave, and a dark cloud was overshadowing the cave. The midwife said, "My soul is magnified today, for my eyes have seen a mystery: a Savior has been born to Israel!" 4. And immediately the cloud withdrew from the cave, and a great light appeared in the cave so that their eyes could not bear it. 5. After a while the light withdrew, until the baby appeared. It came and took the breast of its mother Mary; and the midwife cried out, "How great is this day, for I have seen this new wonder!"

20.1. The midwife went in and placed Mary in position, and Salome examined her virginal nature; and Salome cried aloud that she had tempted the living God—"and behold, my hand falls away from me in fire." Then she prayed to the Lord.

2. Behold, an angel of the Lord appeared, saying to Salome, "Your prayer has been heard before the Lord God. Come near and take up the child, and this will save you." 3. She did so; and Salome was healed as she worshiped. Then she came out of the cave. 4. Behold, an angel of the Lord spoke, saying, "Salome, Salome, do not report what marvels you have seen until the child has come into Jerusalem."[3]

21.1. And behold, Joseph was prepared to go into Judea. Now there arose a tumult in Bethlehem of Judea, for Magi came saying, "Where is the king of the Jews? For we saw his star in the East, and we have come

---

[3]There is also a more elaborate version of ch. 20 which is found in most of the later manuscripts:

The midwife went in and said, "Mary, get yourself in position, for a great deal of controversy surrounds you." Then Salome tested her virginal nature with her finger; and Salome cried out and said, "Woe is my lawlessness and my faithlessness, for I have tempted the living God. And behold, my hand falls away from me in fire."

Then she bowed her knees before the Lord, saying, "God of my fathers, remember me, for I am seed of Abraham and Isaac and Jacob. Do not expose me to contempt to the children of Israel, but return me to the needy. For you know, O Lord, that I accomplished my healings in your name, and I received my pay from you."

And behold, an angel of the Lord appeared, saying to Salome, "The Lord heard your prayer. Bring your hand near to the child and take him up, and it will be to you salvation and joy." Salome, overjoyed, came to the child, saying, "I will worship him, I will take him up, and I will be healed, for a great king is born to Israel." Immediately Salome was healed; and she came out of the cave justified. And behold, there came a voice saying to her, "Salome, Salome, do not report what marvels you have seen in Bethlehem until the child comes to Jerusalem."

to worship him." 2. Herod, hearing this, was terrified. He sent attendants and summoned them, and they explained clearly to him concerning the star.

3. The Magi departed, and behold, they saw a star in the East, and it preceded them until they came into the cave and stood at the head of the child. 4. Then the Magi, seeing the child with its mother Mary, brought forth gifts from their leather pouches: gold, frankincense, and myrrh. But having been warned by an angel, they went away by a different route into their own land.

22.1. When Herod realized that he had been deceived by the Magi, in his wrath he sent his murderers, telling them to kill all the babies two years old and under. 2. Mary, hearing that they were killing the babies, was frightened, and she took the child and wrapped him and placed him in a cow stable.

3. Now Elisabeth, hearing that Herod sought John, took him and went up into the mountain. She looked around for a place where she might hide him, but there was no place. 4. Then Elisabeth groaned, saying in a loud voice, "Mountain of God, receive a mother with her child"—for Elisabeth was unable to ascend. 5. And immediately the mountain opened up and it received her. That mountain appeared to her as a light, for an angel of the Lord was with them, protecting them.

23.1. Herod sought John, and he dispatched attendants to the altar to Zacharias, saying to him, "Where have you hidden your son?" 2. He answered, saying to them, "I am a ministering servant of God, and I serve in the Temple. How do I know where my son is?" The attendants went away and reported all these things to Herod.

3. Angered, Herod said, "His son is going to be king in Israel." Again he sent the attendants, saying to him, "Tell me the truth! Where is your son? You know that you are at my mercy." 4. The attendants went forth and reported these things to Zacharias. In answer he said, "I am a witness of God; pour out my blood. 5. The Lord will receive my spirit, for it is innocent blood you are shedding at the doorway of the Temple of the Lord." 6. About daybreak Zacharias was murdered, and the children of Israel did not know how he was murdered.

24.1. But at the hour of the salutation, the priests went in, and the blessing of Zacharias did not meet them as was customary. 2. The priests stood waiting for Zacharias to greet them in prayer and to glorify the most high God. When he failed to come they were all afraid. 3. But a certain one of them, getting up his courage, went into the sanctuary and saw by the altar of the Lord dried blood; 4. and a voice said, "Zacharias has been murdered, and his blood will not be wiped away until his avenger comes."

5. When he heard these words he was afraid, and he came out and

reported to the priests what he had seen and heard. 6. They took courage and went in, and they saw what had taken place; 7. and the wall panels of the Temple cried aloud, and they split in two from top to bottom. 8. They did not find his corpse, but they found his blood, which had become like stone.

9. They were filled with fear, and they went out and reported that Zacharias had been murdered. All the tribes of the people heard it, and they mourned and lamented him three days and three nights.

10. Now after the three days, the priests deliberated on whom they would set up in the place of Zacharias, and the lot fell on Simeon. This was the one to whom it had been revealed by the Holy Spirit that he would not see death until he saw Christ in the flesh.

25.1. Now I, James, who wrote this history in Jerusalem, there having arisen a clamor when Herod died, withdrew myself into the desert until the tumult in Jerusalem ceased. 2. Now I glorify the Lord who gave me the wisdom to write this history. And grace will be with all who fear the Lord. Amen.

Part 2

GREEK, JEWISH, AND ROMAN PARALLELS ILLUSTRATING THE MILIEU OF THE GOSPELS

Part 2 is a collection of excerpts from a wide variety of religious traditions contemporaneous with early Christianity. The theme of this collection might well be the statement of Justin Martyr quoted in the Introduction, "We (Christians) introduce nothing new (about Jesus Christ) beyond (what the Greeks say) regarding those whom you call sons of Zeus" (above p. 16). We have broadened the scope somewhat to include Jewish and Roman material as well. Numerous Savior Gods are represented, but also other material. The idea has been to combine the parallels in sections roughly corresponding to the major parts of the gospel narratives in the New Testament.

The Sacred History of Asklepios

Introduction: Sometime during the second century A.D. an unknown author in Memphis, Egypt, undertook to translate an ancient Egyptian sacred scroll into Greek. Apparently, the sacred history had to do with the Egyptian healing God Imouthes, whom the Greeks identified with Asklepios. This Imouthes differed from most Egyptian deities in that he was part human, part divine; i.e., his father was the God Ptah, but he had a human mother. The original spelling of his name was Imhotep, and he was the famous Grand Vizier, architect and physician of Pharoah Zoser (c. 2700 B.C.).

The fragment given here is all that exists of this book, i.e., its preface. The king Nectaneibis mentioned at the outset was a king well-known to the Greeks, having been the last independent ruler of Egypt (c. 380–363 B.C.).

Who the "I" of the third paragraph was is unknown. However, he apparently had found a very ancient scroll and the "mighty miracles" described in it seemed to him to be similar to those performed by the Greek God Asklepios. Consequently, he desired to translate—or rather to *paraphrase*—its contents to the glory of Asklepios. It is for this reason that he prefaces his translation with a personal experience of healings by Asklepios to authenticate his spiritual preparedness to undertake this great task.

The selection is of prime importance for several reasons. First many terms familiar to us from early Christian literature are also found here: kerygma, divine scripture, holy book, prophecy, myth, etc. Secondly, this is a rare case of a *translation* of a sacred scripture into a foreign tongue (although one might well ask which religion, Egyptian or Greek, is really being "proclaimed"). Third, this shows quite vividly how this kind of task was approached at least by this man—he had to be certain he was inspired, and, once he had satisfied himself of this, he unhesitatingly passed on to the reader the evidence of his divine inspiration. Fourth, it is obvious that what he was "translating" into Greek was in fact a much abbreviated, stylistically improved *paraphrase* of the original, and not at all a slavish translation. In other words, it was clearly part of his idea of "divine inspiration" to depart from the original wording whenever and wherever considerations of simplicity and clarity required it—always under the guidance of Asklepios himself, of course. The author clearly thought he was getting across the gist of the original, and that was his primary consideration. One might recall at this point

Josephus' monumental job of abbreviating and paraphrasing the Hebrew scripture in his *Antiquities of the Jews* (though probably he was not translating). Again, if Damis's notebooks actually existed, Philostratus had something of the same task in boiling them down into elegant literary Greek. Conversely, it would prove exceedingly difficult to reconstruct the source material from these writers' final products, it had been so heavily rewritten. Such, for instance, seems to be the case with the Gospel of John.

Papyrus Oxyrhynchus 1381

". . . When Necteneibis heard this he also became exceedingly furious at those (priests) who had deserted the temple (of Asklepios). Therefore, he wished to determine quickly the (original) number (of priests) from the writing, so he ordered Nechautis, who served at that time as Archdicast (Head Judge?), to search through the book (which had been found), taking no more than a month if possible. But he pursued it very zealously so that he provided (the list) for the king, having spent only two days instead of thirty.

When the king read it he was amazed indeed at the divinity (*theia*) of the history (*historia*), and when he discovered that there had been twenty-six priests who had escorted the God's statue from Heliopolis to Memphis, he distributed to their descendants the (position of) prophecy befitting each one. Not only that, after he had restored (the condition of) the book, he enriched Asklepios himself with 330 more *arurae* of tillable cornfields, especially when he heard through the book that the God had been particularly resorted to in worship by Pharoah Mencheres.

Now I often began the translation of this same book into the Greek tongue (without success) when I finally learned how to make it known (*keryxai*). But then in the midst of pouring forth my words, my eagerness was restrained by the greatness of the story (*historia*) because I was about to (unlawfully) take it (to give to those) outside (Greek unclear), for to the Gods alone but not to mortals (is it permitted) rightly to describe (*diegeisthai*) the powers (*dynamai*) of the Gods. For if I failed, not only would I be disgraced before men but also (warnings-oracles descending (from above) prevented me . . . [text has a break here]. . . . through his anger and his immortal virtue (assisting) my weakness to complete the writing. But if I succeeded, my life would be happy and my fame undying. For the God (Asklepios) is always ready to help (as we can see by the fact that) he often saves people after all medical efforts have failed to (liberate them) from the diseases binding them, if only they turn to him in worship, however briefly.

On this account, then, I fled from my rashness and restrained myself until the right moment in old age. For I was delaying in (making good) my promise[1] since youth especially is apt to be indiscreet when its enthusiasm rises quickly and aggressiveness leads the way to sieze the thing wanted. When a period of three years had elapsed during which I was still not sick, but during which the God made (his punishment) fall on my mother, afflicting her with quartan fever or chills (malarial fever), at length we came to our senses and appeared before the God entreating him to grant my mother recovery from the disease. He who is kind (*chrēstos*) toward all in every way appeared to her in dreams and cured her by simple remedies while we returned fitting thanks through sacrifices to our Savior. When I also was suddenly afflicted not long after with a pain in my right side, I quickly hastened to the helper of human nature and again he was more than ever prepared to bestow his mercy (upon me), demonstrating more effectively his unique power for good (*euergesia*), which I would give my personal testimony to at this point before I announce (*apangello*) his frightening powers (in the book translated below).

It was night when every living thing except those in pain is asleep but when the supernatural (*to theion*) manifests itself more effectively. An exceedingly hot fever burned me and I was convulsed with pain in my side because of constant coughing and choking. Groggy from suffering, I was lying there half-asleep and half-awake, being tended by my mother as if I were still a baby for she is by nature affectionate. She was sitting (by my bed) extremely grieved at my agony and not able to get even a little sleep, when suddenly she saw—it was no dream or sleep for her eyes were open immovably, although (admittedly) she was not seeing very distinctly since a supernatural and terrifying vision (*phantasia*) came to her which easily prevented her from observing the God (Asklepios) himself or his servants, whichever it was. In any case, it was someone of superhuman size, clothed in shining linen and carrying a book in his left hand. He only examined me from head to foot two or three times and then vanished. When she had recovered, still quaking (with fear) she tried to rouse me. But she discovered that my fever was gone and sweat was pouring off of me, so she gave glory to the God for his appearance and dried me off and woke me up. Now when she began to tell me of the virtue (*aretē*) of the God just revealed, I interrupted her and announced (*apangello*) everything to her first, for what she had seen through her vision I had imagined through dreams. The pain in my side had abated, for the God had given me still one more healing cure, so I

[1] He must have promised this translation to Asklepios in an earlier part of the text now missing.

proclaimed (*kēryssō*) his benefits (*euergesiai*).

But when we were again seeking his favor by offering all the sacrifices we could afford, he demanded, through the priest who was serving him, the fulfillment of the promise I had long before given him. We knew that we did not lack sacrifices or votive offerings, nevertheless we besought him again with these. But after he repeatedly said that he would not be pleased by these but by that which I had sworn previously, I was quite at a loss, for he was subjecting me to the supernatural duty (*to theion chreos*) of (finishing the) book—a task I scarcely took lightly.

However, as soon as Thou recognized, O Master, that I was neglecting Thy divine book (*theia biblos*), I invoked Thy providence and, being filled by Thy divinity (*theiotēs*) I eagerly hastened to the Heaven-sent prize of Thy narrative (*historia*). For I hope to make Thy intention widely known through my prophecy. In fact I have already written a plausible explanation of the story (*mythos*) of the creation of the world (by turning it into) natural concepts (*physikō logō*) closer to the truth.

Throughout the writing I added what was lacking and removed what was superfluous so that I wrote briefly an overly wordy narrative (*diēgēma*) and told once a repetitive story (*allattologos mythos*). Accordingly, O Master, I deem the book to have been finally completed according to Thy kindness and not according to my intention. A writing (*graphē*) such as this suits Thy divinity, O Asklepios, for Thou hast disclosed it! Thou, greatest of Gods and Teacher, shalt be made known by the thanks of all people. For every gift of a votive offering or a sacrifice lasts only for the moment, and immediately perishes, while scripture (*graphē*) is an undying thanks (*athanatos charis*) since it rejuvenates the memory (of God's kindness) again and again. And every Greek tongue shall tell of Thy story (*historia*) and every Greek man shall worship Imouthes of Ptah.

> Come forward, all ye men who are kind and good!
> Depart, ye evil and impious ones!
> Come forward . . . all ye who have
>   by serving the God been healed of diseases!
> Ye who are versed in the knowledge of healing!
> Ye who labor as zealous devotees of virtue!
> Ye who are blessed with a great abundance of good things!
> Ye who have been saved from dangers at sea!
> (All hail!) The saving power (*dynamis sōtērios*)
>   of God is gone out into every place,
> I am about to announce (*apangellō*) his

miraculous appearances, the greatness
of his power and the gifts of his benefits.

(Then the story begins, and after a few sentences the papyrus breaks
off.)

Two Prefaces from Arrian

Introduction: A native of the province of Bithynia, Arrian was born
near the middle of the first century A.D., and eventually rose to become
governor of the province of Cappadocia under Hadrian (emperor A.D.
117–138). He was a student of the Stoic philosopher Epictetus, and
saved for posterity a valuable verbatim transcript of his *Discourses* (see
below, pp. 146ff). He also wrote on historical subjects, most importantly
a narrative describing Alexander the Great's expedition to conquer
Persia. Below are Arrian's own comments on each of these writings.

Arrian, *Letter to Lucius Gellius*

Arrian to Lucius Gellius: greetings.

I did not compose "The Words of Epictetus" as one usually composes
such a book, nor did I myself present them to humanity (i.e., publish
them). I declare that I did not "compose" them at all. Rather, whatever I
heard him say I wrote down verbatim, this writing a memoir
(*hypomnēmata*)[1] to endure for myself, to preserve his thoughts and bold
(speech).

These words are thus an example of remarks such as someone might
make extemporaneously to another; they are not what someone would
write to be read for posterity. As such, I do not know how without my
control or knowledge they fell into men's hands.

To me it is no great concern if I appear incapable of composition; and
to Epictetus it would be no concern at all if someone were to despise his

[1]The Christian gospels are called "memoirs of the apostles" by Justin Martyr, *Apol.* I.
66–67.

words, since he, when he said them, desired nothing other than to excite the thinking of those who heard them to the best things. . . . Farewell.

The Expedition of Alexander, Preface

Wherever Ptolemy the son of Lagos and Aristoboulos the son of Aristoboulos have both written the same things concerning Alexander the son of Philip, these I have written as being completely true.[2] But those things (they wrote) that are not the same, I chose (from one or the other) those things which seemed to me more believable and at the same time more interesting.

Many other writers have written things about Alexander, nor is there anyone about whom more discordant things are written. But to me Ptolemy and Aristoboulos seem more credible to use in my own account because Aristoboulos fought beside King Alexander while Ptolemy besides fighting with him, was king later on, and for him to lie were even more shameful than for Aristoboulos . . . There are still other writings I have used, which contain things that seemed to me to be worth telling, and are not completely incredible. These I included as "rumors about Alexander."

Isocrates

Introduction: Isocrates (c. 436–338 B.C.) was a famous orator of Athens. Evagoras was king of Salamis (435–374/3 B.C.). This panegyric is a model of its type.

Evagoras

King Nikokles, when I saw you honoring the tomb of your father Evagoras not only with many and beautiful offerings, but with dances and music and athletic contests, and yet more with horse and boat races, and letting no one go beyond you, I thought that Evagoras, if there is any perception among the dead as to what happens here, would receive

[2]The men named here were two of Alexander's top generals.

these well and rejoice at seeing the care expressed toward him and your splendor. But still more than any other man he would have joy in someone who could worthily tell of his life's principles and his dangerous deeds. For we find that those among men who love honor and greatness of soul not only want to be praised for such things, but prefer to die gloriously than to live, and they seek glory more than life. They do all in order to leave behind an immortal memory of themselves.

Extravagance does nothing of these things; it is only a sign of wealth. Those who are devoted to music and other contests, some showing their strengths, others their skills, win greater honors for themselves. But the speech which should sufficiently tell of his deeds would make the virtues of Evagoras eternally remembered among all men.

> Isocrates praises the life of Evagoras as an example to the new king, Nikokles. Throughout the oration Isocrates emphasizes that his *encomium* is given so that others may follow Evagoras' life as an example.

Thus, if any men of the past are immortal because of virtue, I believe Evagoras to have become worthy of this gift. The signs of this are that he lived, while here, a life more fortunate and blessed by the Gods than did they.

For the greater number and most famous of the demi-Gods, we shall find, were beset by very great calamities. But Evagoras sustained not only the most marvelous but the most enviable life from its beginning.

What did he lack of complete happiness? He had ancestors who were like those of no other men, unless it was someone who had the same family. And he had such greatness of body and mind over others that he was not only worthy to rule over Salamis but also over all Asia . . . although born a mortal he left behind the immortality of his memory . . .

. . . thus, if any of the poets used hyperbole concerning any man of the past, saying that he was like a God among men or a mortal divinity (*daimōn*), any such things to be said about his character would harmonize, especially in respect to (what is said about Evagoras).

For these reasons, I have set my hand to write this piece; that it would be the very best encouragement to guide you and your children and all the other descendants of Evagoras, if someone were to put together his virtues, adorn them by speech and hand them down to you to study and to pass the time with them.

For we urge men to philosophy by praising others, in order that they may emulate those who are eulogized and they may desire their virtuous lives . . .

The Birth of Plato (1)

Introduction: This author, more a collector of opinions about the philosophical schools than a philosopher himself, lived during the first half of the third century A.D., possibly in Alexandria. His account of the life and teachings of Plato (c. 429–347 B.C.) reflects the enormous veneration felt toward this philosopher in Diogenes' day, including this belief in Plato's miraculous (but hardly virgin) birth, an account which can be found in many other writers from the Roman period.

Diogenes Laertius, *Lives of Eminent Philosophers* 3.1–2, 45

Plato, the son of Ariston and Periktione (or Potone), was an Athenian. His mother's family went back to Solon. He was, moreover, a brother of Dropides, the father of Kritias, the father of Kallaischros, the father of Kritias (one of the Thirty) and Glaukon, the father of Charmides and Periktione, who with Ariston were the parents of Plato, the sixth generation from Solon. Solon, moreover, traced his ancestry back to Neleus and Poseidon. And they say his father's ancestry goes back to Kodros the son of Melanthos, who, according to Thrasylos' account, are descended from Poseidon.

Speusippos,[1] in his writing "The Funeral Feast of Plato," and Klearchos, in his "Encomium on Plato," and Anaxilaides, in the second book "On the Philosophers," all say that there was at Athens a story that when Periktione was ready (to bear children) Ariston was trying desperately but did not succeed (in making her pregnant). Then, after he had ceased his efforts, he saw a vision of Apollo. Therefore he abstained from any further marital relations until she brought forth a child (from Apollo).

And Plato was born, as Apollodoros says in his "Chronology" in the 88th Olympiad, on the seventh day of Thargelion, which was the day the Delians say Apollo was born . . .

Plato's genealogy is here traced back to divine ancestors, through one of the preeminent fathers of Athens. Note also the fixing of the date of birth according to general Greek history (cf. Luke 3:1f.). To show that Diogenes

[1]Plato's nephew, and close friend.

129

Laertius fully intends his reader to understand that Plato was the son of Apollo, let us hear one of the "epitaphs" he composed for Plato:

"If Phoebus[2] did not beget Plato in Greece,
How did he heal men's souls with words?
For as Asklepios, also begotten by Apollo,
Is a physician of the body,
So Plato makes the soul immortal."

The Birth of Plato (2)

Commented on by a Christian

Origen, *Against Celsus* I. 37

It is not absurd to use Greek stories (*historiai*) when talking to Greeks in order that we might not seem to be the only ones to be using such an incredible story (*paradoxēs historia*) as this one (viz., about Jesus' birth from a virgin). For it seemed proper to some people to record—not concerning the ancient histories of the heroes but even of men born rather recently—as if it really happened that Plato was born of (his mother) Amphiktione while (her husband) Ariston was prevented from having sexual intercourse with her until she had given birth to the offspring of Apollo (*ton ex Apollōnos sparenta*). But these stories are really fables (*mythos*). People just fabricate such things as this about a man whom they regard as having greater wisdom and power than most others. So they say he received at the beginning of the composition of his body a superior and more divine sperm, as if this were appropriate for those who surpass ordinary human nature.[1]

---

[1]For further references to Plato's miraculous birth, see H. Chadwick, *Contra Celsum* (Cambridge: Cambridge University Press, 1955), p. 321, note 12.
[2]Phoebus Apollo was worshiped as a God of divine wisdom and bodily health.

The Birth of Alexander the Great

Introduction: Within Alexander's own lifetime, it was widely believed that Olympias, Alexander's mother, had conceived him through the agency of one of the Gods, namely Zeus. Not the ordinary Zeus of the Greek homeland, however, but the exotic Zeus-Ammon, whose world-famous shrine was in faraway Siwa, Cyrene, deep in the Sahara. Writing some four hundred years after his death, Plutarch records the generally accepted account concerning Alexander's true divine origin, but he also included the skeptical minority viewpoint.

Plutarch, *Parallel Lives,* Alexander 2.1–3.2

Alexander was a descendant of Herakles, on his father's side, through Karanos; on his mother's side he was descended from Aikos through Neoptolemos; this is universally believed. It is said that Philip (Alexander's father) was initiated into the mysteries at Samothrace with Olympias (Alexander's mother). He was still a youth and she was an orphan. He fell in love with her and conjoined a marriage, with the consent of her brother, Arumbas.

The bride, before the night in which they were to join in the bridechamber, had a vision. There was a peal of thunder, and a lightning bolt fell upon her womb. A great fire was kindled from the strike, then it broke into flames which flashed everywhere, then they extinguished. At a later time, after the marriage, Philip saw a vision: he was placing a seal on his wife's womb; the engraving on the seal was, as he thought, in the image of a lion. The men charged with interpreting oracles were made suspicious by this vision and told Philip to keep a closer watch on his marital affairs. But Aristander of Telmessus said (the vision meant that) her husband had impregnated her, for nothing is sealed if it is empty, and that she was pregnant with a child whose nature would be courageous and lion-like.

On another occasion, a great snake appeared, while Olympias was asleep, and wound itself around her body. This especially, they say, weakened Philip's desire and tenderness toward her, so that he did not come often to sleep with her, either because he was afraid she would cast spells and enchantments upon him, or because he considered himself discharged from the obligation of intercourse with her because she had become the partner of a higher being.

. . . After the vision (concerning the snake), Philip sent Chairon of

Megalopolis to Delphi (to learn its meaning). He brought an oracle to Philip from Apollo: Philip was henceforth to sacrifice to Zeus-Ammon and worship that God especially. Furthermore, he was to put out the eye which spied on the God through the crack in the door, the God who, in the form of a serpent, had lain with his wife. And Olympias, as Erastosthenes says, when she sent Alexander on the campaign (against the Persians), told him alone the forbidden secret of his conception, ordering him to act worthy of his birth. But others say that she just dismissed him remarking (to her friends), "Alexander never stops lying about me to Hera" (i.e., by claiming Zeus had been unfaithful to Hera, his wife).

The Birth of Augustus

Introduction: Suetonius' *Lives of the Caesars* was published A.D. 121. Although Suetonius is noted for his assiduous collecting of data for his books, he is not usually credited as having a critical faculty when dealing with his material.

Suetonius, *Lives of the Caesars* II.94.1–7

1. . . . It is not out of order to add what came to pass concerning Augustus before he was born, on the very day of his birth, and after, by which one could foretell his great future and continual happiness.
2. Long ago, when a part of the wall of (his home town) Velitrae was struck by a lightning bolt from heaven, it was interpreted that a citizen from Velitrae would rule the world someday. Led by this belief, the Velitrians at once made war on the Roman people, and, after that, they often did so almost to their own extinction. At long last this proved that (the omen) portended the reign of Augustus.
3. Julius Marathus is the authority that, a few months before Augustus was born, a portent occurred in public which warned that nature was about to give birth to a king for the Roman people. The frightened

Senate resolved that no boy born that year should be trained (for public life); those who had pregnant wives, because each applied the prophecy to his own family, took care that the Senate's decree was not really obeyed.

4. In the book, *Theologumenon* by Asclepias of Mendes, I read that when Atia (Augustus' mother) had come in the middle of the night to the solemn rite of Apollo, when her litter had been set in the temple, and while the other women slept (or, went home),[1] she slept. A snake slipped up to her and, after a little while, went out. When she awoke, she purified herself as if coming from her husband's bed. And immediately on her body there appeared a mark colored like a snake, and she could never get rid of it. Therefore, she always avoided the public baths. Augustus was born in the tenth month after this and because of this was considered the son of Apollo.

Atia herself, before she gave birth to him, dreamed that her womb was carried up to the stars and spread out over all the earth and sky. Octavius, the father, dreamed that the radiance of the sun rose from Atia's womb.

5. . . . When Octavius led an army through the remote regions of Thrace, he consulted about his son with barbarian rites in the grove of Father Liber. (Augustus' future reign) was confirmed by the priests, because when the wine was poured on the altar such a great flame shot up that it went beyond the roof of the temple to the sky. Only in the case of Alexander the Great, when he offered a sacrifice on the same altar, did a like portent occur.

6. . . . When Augustus was a baby, as the writing of C. Drusus reports, in the evening his nurse set him in the cradle, which was on the ground floor. The next morning he had disappeared. After a lengthy search, he was found on a very high tower with his face turned toward the sun's radiance.

7. When he first began to talk at his grandfather's country home, he ordered to be silent some frogs who were making a great racket. And from that time, it is said, no frog ever croaked there . . .

---

[1] *dormirent* or *domum irent?*

The Birth and Childhood of Pythagoras

Introduction: It has been said that, one hundred years after his death, around 497 B.C., hardly anyone at Athens still remembered anything of Pythagoras of Samos; seven hundred years later, his followers knew everything about him including the secret recipe of his favorite honey cakes. The author of this account of Pythagoras' ancestry and birth, the Neo-platonic, Syrian philosopher Iamblichus, was just such a follower. Living in the fourth century A.D., he was a vigorous opponent of the newly emerging Christian religion, writing many books on Pythagoras and his teachings.

Iamblichus, *The Life of Pythagoras*, 3–10

3. It is said that Ankaios who lived in Samos in Kephallenia was begotten by Zeus. Whether he received this repute because of virtue or a greatness of soul, he exceeded the wisdom of the other Kephallenians. An oracle was given about him by the Pythian oracle (Apollo of Delphi) to gather a colony from among the Kephallenians and the Arcadians and the Thessalians . . .   4. They say that Mnesarchos and Pythais who were the parents of Pythagoras were descended from this house and were of the family of Ankaios . . .   5. Once when his nobility of birth was being celebrated by the citizens, a certain poet from Samos said he (Pythagoras) was begotten by Apollo . . .

> 5. Iamblichus goes on to show that this is really simply rumor, at least as far as Apollo's physically being the father of Pythagoras is concerned, i.e., by Apollo's impregnating the philosopher's mother. . . .

8. However, the soul of Pythagoras came from the realm of Apollo, either being a heavenly companion or ranked with him in some other familiar way, to be sent down among men; no one can deny this. It can be maintained from his birth and the manifold wisdom of his soul. 9. . . . He was educated so that he was the most beautiful and godlike of those written about in histories. 10. After his father died, he increased in nobility and wisdom. Although he was still a youth, in his manner of humility and piety he was counted most worthy already, even by his elders. Seen and heard, he persuaded everyone (to his way of thinking), and to everyone who saw him he appeared to be astonishing, so that, reasonably, he was considered by many to be the son of a God.

The Birth of Herakles

Introduction: Diodorus' account of the life or deeds (*praxeis*) of Herakles is taken from a lengthy "Universal History" in forty books, written by an otherwise unknown Sicilian historian of the first century B.C. Less than half of the work is still extant. The "Universal History" reflects the Stoic notion of "one world / one society / one humanity." As a result, Diodorus goes back to the origin of the Gods and the creation of the world in his opening books. He then carefully treats the mythical heroes or demigods of each nation (Egypt, Assyria, India, Ethiopia, Atlantis, Greece, etc.) until he comes to more contemporary times.

The object of all this is to demonstrate that all the nations' histories sprang up from the universal activity of Divine Providence for the mutual benefaction of the whole world. Our account comes from Diodorus' treatment of the Greek mythical heroes.

Aware that his readers might be skeptical of his description of Herakles, Diodorus warns his readers not to judge Herakles by their own weaknesses, lest they "forget the good deeds he bestowed upon all humanity, belittling the praise he used to receive for the noblest deeds . . . (and thus) no longer preserve the religious veneration for this God which has been handed down from our fathers."

Diodorus' account of the birth and labors of Herakles probably was greatly dependent upon an earlier writing entitled, *In Praise of Herakles* by Matris of Thebes. Matris lived in Alexandria during the second century B.C.

Diodorus Siculus, *Library of History* 4. 9.1–10

They say that Perseus was the son of Danae, who was the daughter of Akrisios and Zeus. Andromeda, Kepheos' daughter, lay with him (Perseus) and bore Elektryon; then Euridike, daughter of Pelops, cohabited with him (Elektryon) and gave birth to Alkmene. Alkmene was taken by Zeus, through a deceit, and she bore Herakles. Thus, the root of his family tree, through both his parents, is said to go back to the greatest of the Gods (i.e., Zeus), in the way we have shown.

The excellence (*aretē*) begotten in Herakles is not only seen in his great acts (*praxeis*), but was known before his birth. When Zeus lay with Alkmene, he tripled the length of the night, and, in the increased length of time spent in begetting the child, he foreshadowed the exceptional power of the child who was to be begotten. All in all, this union was not

135

done because of erotic desire, as with other women, but more for the purpose of creating the child. Because he wished to make the intercourse legitimate, and he did not wish to take Alkmene by force, nor could he ever hope to seduce her because of her self-control, therefore, he chose deceit. By this means he tricked Alkmene: he became like Amphitryon (her husband) in every way.

When the natural time of pregnancy passed, Zeus, with his mind set upon the birth of Herakles, announced beforehand, with all the Gods present, that he would make the child born that day king of Perseus' descendants. At that Hera became jealous and, using her daughter Eileithyia as her helper, she stopped the labor pains of Alkmene, and brought Eurystheus[1] to light before his full time. Zeus was outwitted, but he wished to confirm his promise and to look ahead to the appearance (*epiphaneia*) of Herakles. Therefore, they say, he persuaded Hera to agree: Eurystheus was to be king, as Zeus promised; but Herakles was to serve under Eurystheus and to complete twelve "labors" which Eurystheus was to devise. When the deeds were done, Herakles was to obtain immortality.

Alkmene gave birth, and, because she was afraid of Hera's jealousy, the child was exposed in a place which to this day is called the Field of Herakles. Now, at the same time, Athena, with Hera, happened to go by and was amazed at the quality of the child. She persuaded Hera to offer her breast. The child sucked on the breast more violently than a normal child, and Hera, suffering great pain, tore the child away from her breast. Athena then took him to his mother and urged her to nurture him . . .

After this, Hera sent two snakes to destroy the baby, but the child did not panic, and he grabbed the neck of each snake in his hands and strangled them.

----

[1] A descendant of Perseus by a different family lineage, and later the king of Argos.

TEACHINGS

Aesop's Fables

Introduction: Everyone knows of Aesop's *Fables,* but no one knows Aesop. There is even some doubt as to the actual existence of Aesop, one of the most widely published authors in Western history. According to legend, Aesop was a slave who lived at Athens in the sixth century B.C. The fables of Aesop probably represent a collection which grew through the centuries. The variety of the contents of the various manuscripts of Aesop's *Fables* demonstrates this. Strictly speaking, a fable is a tale about animals who behave with human attributes. However, the Aesop collection contains other types of story also. Since his animal fables are so familiar, we have included here more of this less-familiar material, as well as a couple lesser-known animal fables. The morals were probably added much later. Therefore, we have listed them separately so that our readers may more easily draw their own morals.

---

1. The Witch-Woman

A witch woman promised many charms and appeasements of religious sins, and she received many payments for her services; from these she made no small living. Because of this, some men accused her of making innovations in the religion; she was dragged to judgment and her accusers succeeded in having her sentenced to death. Someone who saw her as she was led from the courtroom said to her, "Look at you! You promised to appease the wrath of the demons, how is it you cannot persuade men?"

2. Aesop in the Shipyard

Once, Aesop, the fable teller, having some time off, went into a shipyard. The workmen teased him until they provoked him to say, "In olden times there was chaos and water, but Zeus wished to make the element of the earth appear. He ordered that the earth should gulp down the sea three times. The earth began to do so. The first time (she swallowed) and the mountains appeared; then the earth gulped more sea and revealed the plains. If she decides to drink the third time, your boats will be useless!"

3. Prometheus and Mankind

Prometheus created men and beasts at Zeus' order. When Zeus saw that there were many more arational creatures (i.e., beasts) than men, he ordered Prometheus to destroy and to change some of the beasts into men. When Prometheus had carried out this order, the result was that those men who had been transformed from beasts had the form of men but the souls of beasts.

4. The Rich Man and the Tanner

A wealthy man came to live by a leather tanner. Since he could not stand the stink, he constantly urged the tanner to move. The tanner pretended to agree, saying he would move in a little while. After their debate went on for some time, the rich man got used to the stench and it no longer annoyed him.

5. The Money Lover

A money lover turned all his possessions into gold bars. He then buried the treasure by a wall, and continually came and checked on it. A certain workman watched his arrivals carefully and discerned the truth. When the rich man left, he stole the gold. The money lover came and found his cache empty; he cried and wept tearfully. Someone saw him grief-stricken and learned the cause. He said to the hoarder, "Do not grieve. Take the stone cover (of the cache) and put it back in its place and think hard that the gold is still there. You could not use it better when it was really there."

6. The Enemies

Two enemies sailed in the same boat. They wished very much to avoid each other, so the one sat in the bow and the other in the stern, and they stayed there. A great storm came up, and the boat was in grave peril. The man in the stern asked one of the sailors which part of the boat would sink first. The sailor said "the bow." "Now death is no longer a grief for me, for I will get to see my enemy die first," replied the man.

7. The Cat and the Birds

A cat heard that there were some sick birds in a certain roost, so he disguised himself as a physician and, taking some instruments and medicine, he went there. He stood before the roost and asked them how they were. "Fine," they replied, "if you go away."

(Some tales are attributed to Aesop in a few manuscripts, but are probably spurious. Here are two examples.)

8. The Mule

There was a certain mule who had grown fat from grain. It was enjoying running around (the field) and said to itself, "My father is a fast racehorse, I am in all respects like him." And then one day it was necessary suddenly for the mule to compete in a race. When the race was ended, it had learned that its father was only a jackass.

9. The Man Who Promised the Impossible

A poor man was sick, in very bad shape. Since he was a lost cause as far as the physicians were concerned, he turned to the Gods and promised a costly offering and expensive sacrifices if they would save him. When his wife, who was standing by him, asked, "Where are you going to get all these things?", he replied, "Do you think I intend to get well again in order that the Gods can get all these things from me?"

Morals

1. This story is for cheaters and those who make big promises, since they are revealed as what they are by little things.

2. This tale clearly shows that those who scoff at their betters will get back from them more than they expected.

3. This tale is applicable to crooked and bestial men.

4. This tale clearly shows that familiarity soothes irritations.

5. This tale clearly shows that to own something is worthless if you do not use it.

6. Thus, some men, on account of ill will toward a neighbor, will find some occasion for their own suffering to see the ill fortune of the enemy. Or, this fable shows that many men think nothing of their own injury, if they only can see their enemy come to harm before them.

7. Thus, the evils of men are clear to wise men, even if the evildoers make a disguise of being good.

8. This tale shows clearly that it is necessary, if the circumstances bring something to mind, not to forget one's origin; for this life is uncertain.

9. This tale shows clearly that men make promises easily which they have no intention of keeping.

Rabbinic Parables

Introduction: A parable is usually a brief and easily understood narative which either makes or illustrates a point. Most rabbinic parables are exegetical, intended either directly to explain a scriptural passage (1) or to illustrate an interpretation already given (2 and 3).

---

1. "Thus the people cried out to Moses" (Num. 11:2).—But what had Moses done? Would it not have been more appropriate to say "And the people cried out to God?" Thus why does the passage say, "And the people cried out to Moses?" R. Shime'on says: "There is a parable. To what can this be compared? To the case of a human king who was angry with his son. That son went to his father's friend and said to him: 'Go and plead for me before my father.' Thus Israel went to Moses and said to him: 'Plead for us before God' " (Sifre Num. 86).

2. "Happy are you, O Israel" (Deut. 33:29).—All Israel gathered together before Moses, and they said to him: "Moses, our Master, tell us what good the Holy One, blessed be he, is about to give to us in the coming eternity." He said to them: "I do not know what further to say to you. Happy are you in the way prepared for you." It is like the case of a man who turned his son over to a tutor. He (the tutor) was taking him around and showing him, and he said to him: "All these trees are yours, all these grapevines are yours, all these olive trees are yours." When he grew tired of showing him, he said to him: "I do not know what further to say to you. Happy are you in the way that is prepared for you." Thus Moses said to Israel: "I do not know what further to say to you. Happy are you in the way that is prepared for you: 'How abundant is thy goodness, which thou hast laid up for those who fear thee' " (Ps. 31.19; Sifre Deuteronomy 356).

3. Another interpretation of "the mind of Pharaoh and his servants was changed toward the people" (Exod. 14:5).—They said: "Has not much good come to us because of them (the Israelites)?" R. Yose the Galilean says: "There is a parable. To what can this be compared? To the case of a man who inherited a field and who sold it for a pittance. The buyer went and opened up wells in it, and he planted in it gardens, trees, and orchards. The seller then began to be choked with grief. Thus it happened to the Egyptians who sent (the Israelites) out without

knowing what they sent out. Concerning them there is an explicit statement in the traditional writings: 'Those whom you sent out are an orchard of pomegranates,'" etc. (Song of Solomon 4:13; Mekilta Beshallah 2).

Sayings of Thales, Aristippos, and Aristotle

Diogenes Laertius, *Lives of Eminent Philosophers* 1.35–37; 2.68–81; 5.17–18

Thales, c. 636–546 B.C., Philosopher; One of the Seven Sages

1. 35. He said there is no difference between life and death. Someone said, "Then, why do you not die?" "Because," he said, "there is no difference." 36. To the question as to which is prior, night or day, he said, "Night is one day older." Someone asked him if a man who did evil could escape from the Gods. "Not even one who thinks evil," he said. To the adulterer who asked if he should deny that he committed adultery, he said, "Perjury is no worse than adultery." He was asked what is difficult to bear? He said, "To know oneself." What is most easy to bear? "To advise someone else." What is most pleasant? "To succeed at something." What is divine? "That which has neither a beginning nor a completion." What was the strangest thing he had seen? He said, "An old dictator." How can someone best bear troubles? "If he should see his enemies faring worse." How may we live a most excellent and just life? "If we do not do what we accuse others of doing." 37. Who is happy? "The man who has a healthy body, a resourceful soul, and a well-trained nature." He said to remember friends both present and absent, not to be pretentious about appearance, but to be beautiful in the pursuits of life. "Do not gain riches by evil means," he said, "and do not let a word cause you to distrust those who have joined with you in trust." "You may expect from your children the same kindnesses you show to your parents."

Aristippos, c. 450–365 B.C.
Companion of Socrates; Professional Rhetorician

2. 68. Diogenes (the Cynic), who was washing his vegetables, saw him going by and said, "If you learned to stomach these, you would not have to flatter the courts of tyrants." Aristippos replied, "If you knew how to get along with people, you would not be washing vegetables." He was asked what advantage he had gotten from philosophy; he said, "To be able to get along confidently with everyone." Once he was castigated for his rich living. "If this is wrong," he said, "luxury would not be found at the feasts of the Gods" (i.e., with their permission). Once he was asked what advantage philosophers have; he said, "If all the laws are repealed, we shall live as we do now."
69. . . . Once he was going into the house of a courtesan. When one of the youths with him blushed, he said, "It is not entering that is troublemaking, but being unable to come out." 70. Someone showed him a very difficult riddle and said, "Solve it." "You idiot," he said, "why do you want me to solve it? It gives us enough trouble as it is." He said, "It is better to be a beggar than to be uneducated; the beggars must have money, the others need to be made human" . . .   71. Once he sailed for Corinth. A great storm came up and he was very afraid. Someone said to him, "We common people are not afraid, why are you, a philosopher, so afraid?" "You and I are not frightened for comparable lives," he said . . .   74. He said, to someone who accused him of living with a whore, "Is there a difference between living in a house in which many have lived, or in which no one has lived?" The questioner said, "No." He continued, "What is the difference between sailing in a ship in which ten thousand have sailed, or in which no one has sailed?" "No difference." "Then," he said, "there is no difference between living with a woman many have used or one no one has used."
81. A prostitute told him, "I am pregnant by you." "You no more know that," he said, "than if after running through the bushes you knew which one stuck you." Someone accused him of casting out his son just as if he were not his own child. He said, "Phlegm and lice we know are from our own begetting, but, because they are useless, we throw them as far away as we can."

Aristotle, 384–322 B.C.
Philosopher and Scientist

5. 17. When he was asked what is the gain for those who tell lies, he said, "When they speak the truth, no one believes them." He was once rebuked because he gave money to an evil man, "It was not his life-style, but the man I pitied." He constantly said to his friends and students, whenever and wherever he lectured, that, as sight takes in the light from the (air) around it, so does the soul from mathematics. Many times and lengthily he said the Athenians discovered both wheat and laws, but they used the wheat, not the laws.

18. He said, "The roots of education are bitter, but the fruit is sweet." He was asked what ages very quickly. "Gratitude," he said. Having been asked what hope is, he said, "A dream by one who is awake." When Diogenes wished to give him some dried figs, he knew, if he did not take them, Diogenes would have ready a witty put-down, so he took the figs and said that Diogenes had lost both the figs and the witticism. Another time, when some figs were offered, he took them, held them up as you do with children, and said, "Diogenes is terrific!"—and gave them back. He said three things are essential for education; natural ability, study, training. He heard that he was being slandered by someone. "He may even whip me," he said, "in my absence."

Sayings of Alexander and Others

Introduction: The Greek biographer and historian, Plutarch, amassed an enormous amount of information about all sorts of famous Greek, Roman, and foreign people. Two of his most famous publications were a multi-volume collection of miscellaneous sayings, observations, and bits of lore, Greek and Roman, called *Morals.* A second, much more ambitious work, was his *Parallel Lives of Greeks and Romans,* containing some fifty matched biographies. In the earlier writing, the *Morals,* Plutarch had several collections of famous sayings: "Sayings of Kings," "Sayings of Romans," "Sayings of Spartans," and "Sayings of Spartan Women." Here is a brief excerpt illustrating this kind of literature.

Alexander the Great (Plutarch, *Morals* 179D–181F)

179D. While Alexander was still a child and Philip was accomplishing many things, Alexander was not happy but said to his playmates, "My father will leave nothing for me (to do)." The boys said, "He is getting all this for you." "What good is this," he said, "if I have many things, but do nothing?"

He was quick and fast, and his father said that he ought to run in the Olympics. "I would run," he said, "if I were going to have kings as opponents."

179E. A young girl was brought to him in order that she would sleep with him. He asked her, "Why have you come at this (late) hour?" She said, "I had to wait until my husband went to bed." He bitterly reproached his servants, because he had nearly become an adulterer because of them.

Once he was offering incense to the Gods lavishly and picking up handfuls of the frankincense (to throw into the fire). Leonidas, his teacher, who was there, said, "My boy, you may offer incense in this lavish way when you conquer the land which supplies the frankincense." When Alexander conquered the land, he sent a letter to Leonidas, "I have sent you one hundred talents[1] of frankincense and cassia, so that you no longer will be stingy toward the Gods, since you know that we have conquered the land which produces these fragrances."

180B. Once, all was ready for battle and his generals asked him what else they should do. "Nothing," he said, "except to shave the Macedonians' beards." Parmenio was astonished at this strange order. "Do you not know," Alexander said, "that there is nothing better to grab hold of in a battle than a beard?"

180C. Darius (begged for peace and) offered him 10,000 talents and also half of Asia Minor. Parmenio said, "If I were Alexander, I would (not fight any more but) take it." "So would I, by God," he said, "if I were Parmenio." But he answered Darius that the earth could not stand two suns nor Asia two kings.

180E. One of Alexander's (more stingy) friends was entertaining him during a cold winter. The host brought in a small brazier with a tiny fire in it. Thereupon Alexander ordered him to bring either firewood or frankincense.

180F. Once Antipatrides brought a beautiful harp player to dinner. Alexander fell in love with her at first sight. He asked Antipatrides if he was in love with her, too. He confessed that he was. "You louse," said Alexander, "get her away from the party immediately."

181D. Once (Alexander's forces encountered) a king who held a rock fortress which seemed to be unconquerable, but he nevertheless surrendered himself and his fortress to Alexander. Thereupon Alexander ordered him to continue to rule and actually gave him more land, saying, "The man seems to me to be wise, entrusting himself to a good

[1]Approximately $100,000 value.

man rather than to a fortified place."

181E. He sent fifty talents to Xenocrates, the philosopher. The latter would not accept them, saying he did not need the money. Alexander asked if Xenocrates did not have a friend (who wanted it), and said, "In my case, all the wealth of Darius was scarcely enough for my friends."

181F. When he was dying, he looked at (all) his companions, "I see that my funeral will be a big one," he observed.

Miscellaneous

172B. Artaxerxes, the Persian king . . . considered it as much the attribute of a king and lover of mankind to accept small gifts graciously and eagerly as to give great gifts to others. So, when he was once traveling down a road, a laborer, having nothing else of his own, took water from the river with his two hands and offered it to the king. Artaxerxes accepted it happily and smiled. It is by the eagerness of the giver, not by the usefulness of the gift, that the favor is measured.

173B. Semiramis[2] erected a tomb for herself and inscribed on it, "Any king who has need of money, let him break into this tomb to take whatever he wishes." Darius, therefore, broke into it. He found no money, but he did find another inscription there which said, "If you were not an evil and greedy man, you would not be disturbing the resting place of the dead."

175C. Hiero[3] was reviled by someone because he had bad breath and asked his wife why she had not told him about it. She said, "I thought all men smelled that way."

Epictetus

Introduction: Epictetus was a famous Stoic philosopher, who lived during the late first and early second century in Rome. In this selection from his Discourses, he describes different aspects of the divine mission of the Stoic "scout." (For the prefaces of these memoirs, see above, pp. 125f.)

---

[2]Mythical queen of Assyria, and founder of ancient Babylon.
[3]King of Syracuse, 478–467 B.C.

Arrian, *Discourses of Epictetus* 3.22.1 ff

1. One of (Epictetus') acquaintances who seemed to lean toward the Cynic's calling, asked, "What kind of man ought a Cynic be, and what is the basic conception of his vocation?" Epictetus said, "We will look closely at this at leisure. 2. I can tell you this, the man separated from God who takes up so great a calling is hateful to God, and he wishes (for himself) nothing other than public disgrace. 3. For no one in a well-run household comes along and says to himself, 'I ought to manage this house.' If he does, the lord of the house, when he turns and sees him pompously giving orders, will drag him out and squeeze him dry.

4. "It is the same way also in this great city (the world). There is also here a Lord of the house who gives orders to each. 5. You are the sun. You are able to circle the heavens, to make years and to nourish and to make the crops grow. You can move the winds and calm them, and to give even warmth to human bodies. Arise, orbit and thus move everything from the greatest to the tiniest.

"You are a calf. When a lion appears, do what is yours to do. If you do not, you will lament.

6. "You are a bull, come and fight. For this is given to you; it fits your being, and you are able to do it.

7. "You can lead the army against Ilium; be Agamemnon. You can fight Hector; be Achilles. 8. But if Thersites had come along and assumed command, he would not have got it, or he would have shamed himself before a host of witnesses.

9. "So you consider your vocation carefully; it is not what it seems to you, 10. (who says) 'I wear a hair cloak now, and I shall continue to do so. I have a hard bed now, and I shall continue to sleep on it. I shall carry a bag and a staff, and I shall start to wander around and beg from those I meet—and revile them. If I see someone using a depilatory or with a fancy haircut or walking around in scarlet, I will remonstrate with him.'

11. "If you imagine the calling to be like this, get far away from it. Do not approach it; it is not for you.

12. "But if your imagination is correct, and you do not consider yourself unworthy, consider the greatness of the calling which you are taking in hand.

13. "First, you must completely change everything about you from your current practices, and you must blame neither God nor man. You must obliterate yearnings and turn your tendencies toward moral considerations alone. You must never feel wrath, nor anger, nor envy, nor pity; no little girl should seem pretty to you, nor should a petty reputation, nor a little boy as a lover, nor little sweet cakes. 14. You need to know

this: other men have the cover of their walls and houses and the darkness when they make use of these things, and they have many secrets. A man closes the door, stations someone outside the bedroom (and says), 'if someone comes, tell him, "he is gone out, or he is not at leisure." '

15. "But the Cynic, opposed to all this, ought to be protected by his own honor; if he does not, he will be shamed naked and in the open. This is his house, his door; this is the guard before his bedroom; this his darkness. 16. He should not want to hide anything of himself—lest, if he does, he should destroy the Cynic, do away with the open man, the free man; he has begun to fear externals; he has begun to have need of his concealment—nor if he wishes, should he be able to do so. Where will he hide himself, or how?

17. "If by chance this instructor of the masses, this 'professor' be exposed, what must he suffer? 18. Can one who is afraid of all this continue with his whole soul to oversee other men? It cannot be done; it is impossible.

19. "First, you must make pure the governing principle of your life, and have this plan: 20. 'From now on, my mind is my raw material, as wood is to the builder, as leather to the shoemaker. My job is to use my information correctly. 21. My body means nothing to me; its parts are nothing to me. Death? Let it come when it will, either the death of all or a part of me. 22. Exile? To where can anyone expel me? He cannot send me outside the world. Wherever I go, there is the sun, there the moon, there the stars, dreams, omens, communion with the Gods.' "

23. "Next, after he is thus prepared, the true Cynic cannot allow this to suffice, but he must know that he has been sent as a messenger from Zeus to men to show them about good and evil things, that they have strayed off and are looking in the wrong places for the essence of good and evil. They look where it is not; where it is they have no idea. He must be a spy, as Diogenes was when he was taken off to Philip after the battle of Chaironeia. Truly the Cynic spies out what is beneficial and what is harmful to men. He must spy accurately and, when he comes back, he must report truthfully. He must not become panic-stricken, so that he identifies as enemies those that are not, nor in any other way should he be troubled or mixed-up about his information.

53. "Consider carefully. Know yourself. Ask God. Without God, do nothing. If he thus counsels you, be certain that he wants you to become great, or to receive many beatings. For mixed into the Cynic's life is this all too sweet refinement; he must be beaten like a donkey, and, while he is beaten, he must love the floggers as if he were the brother or father of them all. Not you, however. If someone beats you, you go into the middle of the town and shout, 'O Caesar, in your peaceful reign, why do

I suffer? Let us go to the proconsul.' But to a Cynic, what is a Caesar or a proconsul, or anyone else other than he who sent him and whom he serves, namely, Zeus? Does he call on anyone except Zeus?

81. "Friend, (the Cynic) is the father of all men; he has mankind as sons, womankind as daughters. This is the way he comes to all; thus he cares for all. Or do you think he chastises everyone because he is a meddler? He does this as a father, as a brother and as a servant of Zeus, the Father of us all.

95. ". . . every thought he thinks is as a friend and servant to the Gods, as a sharer in the reign of Zeus. He always has this motto before him: 'Lead me on, O Zeus and Destiny!,' (Cleanthes), and, 'if he pleases the Gods, let it be thus' (Plato, *Crito*, 43D). Why should he not be bold so as to speak openly to his own brothers, to his children, succinctly, to his kin?"

Two Stories from Epictetus

Introduction: Epictetus and his students were discussing one day the curious way different people will accept different degrees of bondage to others. Why is there this difference between people? Why do "different people sell themselves at different prices?" Taking off from this point, Epictetus urges his students—who were mostly young men about to enter public affairs—each to discover who he really was and to live his life in a manner appropriate to his own true nature. Likening himself to the purple strip around the border of the toga, which lent grace and beauty to the whole garment and without which it would look quite plain, he told two stories of men who also believed their nature was to stand out against the mass of people.

Arrian, *Discourses of Epictetus* 1.2.19–29

Priscus Helvidius indeed saw this (same point), and having seen it, acted upon it. Once Vespasian sent him an order not to come to the Senate, but he answered, "You have the power not to permit me to be a senator, but as long as I am one, I must come to the meeting." "All right, go, but when you attend, be silent." "Do not call on me during roll call, and I will be silent." "But I have to call the roll." "And I must speak what appears to be right." "But if you speak, I shall kill you." "When, then, did I say to you, 'I am immortal?' You do your job and I will do mine. Yours is to kill, mine to die unafraid. Yours is to banish, mine is to go into exile without grieving."

What of profit did Priscus do, who was just one man? How does the purple strip help the toga? What except to stick out in it as purple and to the rest to be exposed as a good example? Another man in such circumstances, when Caesar told him not to come to the Senate, would have said, "Thank you for excusing me." In fact, Caesar would not have prevented that kind of man from coming, but would have known that either he would sit (silently) like a jug, or, if he spoke, he would say what Caesar wished, and he would pile it on.

A certain athlete once behaved in the same way. He was going to die unless his genitals were amputated. When his brother, who happened to be a philosopher, came to him and said, "Well, brother, what are you going to do? Shall we cut off this part and again go forth (to exercise) in the gymnasium?" He did not submit, but stood firm and died. Someone asked (Epictetus), "How did he do this? As an athlete or as a philosopher?" "As a *man*," Epictetus replied, "a man who had been proclaimed at the Olympics and competed in them, who had lived in such places, not simply had a rubdown at Bato's Wrestling School. Another would have had his neck cut off, if he were able to live without a neck."

Asklepios

Introduction: The origin of the worship of Asklepios as a healing God is unclear, but it seems to have arisen after the time of Homer, who only spoke of him as a mortal physician. Later on, legends concerning his divine origin appeared (his father being considered to have been Apollo), and the central cult temple for his healing activity was Epidauros on the Adriatic Sea, although there were many others. It was the custom for the person healed to record the basic facts of his case on a marble plaque, and leave this at the temple as a memorial. The following accounts are taken from just such plaques, found in the temple at Epidauros. These were inscribed mostly during the fourth century B.C.

The Epidauros Inscriptions

Cleo was pregnant five years. She, already five years pregnant, was brought prostrate in bed to the God as a supplicant. Immediately as she came from him and from the temple, she bore a boy; as soon as he was born, he washed himself in the spring and walked around with the mother. After she had accomplished this, she wrote about it on the votive offering. One should be amazed not at the greatness of the tablet, but at the God. Five years Cleo bore the burden in her womb until she slept in the temple and she became healthy.

A man who had the fingers of the hand crippled except one came to the God as a supplicant. But seeing the tablets in the temple, he disbelieved in the healings and he sneered at the inscriptions. While sleeping he saw a vision. It seemed he was casting the bones (in the crypt) under the temple[1] and as he was about to cast the bones, the God appeared and seized upon the hand and stretched out its fingers. As it turned out, he seemed to bend the hand to stretch out the fingers one by one. When he straightened all of them, the God asked him if he still disbelieved the inscriptions upon the tablets of the temple. He said, "No." Asklepios replied, "Because formerly you did not believe those things which are not unbelievable, may you henceforth be named 'Unbeliever.'" When it was day, he came out, healthy.

[1] I.e., throwing the sacred dice to gain a favorable omen that he would be healed.

Ambrosia from Athens had one good eye. She came, a supplicant, to the God. But, as she walked around the temple of healings, she mocked some things as incredible and impossible, that the lame and blind could be healed at only seeing a dream. While lying there, she saw a vision. It seemed the God stood over her and said to her that he would make her healthy, but it was necessary that she set in the temple a silver pig as a reward, that is, as a remembrance of her stupidity. While saying these things, he cut into the place where her other eye was diseased and poured in some medicine. When it was day, she went out healthy.

There was a child who could not speak. He came to the temple for a voice. He sacrificed and performed the customary rituals. After this, the child, while he was bringing a torch to the God, was commanded, as he was looking at his father, to wait one year, and when he had gotten what he wanted, to come back and offer the thank offering. The child suddenly said, "I will wait." And the father, astonished, ordered him to speak again. He spoke again. From this time he was healed.

Pandaros of Thessaly had brand-marks on his forehead.[2] While he lay there, he saw a dream. It seemed the God bound the brand-marks with a cloth and ordered him, since he was outside the holy ground, to remove the band as an offering to the temple. In the morning, he went forth and removed the band, and his face appeared empty of the brand-marks. He presented the cloth band as an offering to the temple. It had upon it the marks from his forehead.

(This is how) Echedoros received brand-marks from (his fellow slave) Pandor as well as from his master. He took money from Pandor to offer as a gift to the God in Epidauros for him. But he did not make the offering. As he slept he saw a dream. It seemed the God was standing over him and asking if he had some money from Pandor in Athens as a gift to the temple. He denied he received any such thing from him, but said that if he would make him healthy, he would set up a statue to him with an inscription on it. After this the God ordered him to wrap the band of Pandor around his brand-marks, then go out from the holy ground, remove the band and wash his face in the spring and to look at himself in the water. In the morning he went out from the holy place and took off the band; it did not have writing. Looking down into the water he saw his face with its own brand-marks still on it and it had also received the brand-marks of Pandor.

[2]Customarily put on slaves by their owners as a means of identification.

A good omen concerning a child of Epidauros. Suffering from a skin rash he went to sleep. It seemed the God stood over him and said, "What will you give me if I make you well?" He said, "Ten dice throwings." The God laughed and said, "Now stop that!" In the morning he came out healed.

Pythagoras

Introduction: Iamblichos' *Life of Pythagoras,* in addition to a collection of his teachings also employs a traditional collection of miracles said to have been performed by Pythagoras. We here present a few of them to illustrate how this kind of story was used to honor this kind of "divine man."

Iamblichos, *Life of Pythagoras,* 36, 60–61, 134–36

36. At that time (Pythagoras) was going from Sybaris to Krotona. At the shore, he stood with men who were fishing with nets; they were hauling the nets weighed down with fish from the depths. He said that he knew the number of fish they hauled in. The men agreed to do what he ordered if the number of fish was as he said. He ordered the fish to be set free alive after they were indeed counted accurately. What is more astonishing, in the time that they were out of the water being counted, none of the fish died while he stood there. He paid (the fishers) the price of the fish and went to Krotona. (The fishermen) told the deed everywhere; they had learned his name from some children.

60. If we can believe so many ancient and worthy historians, Pythagoras had in (his) *logos* something analytical and admonishing which (affected) even arational animals; through this it is shown that, in learning, all are overcome by those who have intellect (*nous*); even wild animals and those thought to be without *logos* (are overcome).

It is said that he mastered the Daunian bear, which had severely harmed the inhabitants. He stroked it with his hand for a long time; he fed it with maize and acorns; then he compelled it by an oath not to touch any living thing, and he sent it away. The bear went straight to the mountain and into the woods, into hiding, and from that time was never seen to attack an arational creature. 61. Seeing an ox in Tarantum eating green beans in a field, he approached the ox keeper and told him to tell the ox to stop eating the beans. The ox keeper laughed at him because Pythagoras said, "Tell (the ox)," and he said that he did not know how to speak "ox language," but, if Pythagoras knew, it was in vain to order the ox keeper to do the talking but fitting for Pythagoras to advise the ox. Pythagoras approached the ox and whispered in its ear for a long time. The ox then not only refrained from beans, but never again, it is said, tasted them.

This ox lived for a long time in Tarantum by the temple of Hera, remaining there when it was old. The sacred ox was called "Pythagoras' Ox," and it was fed human food by those who came to it.

When he was speaking to his disciples about bird omens, symbols, and signs—that they are messengers from the Gods sent to those whom the Gods truly love—an eagle is said to have come down, and, after it was stroked, it went up again. Through all these things and many more, he demonstrated that he had the ruling power of Orpheus over beasts, and that he could charm and hold them by his voice.

134. . . . Once, crossing the Nessos River with his companions, he spoke to it by voice, and the river answered, loudly and clearly so that all heard, "Hail, Pythagoras." Also, on one and the same day (he was present) both in Metapontus of Italy and Tauromenius of Sicily and conversed in common with his companions in both places; this is asserted strongly by all (his biographers), even though there are many miles between the two cities by land and sea, and no one can pass from one to the other in many days . . .

135. . . . myriad other divine signs and wonders are recorded without error and uniformly by the historians about this man: infallible earthquake predictions; he got rid of plagues rapidly and stopped strong winds; he caused hail to stop at once; he calmed rivers and seas so that his companions might cross over easily . . . 136. . . . it is said also that he predicted an earthquake from well water which he tasted and that a ship sailing with a fair wind would sink.

Vespasian

Introduction: During the winter of A.D. 69 Vespasian, one of Rome's leading generals, was in Alexandria waiting out the period of civil war in Italy that had erupted after Nero's suicide in 68. His army was blockading Egypt's grain supply which Rome badly needed. Before long, he was able to gain control of the Empire.

Tacitus, *Histories* 4.81

Throughout those months in which Vespasian was waiting in Alexandria for the season of the summer winds and a calm sea, many miracles happened, by which were exhibited the favor of Heaven[1] and a certainleaning toward the divine in Vespasian. One of the commoners of Alexandria, who was known for the loss of his sight, threw himself before Vespasian's knees, praying to him with groans for a remedy for his blindness, having been so ordered by the God Serapis, whom the nation, being most pious, worships more than all others. And he prayed to the emperor that he should stoop to moisten with his spit his cheeks and the eyeballs. Another, whose hand was useless, ordered by the same God, prayed that Caesar should step on it with his foot. Vespasian at first laughed; then, at the same time, he was moved to fear by the thought of the infamy of failure and to hope by the prayers of the men and the voices of flattery. Finally he ordered it to be determined by physicians if such blindness and debility could be conquered by human powers. The physicians handled the two cases differently: in one, the power of sight had not been destroyed and would be restored if the obstructions were removed. In the other, the joints had fallen into deformity; if a healing force were applied, it would be possible to restore them. This was perhaps the wish of the Gods, and the emperor had been chosen for divine service. At any rate, if the healing was achieved, Caesar had glory; the onus of failure would belong to the poor beseechers. Therefore, Vespasian, sure that his good fortune was able to achieve anything and that nothing was incredible, with smiling face, standing amid the excitement of the tense multitude, did what he was asked. Immediately the hand was changed to a useful one and the day shone again for the blind man. Both cases are told by those who were present, and even now when lying has no reward.

---

[1]As we might suppose, Tacitus was a "court historian."

A Syrian Exorcist

Introduction: This brief excerpt is taken from a satirical dialogue by the second-century A.D. Syrian author, Lucian of Samosata, dealing with the way people readily believe all sorts of things concerning the supernatural world.

Lucian, *The Lover of Lies* 16

"You act ridiculously," Ion said to me, "by your constantly doubting everything. I would like to ask you what you say about those who free the demon-possessed from their terrors, thus plainly exorcising the ghosts. I hardly need to go into it—everyone has heard of the Syrian from Palestine,[1] so skilled was he in these things. Whomever he received, those who were moonstruck and rolled their eyes and filled their mouths with foam, they arose, when they were free of the terror, and he sent them away healthy, for a large fee. When he stands by them as they lie there, he asks (the demons) from whence they came into the body. The sick man is silent, but the demon answers in Greek or some barbarian tongue, or in the language of the country from which he comes, how and from whence he came into the man. The Syrian then levels oaths at him (to drive him out), but if the demon is not persuaded, he threatens [even worse punishments] and expels the demon. I actually saw one coming out, black and smoky in color."

"It is nothing for *you* to see such things, Ion," I replied, "to whom the Eternal Forms plainly appear, which the father of your school, Plato, points out; but to us with weak eyes these things are rather vague!"

---

[1] The identity of this healer is unknown.

Chanina ben Dosa

Introduction: Rabbi Chanina ben Dosa lived in Palestine in the mid-first century A.D., and was a friend and colleague of Yohanan ben Zakkai, the founder of the Academy at Yavneh (Jamnia). He was especially famous for his total piety, being considered a completely righteous man (bBer. 6lb); "one for whose sake God shows favor to his entire generation" (bHag. 14a).

Chanina ben Dosa's Healings Through Prayer

Our rabbis say, once upon a time Rabban Gamliel's son got sick. He sent two men of learning to Rabbi Chanina ben Dosa to beg him mercy from God concerning him. He saw them coming and went to a room upstairs and asked mercy from God concerning him. When he had come back down he said to them, "Go, the fever has left him." They said to him, "What? Are you a prophet?" He said, "I am not a prophet nor am I the son of a prophet. But this I have received from tradition: if my prayer of intercession flows unhesitatingly from my mouth, I know it will be answered, and if not, I know it will be rejected." They sat down and wrote and determined exactly the moment he said this, and when they came back to Rabban Gamliel he said to them, "By the Temple service![1] You are neither too early nor too late but this is what happened: in that moment the fever left him and he asked for water!"

Once again when Rabbi Chanina ben Dosa was going to study Torah with Rabban Yochanan ben Zakkai, the son of Rabban Yochanan ben Zakkai became ill. He said to him, "Chanina, my son, ask mercy from God for him and he will live." He put his head down between his knees [2] and asked mercy for him, and he lived. Rabban Yochanan ben Zakkai said, "Now if ben Zakkai fastened his head between his knees all day long, there would not be any attention paid to him." His wife said to him, "What? Is Chanina greater than you?"[3] He replied, "Of course not, but he is like a servant before the king and I am like a prince before the king"[4] (bBerakoth 34b).

---

[1] A kind of oath; "By God!"
[2] Indicating especially strenuous praying.
[3] At this time, ben Zakkai was the Ruler of the people, just after the great rebellion A.D. 67–73.
[4] He can go in with requests anytime.

Ben Dosa's Wife Is Given Bread

Rab Judah[5] said (in the name of Rab),[6] day in and day out a Heavenly Voice[7] goes forth from Mt. Horeb proclaiming, "the whole world is preserved for the sake of Chanina my son and all it takes to sustain *him* from the eve of one Sabbath to the next eve of Sabbath is a handful of carōb-beans!"[8] (To show you how poor he was,) his wife had a habit of burning a fire all during the eve of Sabbath and throwing in leaves to avoid disgrace.[9] Well, there lived in the neighborhood a certain malicious woman who said, "I know full well that they don't have anything and that she is not cooking anything! What is all that smoke for?" So she went and knocked on the door. The wife of Chanina was ashamed (to let her neighbor find out) and hid in the bedroom instead of answering the door. Suddenly a miracle was done for her. Her neighbor peeked in the window and (contrary to her expectations) saw the oven filled with bread baking and the kettle filled with dough. She called out to Chanina's wife, "Hey you! Get the spatula! Quick! Your bread is burning!" Chanina's wife shouted back, "Why do you think I went to the bedroom!" (bTa'anit 24b/25a).

Chanina ben Dosa's Sinlessness

Our rabbis say, once upon a time a poisonous snake was injuring people. They went and made it known to Rabbi Chanina ben Dosa. He said to them, "Show me its burrow." They showed him its burrow and he placed his heel upon the mouth of the hole. It came forth and bit him—and it died. He put that snake on his shoulders, went to the House of Study (*beth ha-midrash*), and said to them, "See, my sons; it is not the snake that kills but sin that kills." Then they said, "Woe to the man a snake attacks and woe to the snake which Rabbi Chanina ben Dosa attacks!"[10] (bBerakoth 33a).

---

[5]A Palestinian sage who lived about A.D. 300.

[6]Rab, otherwise known as Abba Arika the Tall, died A.D. 247, was one of the most important of the early Babylonian rabbis.

[7]Or *Bath Qōl*, a constant aspect of rabbinic stories; cf. John 12:28, "Jesus said, 'Father glorify thy name.' Then a Voice came from Heaven saying, 'I have glorified it,' " etc. The *Bath Qōl* provides Heaven's point of view in the stories.

[8]A hilarious exaggeration. The carōb was a kind of common bean eaten only by the poverty-stricken. This story tells how ben Dosa's proud wife tried to hide their abject poverty—and was unexpectedly helped.

[9] The smoke would make it look as if she was cooking food in preparation for the Sabbath like everyone else. Since the Sabbath was a day of rest, no housework could be done on that day, and all food had to be ready ahead of time.

[10]The same story is also found in Tosef. Ber. 3.20, only there it is a scorpion that bites him during prayer—and dies.

A Jewish Boy Calms the Sea

Rabbi Tanchuma (c. A.D. 350) said, "Once upon a time a certain cargo ship belonging to Gentiles was crossing the Great Sea in which there was a certain Jewish boy. A great tempest rose up upon the seas, and every single one among them arose and bowed down, taking his idol in his hand and crying out in prayer, but to no avail. Then, when they saw it was no use, they said to the Jewish boy, 'Come, my son. Call to your God. He will hear us, for he responds to you when you complain to him, and he is strong.' So the boy got up and begged with all his heart, and God received his prayer and quieted the sea. Then as they came to the shore, they all went down to buy things they needed. They said to him, the little boy, 'Is there not anything you want to buy for yourself?' He said to them, 'Why do you ask this of me, a poor foreigner?' They said to him, 'You, a poor foreigner? We are the poor foreigners! Some are here and their idols are back home in Babylon, others are here, but their idols are in Rome, and others are here who have their idols with them, but none of them is any help to anyone. But you know every place where you go, your God is with you, as it is written, "What great nation is there that has a God so near to them as our God is whenever we call to him?" ' " (Deut. 4:7; jBerakoth 9.1).

The Rabbis Reject Miracles

Introduction: One day the Jewish sages at Jamnia were debating a legal question (*halachah*), namely whether an oven constructed in sections with sand between them was a "utensil" and therefore subject to the laws of household purity. A dramatic conflict erupted between Eliezer ben Horkanos who argued it was not a utensil but just pieces of tile, and all the other sages, who said it *was* a utensil because the outer shell of cement binding the whole together made it a unified entity used in daily chores. This seemingly insignificant issue became the occasion for a far-reaching conflict between the rabbis over the issue of how best to discern God's will.

On that day, Rabbi Eliezer replied with every legal argument in the world, but the rabbis would not accept them. Thereupon, he said to them, "If the halachah is on my side, let that carōb tree show it!" The carōb suddenly uprooted itself and flew through the air one hundred cubits—some say four hundred cubits. They said to him, "No bringing of proof from a carōb tree!" He said to them, "If the halachah is on my side, then may that stream of water show it!" The stream of water turned around, and flowed backward. They said to him, "No bringing proof from streams of water!" He turned and said to them, "If the halachah is on my side, may the walls of the House of Study we are in show it!" The walls of the House of Study leaned inward, as if about to fall. Rabbi Yehoshua rebuked the walls, saying to them, "If the sages battle each other over halachah, why do you interfere?" They did not fall out of honor for Rabbi Yehoshua, nor did they straighten up out of honor for Rabbi Eliezer; they continue crookedly standing to this day. Again Eliezer said to them, "If the halachah is on my side, let Heaven show it!" A Voice from Heaven (*Bath Qōl*) cried out, "What do the rest of you have against Rabbi Eliezer? The halachah is on his side in everything!" Rabbi Yehoshua leaped to his feet and quoted (Deut. 30:12), " 'It is not in Heaven' ".

What did Yehoshua mean by saying, " 'It is not in Heaven'?" Rabbi Yeremiah explained, "Since the Torah has already been given from Mount Sinai, we do not pay heed any longer to a Heavenly Voice. You yourself, O Lord, wrote in the Torah given at Mount Sinai: 'turn aside after the multitude'."[1]

Later, Rabbi Nathan happened to see the Prophet Elijah. He asked him, "What did the Holy One, Blessed be He, do when we did not pay heed to any of Rabbi Eliezer's miraculous proofs, or the Heavenly Voice?" Elijah replied, "What did he do! God said, 'My sons have defeated me! My sons have defeated me!' "

They say that on that same day, after the debate, all the rabbis gathered everything Rabbi Eliezer had before pronounced clean and burned them with fire,[2] for they had all voted to "bless" him.[3] Then they said, "Who will go make it known to him?" Rabbi Akiba[4] said to them, "I will go, lest an unworthy man go and tell him and cause the destruction of the whole world completely."[5] What did Rabbi Akiba

[1]I.e., "accept the majority view point" in matters of halachah. It is irrelevant to the rabbis' argument that the original meaning of this phrase from Exod. 23:2 has to do with another subject altogether.
[2]Because they were unclean; i.e., all his decisions were now considered null and void.
[3]A euphemistic expression. They voted to excommunicate Rabbi Eliezer.
[4]The successor to Gamliel II and one of the most influential rabbis of this period (90–135).
[5]By provoking Rabbi Eliezer to anger, which he would convey to his God, who would in turn punish the world.

do? He put on black clothing and a black overgarment[6] and came to Rabbi Eliezer, sitting down nearby, four cubits away. Rabbi Eliezer said to him, "Akiba, what happened today?" He said to him, "Master, it seems to me that your brothers have separated from you."[7] Then Eliezer tore his clothing and took off his shoes and sat on the ground, tears dropping from his eyes. Instantly, the world was blighted; one-third of the olives, one-third of the wheat, and one-third of the barley died (. . . A Tanna says, "A great disaster happened on that day, for everything upon which Rabbi Eliezer's eye fell burned up").

Some days later, Rabban Gamliel was traveling in a boat. A tempest rose up and threatened to sink his boat and drown him. He said to himself, "It seems to me this is happening only because of what we did to Rabbi Eliezer ben Horkanos."[8] So he stood up on his feet and cried out: "Master of the World! It is obvious to all and well-known to you that it was not selfishly for my honor that I acted, or for the glory of the house of my father that I acted, but for your honor, in order that divisions of opinion (*Torah*) not increase in Israel."[9]

The waters immediately calmed down.

Summary

The account ends with the story of how Rabbi Eliezer's wife, who was Rabban Gamliel's sister, was terrified what her husband, Eliezer, might do to her brother. Thus she would not allow her husband to pray, lest he pour out his grief to God, and God would severely punish Gamliel. But one day not long after, while her attention was diverted by a beggar's request for some bread, Eliezer went upstairs and began to pray. Thereupon, the story says, news came over from Gamliel's house that he had suddenly died at that very moment (bBaba Mezia 59b).

---

[6]A sign of mourning.

[7]Excommunicated you.

[8]R. Gamliel II was Ruler (*nasi*) at the time, and he apparently was the one primarily responsible for Eliezer's excommunication.

[9]R. Eliezer must have been at the head of a dissident faction of some sort, possibly pro-Christian.

The Murder of Julius Caesar

Introduction: Julius Caesar was assassinated in 44 B.C. by men who bitterly resented his flagrant trampling upon the Senate's authority. But none of the following accounts of miraculous signs of the Gods' sorrow at Caesar's death were written by those men. Virgil and Suetonius, in particular, belonged to the circle of writers dedicated to embellishing the rising glory of Octavian, Caesar's nephew, and the Empire under his control.

Virgil, *Georgics* 1.463–468

. . . the Sun shall give you signs: the story told at evening,[1] the clear skies from whence the wind drives the clouds, and what is the significance of the humid south wind. Who would dare to call the Sun a liar? He, in fact, warns that a secret insurrection is imminent and that deceit and furtive battles are swelling. He expressed mercy for Rome when Caesar was killed; he hid his shining head in gloom and the impious age feared eternal night.

Suetonius, *The Lives of the Caesars* 1.88–89

(Julius Caesar) died when he was fifty-six, and he was registered among the rank of the Gods, not only by means of (the Senate) decree, but also in the conviction of the common people. In fact, at the first games which were established for him by his heir Augustus, a comet shone for seven straight days, rising about the eleventh hour, and it was believed to be the soul of Caesar who had been received into Heaven. It is because of this that a star is placed on the crown of the head of his statue . . .

Hardly any of his murderers lived after him for more than three years, nor did they die a natural death. They were all damned, and they died in various ways, some by shipwreck, some in battle; some killed themselves by the same dagger with which they assassinated Caesar.

Plutarch, *Caesar* 69.3–5

(At Caesar's death) the most astonishing event of human design concerned Cassius. After he was defeated at Philippi, he killed himself

---

[1]Prediction of the next day's weather by the color of the sunset.

with the same dagger which he had used against Caesar. Concerning the events of divine design, there was the great comet—for it shone seven nights after the assassination of Caesar, then disappeared—and the blocking of the sun's rays. For throughout the whole year the sun rose pale, and it had no radiance; and the heat which came from it was weak and effete, so that the air lay heavy, due to the feebleness of the warmth which entered it. The fruits, half-ripe and imperfect, faded and decayed because of the chill of the atmosphere. But especially the ghost that appeared to Brutus showed that the murder was not pleasing to the Gods . . . [2]

---

[2]Here Plutarch is referring to the well-known rumor of his time that a ghost appeared to Brutus the night before his final battle. This apparition predicted his defeat and death.

The Wine Miracle of Dionysos

Introduction: The author of this excerpt was a Greek geographer and traveler who lived during the second century A.D. He composed a lengthy account of his homeland, including especially religious sites, customs, and practices. In describing the province of Elis, he tells of an annual miracle that occurred there in a temple dedicated to Dionysos.

Pausanius, *Description of Greece* **6.26.1f.**

There is an old theater and shrine of Dionysos between the market place and the Menius. The statue of the God is the work of Praxiteles. Of the Gods, the Eleans worship especially Dionysos; indeed they say their God invades the Thyia[1] during the annual feast . . . The priests carry three kettles into the building and set them down empty, when the town citizens and strangers, if they happen to be there, are present. The priests, and any others who wish, put a seal on the doors of the building. In the morning they come to read the signs and when they go into the building they find the kettles filled with wine. These things most trustworthy men of Elis, and strangers with them, swear to have happened. This is by word of mouth; I myself did not arrive at festival time. The Andrians also say that every other year, at the Feast of Dionysos, wine flows of its own accord from the temple. If it is fitting that such things should be believed by Greeks, then one ought to accept, by the same reasoning, what the Ethiopians around Syene[2] say about the Table of the Sun.[3]

---

[1]A temple to Dionysos.
[2]Aswan.
[3]Pausanius does not indicate what miraculous occurrences are meant.

SACRAMENTS

The Salvation of Lucius

Introduction: Apuleius was born c. A.D. 123 in Madauros in Africa. His *Metamorphoses* (the Golden Ass) is the only fully intact Latin novel to have come down to us from Roman times. The work is a rather erotic romp except for the eleventh book which appears to be a serious, perhaps autobiographical, account of an initiation into the mysteries of Isis.

Ill-fortuned Lucius, who tells this tale, suffers through many misadventures due to what he calls his *fortuna collapsa*. At the point we take up the story, his "catastrophic destiny" is that he has been turned into an ass by a witch. Lucius portrays himself as somewhat a Don Juan, and, as he has been tricked into the metamorphosis by his own lust for women and his dabbling in witchcraft, the reader is led to believe that Lucius is paying for his "sins." As book eleven opens, Lucius-the-Ass has run away from his owner and fallen into an exhausted sleep by the sea shore.

Apuleius, *Metamorphoses* 11

Just about the time of the first night-watch, I awakened in a sudden terror. I saw the moon, shining with splendor as she does when she is full, just when she emerged from the sea. It occurred to me that this was the most silent, secret time of the shady night; it certainly was the time when the noble Goddess is most powerful in special grandeur. It came to me that all human things are ruled by her providence. At her nod, not only cattle and wild animals but even inanimate things are made lively by her light and divinity. Earthly bodies as well as heavenly bodies and the sea increase by her waxing and diminish by her waning. I considered then that surely my Fate was satisfied with my many disasters. I found a hope of salvation, although it was late, and I decided to beseech the august image of the risen Goddess.

I rose up with joy, shaking off my weariness. I surrendered to a desire for purification, and walked to the sea. I immersed my head seven times—the number prescribed by the divine Pythagoras as the most efficacious for religious purposes. Then with life and joy, with tearful face, I prayed thus to the powerful Goddess:

"Queen of Heaven (*regina caeli*), whether you are Mother Ceres, the original mothering nurse of all fruitful things, who, after joyfully finding your daughter, abolished the uncivilized nourishment of the ancient acorn and demonstrated a more gentle food—you now decorate the Eleusinian fields; or, whether you are Heaven's Venus, who, at the time of primal origin, coupled together the sexes by the creation of love to bring about the eternal propagation of humanity and are now worshiped at the temples of Paphos; or, whether you are Phoebus' sister,[1] who with soothing medicines relieved birth pangs and brought safely (into the world) so many people and are now worshiped at the shrines of Ephesus; or, whether you are called dreadful Proserpine with nocturnal ululations, who by her triple face, can thwart ghosts and seal and close the cracks in the earth, (those ghosts) who wander in various groves and are worshiped in diverse cults; you who by your womanly light illumines all city walls, by your moist fire nourishes the joyful seed, and as the sun moves, dispenses your changing light—by whatever name, and whatever rite, whatever face you are to be invoked—come; help me now in my terrible need; bolster up my catastrophic destiny (*fortuna collapsa*); draw off the cruelty from my life, and give me peace. Let there be enough of toils, enough of tribulations. Take away (from me) the abominable beast's face, and return me to my own form; return me again to me, to be Lucius.

"But if some angry divine power (*numen*) pursues me with unswerving ferocity, grant me at least death, if I may not live."

In this way, when I had spread forth my prayer and told of my lamentations, sleep returned to my drooping spirit, surrounded me, and pressed me into the very same bed. I had barely closed my eyes in weariness when, behold, a divine face emerged from the midst of the sea; she had features that the Gods would worship. Then the whole body, a most marvelous form, emerged, rising out of the sea, and she stood before me.

> Lucius describes the Goddess, who is divinely beautiful. She wears a crown of flowers, and a jewel representing the moon is on her forehead. She wears a many-colored tunic and a black cloak through which the stars and moon shine. To the cloak clings a garment made up of "all the fruits of growing things." The Goddess carries a sistrum (a musical instrument sacred to her). In her left hand, she carries a vase shaped like a ship—an asp raises its head from the vase's handle.

Such was the Goddess; breathing forth the pleasant spices of Arabia, she deigned to speak to me with her voice:

"I have come to you, Lucius, because of your prayer—I who am the Mother of all nature's things, mistress of all the elements, firstborn of the worlds, the supreme divinity, queen of the world of the dead, first of

[1] I.e., Diana, upon whom women called to lessen the pain of childbirth.

those in Heaven, the singular form of all Gods and Goddesses. With a nod, I regulate the zenith of the heavenly lights, the fair winds of the seas, and the despairing silences of hell. I am she whose singular deity (*numen*) the whole world worships in different ways, by various rites, and by many names.

"The Phrygians, the primal race, call me Pessinuntia, Mother of Gods. The aboriginal races of Attica call me Cecropian[2] Minerva. The Cyprians on their island call me Paphian[3] Venus. The Cretans, the archers, call me Diana Dictynna.[4] The Sicilians, who speak three languages, call me Stygian Proserpine. The Eleusinians call me their ancient goddess Ceres; some call me Juno, some Bellona,[5] some Hecate, some Rhamnusia.[6] Those who are illumined by the morning rays of that God, the sun, the Ethiopians, the Arii,[7] and the Egyptians, who are the best at ancient rituals, all worship me in their ancient rites and call me by my true name, Queen Isis.

"I have come to you in your misery; I have come with comfort and propitiation. Put away your tears, cease your lamentations, dispel your sorrow. Soon, by my providence, the day of your salvation will dawn. Therefore, attend with care to my instructions. That day, a day which shall be born from this night, has been devoted to me by the eternal religion. In this religion, when the winter storms are over, and the sea ceases its upheavals, my priests by custom offer to me a new ship as the first fruits of the year's navigation. You must await this ritual (*sacrum*) with neither anxiety nor with a profane mind.

"At my order, the priest will carry in the sacred procession a wreath of roses next to the sistrum in his right hand. You must push through the throng without hesitation, join the procession, and trust my benevolence. Come close to the priest, as if you wished to kiss his hand, and eat the roses. Thereupon you will put off the beast's skin—a beast I have long abhorred."

Isis then assures Lucius that all will be arranged for this rather unusual sacramental act. She is giving her instructions to the priest (who is in another place) at the same time that she is speaking to Lucius. Further, no one will condemn Lucius for his sudden change from ass to man . . . a metamorphosis that could result in Lucius' being condemned for sorcery. Isis then gives to Lucius a promise and a charge.

"The rest of your life you will be bound to me, and there is no release from this (tie) except death. Consider this no burden, to devote your

[2]Cecrops was the legendary first king of Athens.
[3]Paphos, a city of Cyprus, held a famous temple to Aphrodite.
[4]Dictynna refers to Britomartis, an ancient Cretan Goddess.
[5]The Roman war Goddess.
[6]An epithet for Fate.
[7]The Aryans, inhabitants of Persia.

whole life to her by whose beneficence you shall again become a man. You shall live blessed. You shall live a glorious life under my guidance. And when the season of your life has been traveled, you will go down to the regions of the dead. There I am also in that subterranean semisphere, I, whom you will see shining in the darkness of Acheron and ruling in the Stygian depths. You shall dwell in the Elysian fields, adoring me who has been favorable to you. And if I see that by obedience in dedication, religious devotion, and tenacious chastity you deserve our divine power (*numen*), know that I alone have power to extend your life beyond the limits set by Fate."

> Lucius does as the Goddess orders and is saved from his malicious destiny. There is a long description of the ceremony of initiation into the cult of Isis, a description unique to literature. He stays in the temple as a devotee. When the Goddess finally bids him leave the temple, the following scene takes place.

I prostrated myself then before the face of the Goddess and wiped her feet with my face; with my tears flowing, with repeated sobs interrupting and swallowing my words, I said:

"Most holy and everlasting savior of the human race, always generously cherishing our lives, you who always give the sweet affection of a loving mother to the troubles of the miserable. There is no day or sleep, no instant, which is insignificant to you as you extend your mercy to humanity on sea and land. You dispel the storms of life by stretching out your salutory right hand, by which you unravel even the inextricable twists of Fate. You mitigate the great tempests of Fortune and keep back the injurious course of the stars. The heavenly Gods worship you, and the Gods of the underworld pay homage to you. You turn the globe, light the sun, rule the earth. You tread on Hades. The stars answer to you; the seasons change; the Gods rejoice; the elements serve you. At your nod the winds blow, the clouds nourish, seeds are germinated, and fruits grow. The birds of the heavens, the beasts running on the hills, the serpents hiding in the earth, the monsters that swim in the sea all tremble before your rule.

"But my spirit cannot give you enough praise, and I have not the goods to give you sufficient offering. My voice is not strong enough to say what I think of your majesty, not even if I had a thousand mouths and tongues and an eternal flow of tireless words. Therefore, I will do what I am able, a religious person with poor estate. I will imagine your divine face within my breast, and there, in the secret depths, I will guard your most holy divinity forever."

The Messianic Banquet at Qumran

Introduction: Among the regulations discovered in Cave I was a short fragment setting forth, among other things, the protocol to follow when the Lord sent the priest and the Messiah to Israel. As the *Temple Scroll* vividly demonstrates, the Essenes had radically different ideas in mind for the Temple in Jerusalem, and they were waiting for the Lord to reveal to them the new High Priest after the order of Aaron, who would inaugurate the necessary reforms. The community also expected at any time "a king like David" to be revealed, the future Messiah. The selection given here has to do with the order of precedence at the great banquet to be held when both shall finally have made their appearance.

The Scroll of the Rule (The *Rule Annexe* [1QSa 11–22])[1]

(11) [Concerning the mee]ting of the men of renown [called] to assembly for the Council of the Community when [the Lord] will have begotten (12) the Messiah (cf. Psalm 2:7) among them.

[The Priest] shall enter [at] the head of all the Congregation of Israel, then all (13) [the chiefs of the sons] of Aaron, the priests called to the assembly, men of renown; and they shall sit (14) [before him], each according to his rank.

And afterwards, [the Mess]iah of Israel [shall enter]; and the chiefs (15) of [the tribes of Israel] shall sit before him, each according to his rank, . . . then all (16) the heads of the fa[milies of the Congre]gation, together with the wise me[n of the holy Congregation], shall sit before them, each according to (17) his rank.

And [when] they gather for the Community tab[le], [or to drink w]ine, and arrange the (18) Community table [and mix] the wine to drink, let no man [stretch out] his hand over the first-fruits of bread (19) and [wine] before the Priest; for [it is he who] shall bless the first-fruits of bread (20) and w[ine, and shall] first [stretch out] his hand over the bread. And after[wards], the Messiah of Israel shall [str]etch out his hands (21) over the bread. [And afterwards], all the Congregation of the Community shall [bl]ess, each according to his rank.

And they shall proceed according to this rite (22) at every mea[l where] at least ten persons [are as]sembled.

[1]Translated by A. Dupont-Sommer, *The Essene Writings from Qumran*, trans. G. Vermes, World Publishing Co., Cleveland 1962, pp. 108–9.

APOCALYPTIC PREDICTIONS

2 Esdras 11; 13

Introduction: This work (also called IV Ezra) purports to be visions seen by Ezra after the destruction of Jerusalem in 587 B.C. Actually, the imagery in 2 Esdras refers to the destruction of Jerusalem in A.D. 70–72. 2 Esdras is a Jewish work, probably dating from the late first century A.D. Its strong apocalyptic fervor mirrors the desperation and tension of Judaism as it saw its homeland virtually annihilated by the Roman power.

The Eagle Vision (2 Esdras 11)

10.60. I slept that night and the next, just as he (an angel) bade me.
11:1. And I saw a dream, and behold, an eagle ascended from the sea; the eagle had twelve feathered wings and three heads, 2. and I looked, and behold, he stretched his wings over the whole earth, and all the winds of Heaven blew on him and were gathered together. 3. And I looked, and from his wings there grew opposite wings, and they became small and puny wings. 4. His heads were quiescent, and the middle head was larger than the other heads, but it also rested quietly between them. 5. And I looked, and behold, the eagle flew on his wings and he ruled over the earth and over those things that lived on it. 6. And I saw that all things under Heaven were subject to him, and none spoke against him, nor did any one of the creatures on the earth. 7. And I looked, and behold, the eagle rose up on his claws, and he sent a voice to his wings, saying, 8. "Do not watch everything at once; let each one sleep in his place and watch in (his) time; 9. however, save the heads for last."
10. And I looked, and behold, the voice did not go forth from his heads but from the midst of his body. 11. And I counted his opposing wings and, behold, there were eight. 12. And I looked, and behold, a wing rose up from the right side and ruled over all the earth. 13. And it happened that while it reigned an end came to it, and its place disappeared. And a second (wing) arose and ruled, so that it held (power) for a long time.
14. It happened that while it reigned, its end came, and it disappeared as did the first. 15. And behold, a voice was sent to it, saying, 16. "Hear, you who have reigned over the earth for so long a time; I announce this to you before you disappear: 17. No one after

173

you shall last for as long a time as you did, not even half as long."
18. And the third wing lifted itself and held its reign just as the former ones, and it too disappeared. 19. And it happened to all to govern in turn and then in turn to disappear. 20. And I looked, and behold, in time the wings raised up in order on the right side so that each might hold its reign; and from this group some held power but disappeared immediately. 21. Some others of these raised up but never held power. 22. And I looked after this, and behold, the twelve wings disappeared, so did two little wings. 23. And nothing was left on the eagle's body except the three quiescent heads and six little wings. 24. And I looked, and behold, from six of the little wings two detached and attached themselves under the head which was on the right side. Four remained in place. 25. And I looked, and behold, the four subordinate wings decided to raise themselves and to hold power. 26. And I looked, and behold, one arose but immediately disappeared, 27. and a second also, but it disappeared more quickly than the first. 28. And I looked, and behold, the two which remained, plotted in themselves to reign, 29. and at that, while they were plotting, behold, one of the quiescent heads which was in the middle awoke; this one was the greater of the two (other) heads. 30. And I saw that it made an alliance with the two other heads. 31. And behold, the head turned with those with it and ate the two subordinate wings who had plotted to reign. 32. This head held sway over all the earth, and with much oppression dominated everything that inhabited the earth; it held power over the earth more than any of the wings which had ruled.
33. And after this I looked, and behold, the middle head suddenly disappeared just as had the wings. 34. The two heads remained, however, and they similarly ruled over the earth and over all which inhabited it. 35. And I looked, and behold, the head on the right side devoured the one on the left. 36. And I heard a voice saying to me, "Look in front of you and consider what you see."
37. And I looked, and behold, a lion stirred up out of the woods, roaring, and I saw that it emitted a voice like a man's to the eagle. And he said, 38. "Listen you, I will talk to you; the Most High speaks to you: 39. Are you not the one who remains of the four animals whom I caused to rule over my world and through whom the end of these times would come? 40. And you, the fourth, have come and conquered all the beasts that have passed and have ruled with power and with much fear the world and all the ends of the earth with awful oppression and lived for so long in the civilized world with deceit. 41. And you have judged the earth but not with truth. 42. You have persecuted the meek, and attacked the peaceful, and loved the liars, and destroyed the dwelling places of the fruitful, and knocked down the walls of those who

did you no harm. 43. And your outrageous behavior has ascended even to the Most High, and your arrogance to the Mighty One. 44. And the Most High considered his times, and behold, they are ended, and their desecrations are finished. 45. Therefore, you shall disappear, Eagle, with your horrible wings, and your most wretched little wings, and your malignant heads, and your wretched claws, and your useless body, 46. and the whole earth shall be made fresh again, and freedom from your violence will return, and the earth will hope for the judgment and mercy of him who created her."

The Man from the Sea (2 Esdras 13)

1. And it happened after seven days that I dreamed a dream in the night. 2. And behold, a wind arose from the sea and stirred up all its waves. 3. And I looked, and behold, the wind caused to come out of the seas one like a man, and the man flew up with the clouds of Heaven. Wherever he turned his face and looked, all things upon which he gazed trembled. 4. And wherever the voice from his mouth went forth, all who heard his voice burst into fire, so that the earth quieted, when it felt the fire.

5. And I saw after this, behold, an innumerable multitude of men gathered from the four winds of heaven in order that they should make war on the man who had risen from the sea. 6. And I looked, and behold, he carved out for himself a great mountain, and he flew up on it. 7. I searched to see the region or the place where the mountain had been sculpted, and I could not.

8. And after this, I looked, and behold, all who gathered to him to make war against him were very frightened; however, they dared to make war. 9. And behold, when he saw the attack of the approaching multitude, he did not raise his hand or hold a spear or any other weapon. 10. I saw only that he sent out of his mouth a fiery breath and from his lips a spirit of flame, and he sent out from his tongue sparks and storms. All mingled together, his fiery breath, and the flaming spirit, and a host of storms. 11. And they fell upon the crowd which attacked, which had prepared to make war, and burned them all up. Suddenly nothing could be seen of the innumerable multitude except only ashes and the odor of smoke. I saw, and I was amazed.

12. After this I saw the man himself descending from the mountain and calling to himself another, peaceful multitude. 13. And the faces of many men approached him, some were rejoicing, some mourning, others were fettered, some were leading others whom they presented.

I was sick from a multitude of terrors and, when I awoke I said: 14. "You have shown from the beginning these miraculous things to your servant and have honored me that you receive my prayer. 15.

And now show me the interpretation of this dream. 16. For as I understand in my mind, woe to those who survive in those days, and much more woe to those who do not survive. 17. For those who did not survive were suffering. 18. I know now of things which are reserved for them in the last days and what happens in them. But also of those who survive, 19. because they will come into great perils and many distresses, just as these dreams show. 20. Yet it is easier to enter these perils than to pass away as a cloud from the earth and not to see what things will happen in the last times."

And he (the angel) replied to me, and said, 21. "I will tell you the interpretation of this vision, and I will explain to you about what you have spoken. 22. Because you have spoken about the survivors, this is the interpretation: 23. He who will bring peril in that time will himself guard those who fall into peril, those who have works of faith toward the Most Strong One. 24. Know, therefore, that more blessed are those who survive than those who have died. 25. These are the visions' interpretations. You saw the man ascending from the heart of the sea. 26. He is the one whom the Most High keeps for many ages, who will liberate his creation. And he will decide who is to survive.

27. "You saw wind, fire, and storm come from his mouth 28. and he did not hold a spear or a weapon, but he destroyed the attack of the multitude which came to fight him. This is the interpretation. 29. Behold the days are coming in which the Most High shall begin to free those who are on earth; 30. and he shall bring astonishment to those who live on earth.   31. And they shall plan war against one another, city against city, region against region, and people against people, and kingdom against kingdom.

32. And it shall be, when these things happen, signs will come which I showed you previously. And then my son will be revealed, the man whom you saw ascending (from the sea). 33. And it shall be when all peoples shall hear his voice, each one will leave his own land and his own war which they wage against one another, 34. and an innumerable multitude shall be gathered in one place, wishing to come and to fight him. 35. He, however, shall stand at the peak of Mount Sion. 36. Sion shall come, however, and shall be shown ready and built as you saw, the mountain carved out without hands. 37. My son himself shall accuse those people who come—their impieties are like a storm, on account of their evil designs—with tortures by which they are to be tortured, 38. which are like flames, and he will destroy them easily through the law which is like fire.

39. And you saw him gather to himself the other, peaceful multitude. 40. These are the ten tribes who were taken captive from their land in the days of King Osea, whom Salmanaser, king of Assyria, led to

captivity. And he carried them over the river, indeed they were carried to a foreign land. 41. But they held this council among themselves, that they would leave the multitude of the pagans, and they would depart into a farther land where no race of humans ever lived. 42. There they would actually observe their laws which they had not observed in their own land.

43. "They entered through the narrow entrances of the river Euphrates. 44. The Most High did wondrous signs for them and stopped the sources of the river until they crossed. 45. Through that land there was a long road, one-and-a-half year's journey; the land was called Arsareth. 46. Then they lived there until the last times; and now, when they are about to come out from there, 47. again the Most High will stop the sources of rivers so that they may be able to go across. Thus you saw the multitude gathered in peace.

48. But those who are the survivors of your people, those left in my land (shall be saved). 49. It will happen therefore, when he shall begin to destroy the multitude of those people who are gathered, he shall protect the people who remain. 50. And then he shall show many portents to them."

51. And I said, "Ruler, Lord, show this to me, because I saw the Man ascending from the heart of the sea."

And he said to me, 52. "Just as one cannot examine or know what is in the depths of the sea, so also those on earth cannot see my son nor those with him except in that time. 53. This is the interpretation of the dream which you saw: Therefore you alone have been enlightened. 54. You have forsaken your own concerns, and are free to search my law. 55. You have disposed your life toward wisdom, and you have named understanding as your mother. 56. On account of this, I have showed this to you, as a reward in the presence of the Most High. It will be that after three more days I will speak to you other things, and I will expound serious and wondrous things to you."

A Roman "Messianic" Prophecy

Introduction: Virgil's *Eclogues* (selected poems) cover many pastoral themes. In the fourth, however, he turns to another subject, the coming birth of a boy. The identity of this child is not known. There are many candidates put forward by scholars, but none has been elected by a consensus. The most famous candidate, namely Jesus of Nazareth, is a historical impossibility as the *Eclogues* were written between 12–37 B.C. but was (especially in the Middle Ages) a theological favorite. The "apocalyptic" ring of this poem has drawn the attention of many historians.

Virgil, *Eclogue* IV

Sicilian Muses, let us sing a bit more lofty song.
Arbors and humble tamarisks do not delight everyone;
If we sing of woods, let the woods be worthy of a consul.

The ultimate age of Cumae's song is now come!
The great order is born anew from the line of the ages.
The Virgin has now returned; Saturn's reign has returned;
Now a new offspring is sent from Heaven on High.
You alone grant favor at the birth of the boy by whom the iron age
Shall cease and a golden race shall rise up on the world,
Only you, chaste Lucina; now your own Apollo reigns.

In your consulate, Pollio, yours, this glorious (fulfillment) of the age
Will begin, and the great months begin to process.
During your office, if any vestiges of our wickedness should remain,
Once erased, they shall release the earth from perpetual dread.
He shall have the life of a God and shall see heroes and Gods together,
And he shall be seen as one of them,
And he shall rule a world made peaceful by his father's valors.

But to you, child, earth with no cultivation shall pour out
Its first little gifts: trailing ivy everywhere with cyclamen,
The lotus mixed with smiling acanthus.
Their udders swollen with milk, the goats will come home
Uncalled; the herds will not fear great lions;
Your cradle itself will pour forth flowers to charm you.
The serpent will perish also, and the poisonous, deceiving herb will
    perish.
Assyrian amomum will spring up everywhere.

Yet, as soon as you are able to read the praises of heroes and
The deeds of your fathers, and to know what is virtue,

Slowly the prairie will turn yellow with grain,
The grape will hang reddening from the wild bramble-bushes,
And the hard oaks will exude dewy honey.
A few vestiges of the ancient delusion will remain,
By which to tempt (men) to go to sea, by which to fortify their
Towns with walls and to plow furrows in the earth.
Then there will be another Tiphys and another Argo
Which will carry chosen heroes; there will be another war,
And again a great Achilles will be sent to Troy.

Then, when the strong age will have made you a man,
The trader will leave the sea, the ships of pine will
Exchange no goods; every land will supply all things.
The earth will not feel the rake, nor the vine the pruning hook;
The robust plowman will unhitch the oxen from the yoke;
Wool shall no longer learn to imitate various colors,
But the ram in the field shall change his own fleece,
Now with a sweetly blushing purple, now a yellow saffron.
On its own, vermillion will clothe the grazing lamb.

"Rush on, such ages" the Parcae have said to their spindles,
Speaking in concord with the fixed divine power of the Fates.
Move toward your great honors—the time is now at hand—
Beloved offspring of the Gods, great addition to Jove's family.
Behold the world swaying with its huge dome, the earth and the
Wide sea and the depths of the Heaven,
Behold how all things rejoice at the age to come!

O let the last part of my life which remains be long,
And may I have the spirit to be able to tell of your deeds.
Thracian Orpheus shall not conquer me in song, nor shall Linus,
Though his mother should help the one and his father the other,
Calliope helping Orpheus and fair Apollo helping Linus.
Even if Pan with Arcadia as judge were to compete with me,
Even Pan with Arcadia as judge would declare himself defeated.

Begin, little boy, to greet your mother with a smile;
Ten months have brought protracted weariness to your mother.
Begin, little boy. A child who does not smile at his parent,
Will not be honored at a God's table nor by a Goddess' invitation to her
  bed.

The Footsteps of the Messiah

Introduction: When the Jewish sages of the second century A.D. looked back on the terrible days when Israel had rebelled against Rome (A.D. 66–70) and had suffered the destruction of the Temple for the second time, they often linked a whole series of catastrophic changes to that devastating event. At times, this led them to mention the signs, known as "the footsteps of the Messiah," by which the advent of the Messiah could be recognized. For it was widely thought that as distress and anarchy mounted in Israel, these were sure signs that the Messiah was not far away.

Mishnah, Sotah 9:15

Rabbi Eliezer the Great says, "Since the day when the Temple was destroyed, the Sages began to act like (children's) school teachers, and school teachers like synagogue janitors, and synagogue janitors like the (ignorant) people of the land . . . On whom should we lean? On our Father in Heaven. With the advent of the Messiah,[1] presumptuousness shall wax great and produce shall soar in price; the vine will yield its fruit but the wine will be costly; and the heathen (idol worshippers) will be converted to heresy and there shall be no rebuke . . . The wisdom of the Scribes shall be decadent and those who fear sin shall be hateful to others; and truth shall be absent. The young shall put the elders to shame . . . (as it is written) the son dishonoreth the father, the daughter riseth up against her own mother . . . a man's enemies are the men of his own house (Micah 7:6). . . .And on whom are we to lean?—On our Father in Heaven. R. Phineas ben Jair says, Zeal leads to cleanliness, and cleanliness leads to purity, and purity leads to self-restraint, and self-restraint leads to sanctity, and sanctity leads to humility, and humility leads to the fear of sin, and the fear of sin leads to piety, and piety leads to divine intuition (literally, "the Holy Spirit", *ruah hakodesh*), and divine intuition leads to the resurrection of the dead, and the resurrection of the dead shall come through Elijah of blessed memory." Amen.[2]

---

[1]Literally, "on the heels of the Messiah."
[2]P. Blackman F.C.S., *Mishnayoth,* Vol. III (New York: Judaica Press Inc., 1963), pp. 382–83.

MARTYRDOM

Zeno

Introduction: Zeno, the founder of the Stoic school of Greek philosophy, was an older contemporary of Socrates, coming to Athens from his native island of Cyprus around the year 480 B.C. There are various conflicting stories of Zeno's death. One common account relates that he lived to the extraordinary age of 98 and finally strangled himself out of contempt for his physical frailty. A more popular version, by the time of Diogenes Laertius, had it that he was executed because of his attempts to overthrow a variously identified local king.

Diogenes Laertius, *Lives of Eminent Philosophers* 9.26

Zeno was a great man, both in respect to philosophy and as a politician. His books, at any rate, are full of understanding. He was disposed to unseat the tyrant Nearchos—others say, Diomedon—and was arrested; thus says Herakleides in "The Epitome of Satyros." At that time he was questioned as to the identity of his fellow conspirators and concerning the weapons which he was taking to Lipara. He named all of the tyrant's friends, wishing to leave him without supporters. Then he told the king he had something to whisper in his ear about certain people. When the king leaned over he bit his ear and did not let go until he was stabbed to death, suffering the same death as Aristogeiton, the killer of the tyrant.

Demetrios says, in "Men of the Same Name," that Zeno bit off his (the king's) nose. Antisthenes says, in "Successions of the Philosophers," that after Zeno incriminated the tyrant's friends he was asked by the tyrant if there were anyone else to indict. He answered, "You, the pestilence of the city!" And to those standing by he said, "I am amazed at your cowardice, that on account of the very things which I now endure you are slaves of the tyrant." Finally he bit off his own tongue and spit it at the tyrant. The citizens were so incited that immediately they stoned the tyrant to death. The majority of authors mainly agree in this. But Hermippos says Zeno was thrown into a mortar and butchered.

181

Eleazar

Introduction: This little treatise claims to be a philosophical discussion of "pious reason" (1:1). The following selection is one of the author's examples of the way that this "pious reason" has triumphed in Israel's history. It is clear from the story that "pious reason" also means faith, and loyalty to the Jewish way of life. We include it to illustrate the Jewish belief that a righteous man's death could serve as a vicarious sacrifice to atone for the sins of the less faithful. The setting is during the Maccabean revolt, 166–162 B.C. Antiochus Epiphanes IV, the Seleucid tyrant of Palestine, is portrayed as the villain who is trying to force the Jews to renounce their faith.

---

4 Maccabees 5:1—6:28

5.1. The tyrant Antiochus, with his court, sat upon a certain high place, and, with his fully armed troops around him, 2. he commanded his personal guards to drag in each one of the Jews, and he ordered the Jews to eat pig's meat and foods offered to idols. 3. If any should refuse to eat the abominable meats, they were to be tortured and killed. 4. After many had been forcibly seized, one of the first of the group, an old man named Eleazar who was a priest and trained in the Law's knowledge, who was also well-known to many in Antiochus' court because of the high esteem in which he was held by his own people, was brought before Antiochus.

> 5–38. Antiochus asks Eleazar to save his own life by eating the pig's meat because the meat is a gift of Nature, and one should not reject Nature's gifts. Besides, God will forgive such a sin done under duress. Eleazar refuses to eat the profane flesh and challenges Antiochus to do his worst.

6.1. . . . The guards dragged Eleazar roughly to the torturing place. 2. First, they stripped the old man, so that he was dressed only in the honorable clothes of piety. 3. Then, binding both his arms, they whipped him. 4. "Obey the king's commands!" cried a herald standing by. 5. But the confident and noble man, truly an Eleazar,[1] was no more shaken than if he were being tortured in a dream. 6. The old man kept his eyes raised up to Heaven, as his flesh was torn by the lashes until he

[1] In Hebrew, the name means "God is my helper."

was dripping blood and his sides were gashed. 7. When he fell to the ground because his body could not stand the pain, he still kept his reason unbowed and upright. 8. One of the cruel guards kicked him savagely in the side with his foot to make him get up, 9. but he endured the pain and despised the force, and persevered in spite of the torture. 10. Like a brave athlete, the old man endured the pain. 11. His face was covered with sweat and he was panting; the nobility of his soul astonished his torturers.

12. Then, partly because of compassion for his old age, partly out of sympathy because of their former friendship, 13. and partly from astonishment at his courage, some of the king's men came to him and said, 14. "Why do you irrationally destroy yourself in this awful way, Eleazar? 15. Let us bring you the boiled meats, but you only pretend to eat the pig's meat, and save yourself."

16. Eleazar, as if his tortures were made more painful by their suggestion, cried out, 17. "No! May we children of Abraham never rationalize so evilly, so that with numbed soul we hypocritically play a part unfitting to us. 18. For if we should so reverse ourselves after we have sought the truth up through old age, and have guarded lawfully the honor of such living, that would be wholly irrational. 19. We would become a symbol of impiety to the young, so that we would be an example that they should eat defiled things. 20. It would be shameful if we should live a little more time and yet should be mocked for cowardice by all men during this little time. 21. We would be considered unmanly by the tyrant, and we would not have defended the divine Law until death. 22. Therefore, O children of Abraham, die nobly for piety! 23. Guards of the tyrant, why do you hesitate?"

24. When they saw his greatness in the face of the tortures and that he was unwavering before their compassion, they dragged him to the fire. 25. There they threw him on it, burning him with torture devices, and they poured evil-smelling liquids into his nostrils. 26. When the fire burned to his bones, and he was about to faint, he lifted his eyes to God and said, 27. "You know, O God, that I could be saved, but I am dying from fiery tortures for the sake of the Law. 28. Be merciful to your people; may my torture be a satisfaction on their behalf. Make my blood their cleansing,[2] and take my life as a substitute for theirs."[3] When he said this, the noble, holy man died from the torture, enduring torture unto death for the sake of the Law.

---

[2]From guilt of sin.
[3]His fidelity to the Torah *should* have been rewarded with peace and long life; here he offers his unwarranted death as a substitute to God for the many in Israel who deserved God's wrath for whatever reason.

Rabbi Akiba

Introduction: Akiba ben Joseph is one of the most revered names in all of Jewish history, ranking in importance with Moses and Maimonides. It was largely due to Akiba's leadership in the black days after the destruction of the Second Temple, A.D. 70, that the legal and religious foundations were laid for Israel's long years of expatriation. On the other hand, Akiba was partly the cause of the Jewish exile as well. For, despite the Roman warning against fomenting insurrection, in 132 he openly proclaimed Simeon ben Cosiba (bar Kokhba) to be the King Messiah, the Liberator of Israel, and thus helped spark a full-fledged rebellion which lasted for three frenzied years. After that, the Romans enacted the hateful decree renaming Jerusalem "Aelia Capitolina," and closing it to Jews forever. Indeed, this historic exclusion was not completely overcome until the recent recapture of the Arab sector of Jerusalem during the Six Day War of 1967.

In any case, some time during the fourth or fifth century, long after the tumultuous events of the Bar Kokhba rebellion had subsided, the rabbinic sages in exile in Babylon were examining the meaning of the phrase in Deuteronomy 6:5, "Thou shalt love the Lord thy God with all thy heart, etc." This phrase reminded them of the occasion of Akiba's death at the hands of the Romans, for Akiba had taught, " 'Thou shalt love the Lord thy God . . . with all thy soul'—that is, even if he takes away thy soul (=life)." The following excerpt contains the Babylonian sages' memory of how Akiba lived up to his own teaching.

Our rabbis tell of the time when an evil Kingdom (Rome) forbade Israel to be occupied with Torah. Rabbi Pappos ben Yehudah went and found Rabbi Akiba gathering people (openly) in the streets and instructing them in Torah. He said to him, "Akiba, are you not afraid of the evil kingdom?" He said to him, "I will tell you a parable. To what is it (our situation) similar? It is like a fox who was walking along the bank of the river, watching fishes grouping themselves, first in this spot, then in that. He said to them, 'From what are you fleeing?' They said to him, 'From the nets which the sons of man (*benē ādām*) cast upon us.' He said to them, 'Quick! Come up onto the shore and we will dwell, you and I, in the way my fathers dwelt with your fathers.' They said, 'Are you not he whom they call the smartest of all living things? You are not smart but stupid! If we are afraid in the place where we can live, how much more

184

in the place where we would die?"

18 Not many days later, Rabbi Akiba was arrested and put in jail. They also arrested Pappos ben Yehudah and imprisoned him next to him. Akiba said to him, "Pappos, why are you here?" He said, "Are you not blessed, Rabbi Akiba, for you were arrested on account of the Torah! Woe to Pappos who was arrested on account of nothing!"

When the Romans took Rabbi Akiba out to kill him, it was the time of day appointed to recite the *Shema*.[1] As the soldiers began to tear the living flesh off his bones with hooks of iron, he began to recite the Shema. His disciples said to him, "Master, even here?!" He said to them, "All the days of my life I have been worried by this verse 'with all thy soul'—which means, 'even if He takes thy life.' I used to say to myself, 'When will it be possible for me to fulfill it?' And now the opportunity has come to me. Shall I not fulfill it?" Thereupon he lengthened out saying "On-n-n-ne" until he died, saying "One." A Voice came from Heaven (*bath qōl*) saying, "Blessed are you, Rabbi Akiba, who died while saying 'One.'" But the angels standing before the Holy One, Blessed be He, said to him, "Is that how you repay such devotion to Torah? What about 'Deliver my soul from the wicked . . . from men, by thy hand, O Lord?'"[2] He said to them, "'Their (i.e., the wicked's) portion is (this) life (only).'"[3] A Voice came from Heaven, saying, "Blessed are you, Rabbi Akiba, for your portion is life in the Age to Come!" (bBerakoth 61b).

---

[1]Deut. 6:4, "Hear O Israel. The Lord Thy God, The Lord is One."
[2]Psalm 14:13f.
[3]Psalm 14:13f., i.e., God's answer is a continuation of the same psalm, only reading the second part with hidden meaning, brought out in the text by means of the words in the parentheses.

Romulus

Introduction: The ancient story that Romulus, the legendary cofounder of Rome, was translated to Heaven and became a God was of great importance during the birth of the Roman empire. Romulus was known, in legend, to have been an absolute ruler. To be such also was the desire of the emperors of Rome; they wanted total power in order to bring peace to a chaotic political situation. Julius Caesar and Augustus Caesar consciously sought to project themselves to the public in such a way as to reflect the image of Romulus. Thus, Julius was to be the "second founder" of Rome. However, the tyrannical aspect of Romulus had to be moulded into the image of a Romulus who was a "strong man" but who was benevolent and who had divine sanction. Both Ovid and Livy write to that purpose. Ovid is a poet and Livy a historian, but both were "friends of the court." It is interesting to see how these two points of view deal with the same traditions, which are probably from the poet Ennius. Both exalt the empire, Roman military might, and expansionism.

Ovid, *Metamorphoses* 14.805–851

Ovid tells how Romulus brought peace to his kinsmen, and then ruled them in benevolent fashion until it was time to be taken up to be with the Gods.

Tatius fell, and equally to the two peoples (Roman and Sabine), Romulus, you gave laws. Then, taking off his helmet, Mars spoke to the father of Gods and men (Jupiter), saying, "The time is here, Father, because the Roman state is strong with a great foundation and does not depend on one man's protection, to give the gift promised to me and your noble grandson and to take him from earth and to place him in Heaven. You once said to me in the assembled council of the Gods, for I have remembered and have marked your pious words in my mind, 'one there will be whom you shall lift up into the blue heaven.' Let now the promise of your words be made good." The Omnipotent One agreed, and he hid the sky with dark clouds, and he terrified the earth with thunder and lightning. Gradivus (Mars) knew these were the ratified signs of the booty promised to him, and, leaning on his spear, he boarded his chariot, the horses straining beneath the bloody yoke, and, with a blow of the lash, he shattered the air. Gliding down through the air, he came to rest on the top of the wooded Palatine hill. There, Romulus was giving his friendly laws to the citizens, and Mars caught Ilia's son up. His mortal body became thin, dissolving in the air, as a lead pellet shot by a broad sling will melt away in the sky. Suddenly he had a beautiful form more worthy of the high couches (of the Gods); such a form has Quirinius, now wearing the sacred robe.

Later, his wife was mourning him as dead, when queenly Juno ordered Iris to descend to Hersilia by her arching way, to speak thus to the widowed queen, "O woman of Latium and of the people of the Sabines, glorious, most worthy of all to have been the consort of so great a man, now to (continue to) be the wife of Quirinius, stop your crying, and, if you wish to see your husband, follow me to the sacred grove which is on the hill of Quirinius and which shades the temple of the king of Rome." Iris obeyed and gliding to the earth through her sacred (rainbow) arch, she summoned Hersilia in the words commended to her. Hersilia scarcely raised her eye and, with a sly look, said, "O Goddess, for I dare not say who you are, but it is clear you are a Goddess, lead, O lead, and show me my husband's face. If the Fates grant me to be able somehow to see it, I will have gained Heaven." Immediately, she went to Romulus' hill with the virgin daughter of Thaumas. (When she got) there, a star from Heaven (*ab aethere*) glided down to earth. With her hair flaming from the star's light, Hersilia, with the star, went up into the sky. The founder of Rome's city received her with familiar hands and changed her mortal body and former name. He called her Hora, and now as a Goddess, she is united once more with Quirinius.

Ovid, *Fasti* 2.481–509

> The story is the same, but with some slight difference in the emphasis placed upon details. Here, the story of Romulus' murder of Remus is briefly mentioned. Gradivus (Mars) asks Jupiter to honor his pledge, "Although the other is lost, the one who is left will be enough for me and for Remus" (1.485–6). Jupiter agrees.

489. With Jupiter's assent, both poles (of the earth) shook, and Atlas moved the burden of the sky. There is a place, called by the old ones the marsh of Caprea. By chance, Romulus, you were there giving laws. The sun disappeared, and rising clouds obscured the sky, and a heavy rain shower fell. Then it thundered, the air was torn by flames. The people fled, and the king (Romulus) flew to the stars on his father's (Mars') horses. There was grieving, and certain senators were falsely charged with murder, and that belief might have stuck in the people's mind. But Proculus Julius was coming from the Alba Longa; the moon was

shining, he was not using a torch. Suddenly the hedges on the left shook and moved. He shrank back and his hair stood on end. Beautiful and more than human and clothed in a sacred robe, Romulus was seen, standing in the middle of the road. He said, "Stop the [Romans] from their mourning; do not let them violate my divinity (*numina*) with their tears; order the pious crowd to bring incense and worship the new Quirinius and to cultivate the arts of their fathers, war." He gave the order and he vanished to the upper world from Julius' eyes.

Livy, Book 1.16

. . . when he (Romulus) was holding a maneuver in order to review the army at the field near the marsh of Caprea, suddenly a storm arose, with great lightning and thunder, and it veiled the king in such a dense cloud that his form was hidden from the troops; from that time Romulus was not on earth. The terrified Roman soldiers were finally quieted after the sunlight came back and restored calm and serenity following that hour of wild confusion. But, even so, when they saw the royal seat empty, they remained silent and sad for a long time, as if stricken by the fear of being orphaned, although they readily believed the senators standing nearest him who said that Romulus had been taken up on high by the storm. Then at first a few, then all, joyfully declared Romulus, the king and father of the city of Rome, to be a God, the son of a God. They asked (him) with prayers for peace so that he would always be pleased to wish favor for his children. I believe there were some even then who argued secretly that the king had been torn apart by the hands of the senators. Indeed, this rumor spread also, but very obscurely; the other version was enhanced by men's admiration for Romulus and their panic. Further, the strategem of one man is said to have added to the credibility of the story. For, when the citizens were disturbed by the loss of the king and were hostile toward the senators, Julius Proculus, as it is told, a man of repute—at least he was the author of this important thing—addressed the assembly. "Romulus, O Quirites," he said, "the father of this city, at the first light of this day, descended from the sky and clearly showed himself to me. While I was awed with holy fright, I stood reverently before him, asking in prayer that I might look at him without sin. 'Go,' he said, 'announce to the Romans that Heaven wishes that my Rome shall be the capital of the earth; therefore, they shall cultivate the military; they shall know and teach their descendants that no human might can resist Roman arms.' He said this, and went up on high." It is a great marvel what credence was generated by the man's tale, and how the loss of Romulus, for which the common people and the army grieved, was assuaged by the belief in his immortality.

The Dream of Scipio

Introduction: Marcus Tullius Cicero combined an extraordinarily turbulent, high-level legal, and political career with voluminous literary productivity. His life (106–43 B.C.) encompassed the final years of Rome's republican form of government, as it collapsed into anarchy, opportunism, and autocracy. Cicero hated the new class of political demagogues, as he considered them, and spent the last decades of his life combating them, only to fall victim to the forces of Marc Antony. His lifelong ideal was the old, aristocratic republicanism, and *The Republic,* his greatest political writing, was devoted to expounding its virtues. Cicero chose as the spokesman for these views in *The Republic* a Roman of the old type, a statesman and general of the previous generation from one of Rome's most illustrious families, Publius Cornelius Scipio Africanus the Younger. He carries the main burden of expounding the various subjects throughout the dialogue: the best form of government, Rome's political history, the ideal statesman (or, as we would say, politician), the nature of civil justice, and so forth. But the actual Scipio, despite his high birth, early military success, and political abilities, was never able to cause the Roman Senate to return to the austere, simple ways of the early Republic, and his efforts to do so earned him many enemies (especially Tiberius Gracchus, whose sister was Scipio's wife). He was finally murdered, and the Senate did not seek overly hard to find the culprits, although there were some obvious candidates. Thus it should be noted that Cicero's choice of principal spokesman would have had a startling poignancy for those among Cicero's circle of friends who agreed with his old-time republicanism. And the final scene of his long, six-book "conversation," namely, this "dream" of Scipio's in which Scipio is apotheosized, or brought up to the level of the Gods, looking first into the future and then into Eternity, this scene would have seemed to the same audience a most moving and sublime conclusion to the whole work. Even today, we can still catch the melancholy running throughout, for, to men like Scipio, the world of men within which they are to strive to be honorable is a realm of futility.

Cicero, *The Republic* 6.9–26

9. After arriving in Africa, where, as you know, I was military tribune of the fourth legion under the consul Manius Manilius, my first desire was to meet King Masinissa, who for good reasons was on friendly terms

with our family.[1] When I met him, the old man burst into tears and embraced me. Sometime after, he looked up to Heaven and said, "To you most glorious Sun and to you other Inhabitants of Heaven I give thanks that before I depart this life, I behold within my kingdom and in these halls Publius Cornelius Scipio, whose very name gives me new life; so enduring to me is the memory of that most excellent and invincible man."[2] Then I questioned him about his kingdom, and he in turn asked me about our state, and thus we spent the entire day in protracted conversation.

10. Later, after we had been entertained with royal splendor, we continued our conversation far into the evening; during this time the old man talked of nothing but Africanus, recalling not only all his deeds but his every word. When we departed to rest, a deeper sleep than usual came upon me, as I was weary from my journey and it was late. I had the following dream, induced, I imagine by what we had been discussing earlier; for it often happens that our thoughts and words produce some such effect in sleep, as Ennius recounts with respect to Homer, of whom he often used to think and speak while awake. I dreamed that Africanus was beside me in the form that I knew from his ancestral bust rather than from his person. I shuddered when I recognized him, but he said, "Calm yourself and don't be afraid; commit to memory what I say.

11. "Do you see that city—from a high vantage point that was radiant with stars, he was pointing to Carthage—which, though forced by me to submit to the Roman people, is renewing its former wars and cannot be at peace, to besiege which you now come, though not yet a full-fledged soldier? Within two years you shall be consul and shall overthrow Carthage, and you shall earn by your deeds the surname which you now have as an inheritance from me. When you have destroyed Carthage and have conducted a triumph, you shall be made censor; in the capacity of legate you shall go to Egypt, Syria, Asia, and Greece; you shall be chosen consul a second time in your absence; you shall successfully conclude a great war; and you shall destroy Numantia.[3] But when you ride in state to the Capitol you shall find a republic in turmoil, owing to the counsels of my grandson.[4]

12. "At this time, Africanus, you must show our country the light of your spirit, your character, and your judgment. But here I see that the

---

[1]P. Cornelius Scipio the Younger had gone in 149 B.C. to Africa (=Carthage) as a young tribune to take part in the Third Punic War. There he rejoined an old ally of the Romans, King Masinissa, who had fought at the side of Scipio's grandfather and namesake, P. Cornelius Scipio Africanus the Elder, the Roman general who inflicted the decisive defeat on Carthage to end the Second Punic War.
[2]I.e., P. Cornelius Scipio the Elder.
[3]All these "predictions" Scipio the Younger actually achieved.
[4]i.e., Tiberius Gracchus, the founder of the reform party.

paths of the fates, as it were, are uncertain. For when your life has accomplished seven times eight revolutions of the sun, and these two numbers, each of which for a different reason is regarded as perfect, in Nature's course have made ready for you the time alloted by the fates, the whole state will turn to you and your name alone; the Senate, all the optimates, our allies, the Latins all will look to you, upon you alone the safety of the state will depend, and, in short, you will be called upon as dictator to restore order to the Republic, provided that you escape the impious hands of your kinsmen."[5]

At this juncture Laelius broke into sobs and the others groaned deeply, but Scipio said, smiling gently, "Hush, please don't awaken me; hear me out."

13. "But, Africanus, bear this in mind, in order that you may be more zealous in the defense of your country, all who have preserved, aided, or advanced their country have a definite place in Heaven where the blessed enjoy eternal life. For there is no earthly happening which is more acceptable to that sovereign God who rules all the universe than the councils and assemblies of men joined together by law, which are called states; the rulers and preservers of these go from here and to here they return."

14. Though I was at this point thoroughly frightened, not so much by the fear of death as by the thought of my friends' plotting, I nevertheless asked whether he himself and my father Paulus and the others whom we thought of as dead were still alive. "Those are indeed alive," he said, "who have escaped from the bondage of the body as from a prison; what you call life is in reality death. Do you not see your father Paulus coming toward you?" When I saw him I broke down in tears; he, however, forbade me to weep, all the time embracing and kissing me.

15. When I had stopped my weeping and was able to speak, I said, "If this is indeed life, my sacred and worthy father, as Africanus tells me, why do I tarry upon earth? Why do I not hurry to you here?"

"It cannot be," said he, "for unless that God whose realm is all that you survey, frees you from the prison of the body, you cannot obtain access to this place. For man has been created for this purpose, that he might tend that globe called earth which you see in the middle of this region. And a soul has been given him from the eternal fires that you call constellations and stars, which being spherical and round masses animated with divine impulses, accomplish their cycles and revolutions

[5]This "prediction" is largely gratuitous, for Cicero is heightening the pathos of Scipio's untimely death, which was brought about, perhaps with the aid of his own relatives, before he reached the pinnacle of his career. This is the reason for the others' groans—the "prediction" of Scipio's untimely death evokes sadness from his listeners—much as if someone were to portray a person predicting to the young John F. Kennedy his own glorious political future and sudden assassination.

with amazing speed. Therefore, you, Publius, and all just men, must keep that soul in the care of the body, nor must you depart life without the order of him who gave you that soul, lest you seem to have deserted the post assigned you as mortal by God.

16. "But like your father and grandfather, Scipio, cherish justice and duty, which you assuredly owe your parents and kinsmen, but most of all your country. Such a life is the path to Heaven and to the assembly of those who have ceased to live on earth and who, released from the body, inhabit the place which you see,"—it was the circle that gleamed with the greatest brilliance among the stars—"which you, after the Greeks, call the Milky Way."

When I looked about from there, all else seemed beautiful and wonderful. There were stars which we never saw from earth and the magnitude of each was such as we never imagined. The smallest star was that farthest from Heaven and nearest the earth which shone with borrowed light. The globular masses of the stars, however, far surpassed the size of the earth. Furthermore, the earth itself seemed to me so small that I felt contempt for our empire which covered, as it were, a tiny patch on its surface.

17. While I was gazing still more closely at the earth, Africanus said, "How long will you fix your mind upon the earth? Do you not see what quarters you have entered? The whole is connected by nine circles, or rather spheres. One of them which is the outermost is that of Heaven; it encloses all the rest; it is the supreme God himself, holding and containing the other spheres; in it are fixed the endless revolving courses of the stars. Under it there are seven other spheres which revolve in a direction opposite to that of Heaven. One of these globes is occupied by that star which men on earth call Saturn. Next is that dazzling star called Jupiter which is beneficial and healthful to mankind. Then there is that red star, terrible to the earth, which you call Mars. The next region below almost midway between Heaven and earth contains the sun; he is the leader, chief and director of the lights, the mind and regulating power of the universe, of such magnitude that he illuminates and fills all things with his light. He is followed by Venus and Mercury, as satellites in their orbits, and in the lowest sphere revolves the moon set on fire by the rays of the sun. Beneath the moon there is nothing but what is mortal and perishable except the souls given to the human race by the kindness of the Gods. Above the moon all things are eternal. For the earth which is the ninth and central sphere is immovable and the lowest, and all bodies by their natural downward tendency are drawn toward it."

18. After recovering from my amazement at seeing all these marvels, I said, "What is that sound so loud and yet so sweet which fills my ears?" "That melody," said he, "composed in unequal time which nevertheless

is divided into exact harmony is caused by the impulse and motion of the spheres themselves, and by tempering high with low notes it produces varied harmonic effects; for such great motions cannot be hurried on in silence and nature declares that one extreme produce a low tone and the other a high. For this reason that highest sphere of the starry Heaven whose revolving is more rapid, is stirred with a high and quick sound; while the lowest sphere, that of the moon, is stirred with the lowest sound; for the earth, the ninth sphere, remains motionless and in one position, occupying the center of the universe. The remaining eight spheres, two of which possess the same velocity, produce seven sounds at different intervals, which number is the key of almost everything; and learned men by imitating this harmony with stringed instruments and by singing have discovered for themselves a way for their return to this place as others have done who, endued with brilliant intellect, have cultivated divine pursuits during their mortal lives. Men's ears filled with this sound have become deaf, for you have no duller sense. Thus the people who live near the place where the Nile rushes down from the lofty mountains at the spot called Catalupa have lost their sense of hearing because of the loudness of the sound. But this sound produced by the swift revolution of the whole universe is so great that human ears cannot comprehend it, just as you cannot look directly at the sun because your sense of sight is overcome by its rays." While gazing at these scenes in awe, I nevertheless kept turning my eyes back toward the earth.

19. Then Africanus said, "I see that even now you are contemplating the abode and home of men; if it seems small to you, as it really is, keep your eyes on these celestial things, and despise the earthly. For what renown can you win from the speech of men, or what glory that is worth the striving for? You see that men inhabit only a few, tiny portions of the earth and that between these spots, as it were, there are vast wildernesses. And those who inhabit the earth are so cut off from one another that there can be no communication among them, but some inhabit areas of the earth that are oblique, transverse, and even opposite you; from such you surely can expect no glory.

20. "You are to notice that the same earth is encircled and encompassed, as it were, by certain zones of which the two that are the farthest from one another, under the poles of the Heavens, are stiff from the frost, whereas the central and largest zone is parched by the heat of the sun. Two zones are habitable, of which the southern (whose inhabitants set their footprints in a direction opposite to yours) has no connection with your race. As for the northern zone which you inhabit, see what a small portion of it is yours. For all the earth that you inhabit, narrowing at the poles and broadening from East to West, is but a little island

surrounded by that sea which you on earth call the Atlantic, the Great Sea, or Ocean; and yet its great name notwithstanding, you see how small it is. Has your renown or that of any of us been able to leave these civilized and inhabited lands and cross the Caucasus Mountains there, which you see, or swim the Ganges? What inhabitant of the rest of the East or of the distant tracts of the setting sun or the remote north or south will hear your name? Moreover, how long will those who speak of us continue to do so?

21. "Yet even if future descendants should desire to transmit to their posterity the achievements of each of us, which they have heard from their fathers, yet because floods and conflagrations must occur at appointed times, we are unable to win lasting glory, much less eternal. And of what consequence is it if your name is on the lips of those born after you, when your predecessors never mentioned you?

22. "They were no less numerous and certainly better men; especially as none of those who is able to hear our fame can retain the memory of it for even one year? For men commonly measure the year by the revolution of the sun, this is, of a single star; but when all the stars return to the same point from which they once set out, and bring back after long intervals the same arrangement of all the Heaven, then that truly can be called a full year. I scarcely dare to say how many generations of men are contained in such a year. For as once the sun appeared to men to be eclipsed and extinguished, at the time, when the spirit of Romulus entered these realms, so whenever the sun shall again be eclipsed in the same place and at the same time, then you will know that all the constellations and stars have been recalled to their starting point and that the year is complete. But be assured that the twentieth part of such a year has not yet elapsed.

23. "Accordingly, if you have no hope of returning to this place, where great and preeminent men receive the objects of their aspirations, of what value is your fame among mortals which can scarcely last but a slight part of a single year? Therefore, if you will lift your eyes on high and gaze upon this abode and Heavenly Home, you neither will yield to the gossip of the vulgar nor rest your hopes on human rewards for your deeds; Virtue herself by her own charms should lead you on to true glory. Let others worry about what they may say of you, for talk they will. All such talk, however, is confined to the narrow regions which you see; none concerning any man has endured forever; rather does it die with the man and is erased in the forgetfulness of posterity."

24. When he had spoken thus, I said, "Africanus, if indeed the path to Heaven lies open to those who have served their country well, though from youth I have followed in the footsteps of my father and yourself, yet now with so great a reward set before me I shall strive with much

greater effort." He replied, "Do, indeed, strive and see that it is not you, but your body, that is mortal; for you are not the man that your human form reveals; but the soul of each man is his real self, not the human figure which the eye can see. Know, therefore, that you are a God, if indeed it is a God that has life, sensation, memory, and foresight, and that rules, directs, and moves that body over which it presides just as the sovereign God rules this universe; and just as the eternal God moves the universe which is in part perishable, so an eternal soul moves the frail body.

25. "For that which is ever in motion is immortal, but that which transmits motion to another object and is itself moved from another source must of necessity cease to live when the motion ends. Thus only that which moves itself never ceases to move, because it never forsakes itself; rather it is the source and the cause of motion in other things that are moved. But this cause has no beginning, for all things proceed from a first cause, whereas it cannot be derived from anything else; for that would not be the first cause, if it were derived from another source. And if it never has a beginning, it certainly never has an end. For the first cause, if destroyed, cannot be reborn from any other source nor can it produce anything else itself, because everything must spring from an original source. It follows, therefore, that motion begins with that which is capable of self-motion; this moreover can neither be born nor die; otherwise all Heaven must tumble down and all nature stop; nor will they have any force from which they can be set in motion again.

26. "Since, therefore, it is plain that whatever moves itself is eternal, who can deny that this is the natural property of souls? For everything that is set in motion by an external impulse possesses no soul; but whatever has a soul is impelled by an inner motion of its own; for this is the peculiar nature and essence of a soul. Now if a soul, alone, of all things moves of itself, it assuredly has not been born and is immortal. Employ it in the noblest pursuits. And the noblest concerns are those assumed for the safety of your country; a soul stirred and trained by these pursuits will have a quicker flight to this abode, its own home; and this will be the faster, if even now, while imprisoned in the body, it reaches out and by contemplating what is beyond itself, detaches itself as much as possible from the body. For the souls of those who are devoted to the pleasures of the body and have become slaves to them, as it were, and who under the influence of the desires which are subservient to pleasure have violated the laws of Gods and men, such souls, when they have escaped their bodies, hover around the earth itself, and they do not return to this place until they have been tormented for many ages."—He departed; I awoke from sleep.

———————————————

Apotheosis of Antinous

Introduction: It was widely accepted practice to worship the Roman emperors as Gods, for just as in life so also in the afterlife, they continued to wield great power for good among the peoples surrounding the Mediterranean Sea. It came as something of a surprise, however, when the Emperor Hadrian in A.D. 130 established a cult, not to himself, but to his favorite slave Antinous, adding scandal to shock since this slave had not only been the emperor's pet companion and lover, but he had died suddenly under very suspicious circumstances by accidental (?) drowning in the Nile. Nor did Hadrian's immediate proclamation of the divinization of Antinous and founding temples for his worship, do much to stem the wild rumors that began to circulate. Repercussions of these events were still echoing a century later, when, for example, the Christian theologian Origen of Alexandria considered outrageous the galling insult of his learned antagonist Celsus, who said that the superstitious Christians had invented a new God by divinizing the man Jesus in much the same way that Hadrian had introduced a new deity by ordering everyone to worship his dead lover.

The selections pertaining to the apotheosis of Antinous are of three sorts: Hadrian's own sacred inscriptions proclaiming Antinous to be Osiris, contemporary pagan comment, and contemporary Christian comment.

Hadrian's Memorial to Antinous

These inscriptions on the Pincio Obelisk are very difficult to translate, being composed of extraordinarily confused heiroglyphic phrases written by someone who obviously knew little of the ancient sacred language. But enough can be understood to make some sense of them. The first of the four carvings is an inscription dedicated to Hadrian himself; it is followed by three others which are here given, on the basis of the German translation by A. Erman.

Antinous Before Thoth

Antinous the Holy, he grew up to be a beautiful youth, while he . . . gladdened (?); his heart . . . as that of a strong-armed man; he received the commands of the Gods as . . . All the rituals of the priests of Osiris were repeated in respect to him and all his . . . as unknown. When his book (?) was going forth, the whole land . . . was . . . and

197

. . . never has anything similar been done before to earlier persons as (is done) today, (that is,) his altars, his houses, his titles . . . He breathes the air of life. His glory is in the hearts of all men, like that of the Lords of Hermopolis, the Lords of the hieroglyphs. His soul grows young again as the . . . to their season, during night and day, to each time and each . . .

His love is in the hearts of his servants, his fear (in) all (bellies), his praise is from all men, while they praise him. He sits in the hall of truth. The excellent Enlightened Ones in the company of Osiris in Te-zoser . . . give him justification. They let his words remain in the whole land, their heart is made joyful over him.

He goes to every place where he wants to go. The doorkeepers of the realm of the dead give him every praise (?). They unlock their locks; they open their doors before him, in a million of millions of years, daily . . . his whole life-span, [im]mortal.

Antinous Before Amon

Osiris Antinous, the Holy, who is in Heaven, a . . . will be in his place of . . . made, which names are after his name, for the brave, who are in this land and the helmsmen and . . . of the whole land and likewise all people, who know the place where Thoth is while they . . . give, with wreaths on their head . . . with all good things. One brings offerings there to his altars, one lays fragrant divine offerings (?) before him daily, according to the customs (?) . . . He was extolled by the artists (?) of Thoth as . . . his . . . ; he goes in his place . . . the cities of all lands, for he hears the pleas of those who call him. He heals the sick . . . to him he sends a dream. He accomplishes his work unto men (?); he does miracles (?) . . . his heart, because he is a true offspring of divine seed . . . in his limbs (?) . . . body of his mother (?). He would be . . . in the house of his birth of. . .

Antinous Before (the carving cannot be deciphered)

Antinous, who is in Heaven, who rests in this place which lies in the border field of the Goddess of the pleasures (?) of Rome, he is known as God in the pious places of Egypt. A temple was built to him; he became honored as a God by the prophets and priests of Upper and Lower Egypt, by the residents of Egypt, as many as there are of them. A city was named after his name, the . . . soldiers of the Greeks and those who are in the temples of Egypt, they come to his city . . . their . . . acres and fields are given to them in order to make their life very beautiful. A temple of this God is therein, his name is "Osiris Antinous the Holy." It was built from beautiful limestone, with sphinxes around it and statues and many columns like those that in olden times had been made by the ancients and likewise as had been made by the Greeks. Each God and each Goddess gives to him the breath of life and he breathes in a new youthfulness.

CONTEMPORARY GREEK COMMENT

Dio Cassius, *Roman History* 69.11.2

While Hadrian was in Egypt he rebuilt the city named for Antinous. For Antinous was from the city of Bithynium, a city in Bithynia, which we also call Claudiopolis. Antinous was his darling boy and died in Egypt; he either fell into the Nile, as Hadrian writes, or, what seems to be the truth, he was offered as a sacrifice. As I said, Hadrian was very interested in the magical arts and used all types of divinations and incantations. Thus he gave divine honors to Antinous, either because of his love for him or because he died voluntarily (it apparently was necessary for a life to be freely offered to accomplish what he, Hadrian, wanted). He built a city near the place where he died and he named it after him. He erected statues of him, actually sacred images, almost all over the world. Finally, Hadrian said he had seen a certain star which, it seemed to him, was that of Antinous, and he welcomed the mythical stories of his friends, namely, that the star really was created from Antinous' soul and had just then appeared. He was ridiculed on account of these things and also because, when his sister Paulina died, he did not at once pay her any (divine) honor . . .

Pausanius, *Description of Greece* 8.9.7–8

Antinous also was considered by them[1] to be a God. The temple of Antinous is the newest of the temples in Mantineia. He was a favorite of the Emperor Hadrian. I never saw Antinous personally, but I did see him in statues and pictures. He has sacred honors in other places, and an Egyptian city on the Nile is named after him. He holds the sacred honors in Mantineia for these reasons. Antinous was a native of Bithynia, beyond the Sangarius River. The Bithynians are Arcadians and Mantineians by descent. On account of this, the emperor founded his worship in Mantineia, and mystic rituals are held for him each year as well as sacred games (in his honor) every fifth year.

There is a building in the gymnasium of Mantineia that has statues of Antinous. The building is marvelous to see because of the jewels with which it is decorated and especially because of its pictures. Most of them are of Antinous who is pictured to look like Dionysus . . .

[1]Pausanius is describing the various deities worshiped in Mantineia, a city of Greece, southwest of Corinth.

CONTEMPORARY CHRISTIAN COMMENT

Eusebius, *Ecclesiastical History* 4.8.2[2]

. . . To such men they made cenotaphs and temples even up to the present. Among them is also Antinous, a slave of the Emperor Hadrian. For him the Antinoan games are held, even though he was our contemporary. And Hadrian created a city named for Antinous, and ordained prophets (for him).

Justin Martyr, *Apology* I.29

We think it is not improper to mention among these things also Antinous, our contemporary, whom everyone was coerced to worship as a God on account of fear, although they knew who he was and where he came from.

Clement of Alexandria, *Protrepticus* 4

In Egypt there is another new God, and almost in Greece, too, since the Roman king (Hadrian) reverently elevated to Godhood his lover Antinous, an exceedingly beautiful boy, whom he worshiped, as Zeus did Ganymede,[3] for lust is not easily prevented if it has no fear; and now men celebrate the "Sacred Nights of Antinous," in which those who love shameful things lawlessly stay awake together. Why do you choose for me a God who is to be honored by fornication? And why have you appointed him to be mourned as a son? And why do you go on and on about his beauty? That shameful beauty is withered by wantonness. Do not become a tyrant, my friend, nor act wantonly with the beauty of young boys just grown of age; keep it pure, in order that it may be beautiful . . . But now there is a grave for Hadrian's lover, as well as a temple and a city of Antinous, for graves are held in awe by the Egyptians like shrines; pyramids and mausoleums and labyrinths and other shrines of the dead—as if they were the graves of their Gods.

---

[2]Eusebius is quoting Hegesippus, a Christian writer contemporary with Hadrian. See further for other Christian references, H. Chadwick, *Contra Celsum* (Cambridge: Cambridge University Press, 1965), p. 152 n. 1.

[3]Zeus carried away to be his lover the beautiful little Trojan prince, Ganymede, giving his father in return some remarkable horses; *Iliad* 5.265.

Herakles

Introduction: The twelve "labors" of Herakles were not his only exploits. Diodorus relates several in which Herakles battles king after king who will not give Herakles the hand of their daughters in marriage; the kings claim that Herakles is already married. In each case, Herakles takes the daughter by force after killing the father, or brothers, as the case may be. The last mentioned was Iolê, the daughter of Eurytus, king of a region on the island of Euboea. Following his victory, Herakles sends a servant back to his wife for his sacred clothes in order to make thank offerings to the Gods. She, hearing of Herakles' new paramour, decides to soak the robe in a magic potion which will turn his love toward her. However, the potion was given to Herakles' wife, Deïneira, by a centaur, who is secretly plotting his death. The potion is really a deadly poison. When Herakles puts on the robe, the poisonous fumes attack his flesh, and he begins inexorably to die in horrible torment. We resume the story at this point.

Diodorus Siculus, *Library of History* 4.38.3–5; 39.1–2

38.3–5. As he suffered more and more from his sickness, he sent Likumnios and Iolaos to Delphi to ask Apollo what it was necessary to do to heal the illness. Meanwhile, Deïneira (Herakles' wife) was so overcome by the severity of Herakles' circumstances, and, being aware that it was her fault, ended her life by hanging.

The God delivered the oracle that Herakles was to be carried to Oïte with his battle gear; they were to construct a great funeral pyre near him. The rest, it said, remained for Zeus to do. When these orders were carried out by Iolaos, and he had pulled back a way to see what was to happen, Herakles gave up hope and climbed onto the pyre. He called for each person who came up to light it. When no one dared to obey, only Philoktetes was moved to comply. He received, because of his service, the gift of Herakles' bow and arrows; then he lit the pyre. Immediately, a lightning bolt fell from the heavens; the pyre was completely consumed. After this, those who were with Iolaos came to the bone-gathering, but they found not one bone anywhere. They supposed that Herakles, as the oracle had proclaimed, had crossed over from human circumstances to that of the Gods.

39.1. . . . The Athenians were the first of all to honor, with sacrifices, Herakles as a God, showing, as an example to other men, their piety to the God. Thus they persuaded first the Greeks and, after them, all the men of the inhabited world to honor Herakles as a God.

39.2. . . . after Herakles' apotheosis, Zeus persuaded Hera to make Herakles her son and from that time to regard him with a mother's concern. This (second) birth is said to have happened thus: Hera lay on a couch and took Herakles to her body, letting him fall toward the earth, miming true birth. Even now, the barbarians perform this ritual when they wish to adopt a son. Hera, after the adoption, so the myth-tellers say, united Hebe with Herakles, concerning whom the poet (Homer) says:

> . . . the phantom (of Herakles), he makes merry
> in feasts with the immortal Gods
> and has (as his wife) Hebe of the beautiful ankles
> (*Odyssey* 11.602–3).

They say, therefore, that Herakles was enrolled by Zeus among the twelve Gods, but he did not accept this honor, for it was impossible for him to be enrolled unless first one of the twelve Gods was deposed, and it would have been out-of-place for him to accept an honor which bore dishonor to another God.

Part 3

GREEK AND JEWISH "GOSPELS"

While Part 2 consisted of extracts from longer writings illustrative of different facets of the New Testament Gospels, Part 3 contains whole writings (in abridged form) so that the reader can see how these same facets are combined in sacred biographies written by Greeks or Jews. The focus in this part is shifted to the larger issue, namely, how were these writings written? Are there analogies between the ways in which authors in other religious traditions wrote their spiritual biographies concerning Savior Gods and the way Christian authors wrote about Jesus Christ?

Our use of the word *Gospel* (Greek, *euangēlion* = glad tidings) in the title of this section intends to point to the similarities in function between the Christian Gospels and these writings, mainly to proclaim glad tidings, regarding these saviors (Alexander, of course, excepted). We do not intend to obscure the real differences between these pagan and Jewish proclamations and the Christian Gospels.

The Life of Apollonios of Tyana
Flavius Philostratus

Introduction: A curious feature of the long line of philosophers who claimed descent from Pythagoras of Samos (c. 560–490 B.C.) is the persistent report that many of them, Pythagoras included, possessed more-than-human wisdom. This reputation was certainly enhanced by the few secretive Pythagorean brotherhoods or monasteries which kept themselves under a perpetual blanket of silence, so that hardly anything firsthand became known of their practices. What little information we have today has come from outsiders, and in later times during the Roman Empire, these tended to be romanticists whose reliability was rarely taken seriously.

One of the most famous in this succession of Pythagorean philosophers was a man named Apollonios, of the Greek city of Tyana in the Province of Cappadocia, in what is today eastern Turkey. Although he lived in the second half of the first century A.D., we have little direct information about Apollonios, except for this biography by Philostratus of Lemnos, written much later, i.e., around A.D. 218.

The reason for his writing is noteworthy in itself. When the emperor Caracalla was on his way to capture the territories to the East, he stopped at Tyana to pay tribute to "the divine Apollonios," even donating the funds to build a temple to him there. And Caracalla's mother, Julia Domna, commissioned one of the professional writers in her entourage to publish a fitting account of Apollonios' life.

This conjunction of events suggests that the title of Philostratus' work might best be translated: "*In Honor of Apollonios of Tyana,*" for the entire account from beginning to end consists of carefully constructed praise, using every device known to this well-trained writer. In other words, just as Caracalla's architects built a shrine for Apollonios out of marble, one of his court rhetoricians built a temple out of words—for the same purpose, i.e., to celebrate Apollonios' God-like nature and inspire reverence for him. Thus, Philostratus' narrative is a virtual catalogue of every rhetorical device known to the professional sophistic writers of that time: sudden supernatural omens, minidialogues on the favorite topics of the day, colorful bits of archeological lore, plenty of magic, rapid action scenes, amazing descriptions of fabled, far-off lands, occasional touches of naughty eroticism, and a whole series of favorite "philosophical" scenes: the Philosopher lectures his disciples on being willing to die for truth; the Philosopher is abandoned by his cowardly disciples; the Philosopher confronts the tyrant; the fearless Philosopher is alone in prison unafraid; the Philosopher victoriously defends himself in the court, and so on. On the other hand, Philostratus included enough accurate historical details to give his writing the ring of genuine truth. But mixed in with the real people and places are all sorts of imaginary "official" letters, inscriptions, decrees, and edicts, the whole bound together by an "eyewitness" diary. Finally, to give it the proper supernatural flavor, he has included numerous miraculous and supernatural occurrences: dreams, pre-vision, teleportation, exorcism and finally, vanishing from earth only to reappear later from Heaven to convince a doubting disciple of the soul's immortality.

Guiding Philostratus at each point in constructing his narrative was the reputation of Apollonios as a divine/human Savior God. This understanding of him comes out most clearly in the great speech supposedly composed by Apollonios for his self-defense during his trial before the emperor Domition. Actually written by none other than Philostratus, it is a beautiful example of an *encomium* on Apollonios' life.[1] Forming the high point of Philostratus' whole narrative, it is the moment when Apollonios at last reveals his true supernatural colors:

> "It is thought that the order (*kosmos*) which is dependent upon God the Creator includes all things in Heaven, in the sea, and on the land, in which there is equal participation of men—but according to Fortune. Then there is also another order (*kosmos*) dependent upon the good man which does not transgress the limits of Wisdom; and you yourself, O King, say that it needs a man formed like a God (*theō eikasmenos*). . . . Now I have been thought worthy of much honor in each of the cities which needed me (because I) performed such things as healing the sick, making more holy those being initiated into the Mysteries or offering sacrifice, rooting out pride (*hybris*), and strengthening their laws" (VIII. 7.7). In short, "I do all things for the salvation of men" (VIII. 7.10).

This and many other passages reveals the fact that Philostratus wished to portray Apollonios in the divine/human Savior of the human-race conception, which we can also see in Philo of Alexandria's portrayal of Moses, or, for that matter, in many of the early Christian portrayals of Jesus Christ. Obviously Philostratus was not alone in this view of Apollonios, if we may judge from the circumstances which brought his writing into being.

There is evidence that veneration of Apollonios as a Savior God continued long after Caracalla and Philostratus. About a hundred years later, the provincial governor of Bithynia wrote a tract lambasting the Christians' Jesus and his followers while praising Apollonios and his followers, which moved the Church Father Eusebius to write a scathing

---

[1]On the meaning of encomium, see pp. 255–57.

reply (*Against Hierocles*). During the fourth century when the Emperor Julian the Apostate tried to reinstitute pagan worship, after the Empire had become officially Christian, one of the sophists at his court named Eunapius wrote a book, called *The Lives of the Philosophers,* in which he described Apollonios as someone

"who was not merely a philosopher but somewhere between the Gods and man. For he was a follower of the Pythagorean doctrine and he did much to publish to the world the more divine and effective character of that philosophy. But Philostratus of Lemnos completed a full account of Apollonios, though after he had written a life (*bios*) of Apollonios he should have called it 'The Visit of God to Men'". (*Lives of the Philosophers* 500).

Near the beginning of the fifth century A.D., we find another reference to Apollonios in the *Scriptores Historiae Augustae.* In this curious mélange of fact and fiction concerning the Roman emperors, we read that the Emperor Severus Alexander (ruled 222–235) kept in his private palace chapel several statues of the deified emperors, and certain other "holy souls," including Apollonios of Tyana, Jesus Christ, Abraham, and Orpheus! (*Severus Alexander* xxix.2). Further on in this work, in the account of the Emperor Aurelian (ruled 270–275), this is recorded:

We must not omit one event that enhances the fame of a venerated man. For it is said that Aurelian did indeed speak and truly think of destroying the city of Tyana, but Apollonios of Tyana, a sage of the greatest renown and authority, a philosopher of former days, the true friend of the Gods, and himself even to be regarded as a supernatural being, as Aurelian was withdrawing to his tent, suddenly appeared to him in the form in which he is usually portrayed and spoke to him as follows, using Latin in order that he might be understood: "Aurelian, if you wish to conquer, there is no reason to plan the death of my fellow citizens. Aurelian, if you wish to rule, abstain from the blood of the innocent. Aurelian, act with mercy if you wish to live." Aurelian recognized the countenance of the venerated philosopher and, in fact, he had seen his portrait in many a temple. And so, at once stricken with terror, he promised him a portrait and statues and a temple and returned to his better self. This incident I have learned from trustworthy men and read over again in the books in the Ulpian Library and I have been the more ready to believe it because of the reverence in which Apollonios is held. For who among men has ever been more venerated, more revered, more famous, or more holy than that very man? He brought back the dead to life, he said and did many things beyond the power of ordinary men. If any one should wish to learn these facts, let him read the Greek books which have been composed concerning his life (by Philostratus). I myself, furthermore, if the length of my life shall permit and the plan meet with his favor, will (put into Latin) the deeds of this great man, even though it be briefly, not because his achievements need the tribute of my discourse but in order that these wondrous things may be proclaimed by the voice of every man (*Deified Aurelian* XXIV, trans. D. Magie, Loeb ed.).

Philostratus' work has often been compared to the Greek and Roman novels of his day, and with good reason. As Elizabeth Haight observed, "[Philostratus wrote] with full knowledge of Xenophon's romantic biography of Cyrus the Great as the ideal ruler, of the Greek novels of war and adventure, of the Greek love romances . . . and of the Christian *Acts* with a saint for a hero. [In view of all these possibilities] Philostratus chose to present a *theios anēr*, a divine sage, a Pythagorean philosopher, as the center of his story. To make the life of his hero interesting and to promulgate his philosophy, he used every device of the Greek and Latin novels of the second and third centuries. And the credulity, the discourses, the aspirations of his characters belong as much to the whole first three centuries of the Empire as [just] to the age of the Severi [when he wrote]. Philostratus has written out of the restless cravings of that time another romance to help men escape from the burden of their fears to life's fairer possibilities."[2]

I.1. It is said that Pythagoras consulted with the Gods and learned from them how they are pleased by men and how they are angered, from which he later taught about Nature. Others, he said, only made guesses about the supernatural and gave out contradictory opinions concerning it, whereas Apollo agreed to come and counsel with him as he really is, but that Athena did not so grant or the Muses or other Gods of whom the appearances and names men do not yet know. So whatever Pythagoras would disclose, his disciples considered as law and honored him as one who came from Zeus (*ek Dios hēkōn*). And he ordered them to keep silent about the supernatural (*ho theios*), for he told them many divine and incredible secrets which it were scarcely possible to keep unless they first learn that even being silent is speech (*logos*).

Moreover they say that the great Empedocles of Acragas trod the same path of wisdom, when he said, "Farewell! Now I am unto you an immortal God—no longer mortal"[3] . . . There are many other histories of those who philosophized according to Pythagoras' manner which are not pertinent to my present task. Rather I am eager to proceed with the narrative (*logos*) I have set myself to complete.

[2]E.H. Haight, *More Essays on Greek Romances* (London: Longmans, Green and Co., 1945), p. 111f.
[3]For the whole quote, see above p.15.

I.2. For the practice of Apollonios was akin to theirs, indeed more supernatural (*theioteros*) than Pythagoras was his attainment of wisdom and overpowering of tyrants. But since he lived neither in well-known ancient times nor in our own days, men do not yet know of the true Wisdom that he cultivated in a philosophical and healthy way. Instead now this and now that is praised of the man, while others, since he associated with Babylonian magi and Indian Brahmans and Egyptian wise men, consider him a sorcerer and accuse him of seeming to be wise through trickery, since they understand poorly. For Empedocles and Pythagoras himself and Democritus associated with such soothsayers and uttered many supernatural truths without being lured into the forbidden art. Plato also traveled to Egypt and mixed in with his own teachings many things said by the prophets and priests there, like a painter who adds colors to his sketch, but he was not thought to be addicted to magic even though he was resented for his wisdom more than all men.

Neither should Apollonios' frequent presentiments and foreknowings be suspected as that kind of wisdom, or then even Socrates will be suspected because of the things he would foretell due to his supernatural aide (*daimōn*), and Anaxagoras too because of the things he used to prophesy. For who does not know of the time when Anaxagoras was at the Olympic Games during the dry season and he came into the stadium with a sheepskin on, thus predicting rain, which it soon did, or of the time he foretold that a certain house would fall down and it did? Or what of his predictions that day would turn into night and that stones would fall out of the sky around Aegospotami—foretelling truly? Yet the same people who attribute these feats to Anaxagoras' wisdom deny that Apollonios' foreknowledge came from the same wisdom and claim that he did these things as if by magical tricks. Therefore, I feel I ought to do something about the widespread ignorance of Apollonios by accurately relating the times when he said or did something and the kinds of wisdom as a result of which he succeeded in being considered both supernatural and a divine being (*daimonios te kai theios*).

I have collected some of my source material from cities where he was revered, other material from temples whose rituals at that time were in a state of ruin and were reformed by him, other stories from things people said about him, and the rest from his own letters, for he corresponded with kings, sophists, philosophers, the citizens of Elis and Delphi, with Indians and Egyptians concerning the Gods, customs, morals, and laws—in whatever way someone might be sinning he straightened him out. But the more accurate source material I gathered in the following way.

I.3. There was a man named Damis, not unwise, who used to live in the ancient city of Nineveh. Having joined Apollonios in order to learn philosophy, he kept a record of his journey and says he himself shared it, as well as his opinions (*gnōmai*) and arguments (*logoi*) and whatever he said in the nature of prophecy (*prognosis*). A relative of Damis later brought the notebooks of these as yet unknown memoirs (*hypomnēmata*) to the knowledge of the Empress Julia. Now I happen to be a member of the circle around her—for she indeed welcomes and approves of all the rhetorical exercises—and she commanded me to rewrite these discourses (*diatribē*) and to be careful in the narrative (*apaggelia*) of them for it was narrated by the Ninevite clearly enough but not very well. I have also read the book of Maximus of Aigai which described all the doings of Apollonios at Aigai, and, finally, I am in possession of a *Testament* (*diathēkē*) written by Apollonios himself.

From these sources it is possible to learn how divinely inspired his philosophy was. But do not pay any attention to Moiragenes who wrote a four-part book against Apollonios, since he was ignorant of many things concerning the man. As I said, therefore, I have gathered these scattered sources and taken some care in combining them together. But let the work be to the honor of the man about whom it is written, and for the benefit of those who love learning, for indeed they might learn something here that they do not yet know.

There are many noteworthy features to this preface. First, notice the succession of philosophers back to the divine Pythagoras, who "came from Zeus." Second, observe the defensive tone Philostratus adopts when he comes to Apollonios. His narrative will prove that Apollonios was *not* a swindler or a fake. Finally, notice to what lengths Philostratus goes to assure the reader of the high accuracy of his account. This is the sort of thing educated readers would expect. Now Philostratus is ready to proceed with the first main event: the birth of Apollonios. The reference to Homer is to the *Odyssey* IV. 417–18.

I.4. The home of Apollonios then was Tyana, a Greek city in the land of the Cappadocians. His father had the same name and he came from an old family of the original settlers, richer than others there even though it is a generally wealthy country. While his mother was pregnant with him the shadowy figure of an Egyptian God appeared to her, namely Proteus, who can change his form at will according to Homer. She, not frightened at all, asked him to whom she would give birth. "Me," he said. "But who are you?" she asked. "Proteus," he replied, "the Egyptian God." Why should I describe the wisdom of Proteus to those of you who have heard the poets, how changeful he was and always different and difficult to catch, both knowing and it seems foreknowing all things? But keep this thought of Proteus in your mind,

especially when, as the story (*ho logos*) progresses, it shows Apollonios
foreknowing even more than Proteus and superior to the many perilous
straits and hardships he encountered, especially in the very moment he
seemed to be trapped.

I.5. It is said that Apollonios was born in a meadow near the
temple which was recently dedicated to him there. And the manner in
which he was born should not be left unknown for when the hour of
birth had drawn nigh to his mother, a vision came telling her to go to this
meadow and pick some flowers. Well, she had no sooner arrived when
she fell asleep lying in the grass, while her maidservants wandered over
the meadow picking flowers. Then some swans which dwelt in the
meadow came and formed a ring around her while she slept and as is
their custom suddenly flapped their wings and honked all at once, for
there was a light breeze blowing across the meadow. She jumped up
because of the sound and gave birth, for any sudden panic will cause
birth to take place even before its time. The inhabitants of that area say
that at the same time she was giving birth a bolt of lightening seemed to
strike the earth and then bounce back upward into the air where it
vanished. By this sign the Gods, I believe, revealed and foretold that
Apollonios would become superior to all things earthly, even drawing
near to the Gods and soon.

I.6. Now they say that there is near Tyana a water of oaths to Zeus,a
fountain they call Unquenchable (*Asbamaion*) where the water rises up
cold but it bubbles like a boiling cauldron. This water is favorable and
sweet to those who keep their oaths, but Justice is at hand for those who
have sworn falsely, for it actually attacks eyes and hands and feet, and
they are instantly stricken by swelling of the body and emaciation and
they are unable to go away being held right there next to the fountain
groaning and confessing the false oaths they have sworn. Now the local
people say that Apollonios is a son of this Zeus, although the man calls
himself the son of his father Apollonios.

I.7. When he grew old enough to learn letters, he was already
demonstrating a good memory and power of concentration. Moreover,
he could speak pure Attic Greek for he was not influenced by the speech
of the Cappadocians. Moreover, all eyes were constantly turned toward
him and he was admired by the hour.

Now when he was fourteen years old, his father took him to Tarsus to
Euthydemos the Phoenician. This Euthydemos was a good rhetorician
and began to teach him. Apollonios liked his teacher well enough, but
he began to find the character of the city disgusting and not helpful for
philosophical interests, for more than anywhere else the people of
Tarsus crave luxurious living and joke about everything and constantly
shout insults at each other. They are as worried about fancy clothes as

the Athenians about wisdom. The river Kydnus runs through their city and they sit along its banks like a lot of chattering waterbirds, which is why Apollonios once wrote to them in a letter, "Stop getting drunk on water."

Thus, after asking his father, Apollonios changed to another teacher at Aigai, a town nearby, where it was peaceful as befits the study of philosophy and where he found a more highminded atmosphere. There was even a temple there to Asklepios, where Asklepios himself is manifested to men.

Next, Philostratus will proceed to the customary "precocious brilliance" motif (cf. the similar theme in Philo's *Life of Moses*, pp. 261–62, and Luke 2:41–52).

The various philosophical schools of thought are named in order to emphasize the breadth of Apollonios' youthful education. On the other hand, we should not overlook the fact that these are all *Greek* philosophical positions. This is only the first of many hints that this entire writing will have to do primarily with the dissemination of Greek thought, Greek morals, and Greek wisdom through the efforts of Apollonios. In other words, "Greekness" is here presented as a kind of religion, "good news," if you will. In fact, it is called just that a few sections later, see p. 219.

Philosophizing together with him were Platonists, Chrysippists, and Aristotelians. He also attended to the arguments of Epicurus for not even them did he overlook. But those of Pythagoras he understood with a certain indescribable wisdom. His teacher in the Pythagorean doctrines was not very good, however, nor did he live philosophically but instead constantly gave in to his gluttony as well as to the sexual urge, forming his life according to Epicurus. He was Euxenos from Herakleia in Pontos and he knew the doctrines of Pythagoras the way birds learn things from men, for birds can say "Hello!" and "Good luck!" and "God bless you!" and such like, not understanding what they are saying nor with any feeling of concern for men, but simply because of their trained tongues. Apollonios, however, just as young eagles fly beside their parents while their feathers are soft and are cared for by them in flight, later on are able to mount up, flying above their parents, especially if they notice them greedily skimming along at ground level on the scent of a victim, so also Apollonios remained by Euxenos while he was a child and was led by him through the steps of argument. But when he had advanced to the age of sixteen, he eagerly rushed onward toward a life like Pythagoras, being given "wings" for it by Something Greater. Not that he ceased loving Euxenos, but he asked his father to give him a place outside the town where there were delicate gardens and fountains. "You live there in your way," he said to Euxenos, "but I will live according to the way of Pythagoras."

I.8. Euxenos realized that Apollonios was set on a lofty ambition and he asked him how he was going to start out. "The way doctors do," Apollonios replied; "by cleaning out the intestines, they enable some not to get sick and they heal others." Having said this, he stopped eating food made from animals, arguing that meat was dirty and coarsened the mind. Instead he used to eat dried fruits and fresh vegetables, arguing that whatever the earth herself gives is clean. And he said that although wine is a clean drink, coming to men from so cultivated a plant, nevertheless we should not drink it since it causes the mind to riot by darkening the ether (*aithēr*) in the soul. When he had finished cleaning out his intestines in this fashion he took to going barefoot as his "high fashion" and also put on linen clothing, abstaining from clothing made out of the hair or skin of animals. Moreover he let his hair grow long and began living in the temple of Asklepios. Those who lived near the temple were astonished at all this and even the God Asklepios once told the priest how happy he was that Apollonios was a witness of his miraculous healing of the sick at the temple. People from all over Cilicia and elsewhere gathered at Aigai upon hearing stories of him and the Cilician saying, "Where are you running to? To see the boy?" began to circulate even becoming known as a proverb.

Philostratus now tells two stories which demonstrate Apollonios' uncanny ability to detect false oaths (cf. I.6 above). Then he produces a dialogue supposedly revealing the depth of Apollonios' wisdom at this period.

I.11. He used to philosophize as follows about not exceeding moderation in the matter of sacrifice and temple gifts. Once when many were gathered at the temple not long after the rejection of the wicked Cilician nobleman, he began putting questions to the priest.

"Well, then," he said, "are the Gods just?"

"Indeed, by all means most just," answered the priest.

"Really? And intelligent?"

"Who is more intelligent than the Gods?" the latter replied.

"And do they know the affairs of mankind, or are they ignorant of them?" continued Apollonios.

"But that is especially where the Gods have the advantage over men," the priest answered, "for men, because of weakness, do not even know their own affairs while the Gods are granted knowledge both of ours and their own."

"All excellently said, O Priest, and most true. Since, therefore, they know all things, it seems to me that one who comes before the Gods with a good conscience about his life should pray the following prayer: 'O

Gods! Give to me what you owe me!' For good things are owed to holy people, are they not, O Priest, but to those who are wicked the opposite. And the Gods do well when they find someone healthy and abstaining from wickedness to send him on, crowned not with crowns of gold, to be sure, but all good things. But if they see people spotted with sin and ruined, they will abandon them to Justice (*dikē*) so much do they detest them, particularly since they dare to invade temples in an impure state."

And at once turning his eyes toward the statue of Asklepios he said, "O Asklepios, Thy philosophy is unspoken and natural to Thyself in not allowing wicked people to come here even though they offer Thee all the wealth of India and Sardinia. For they do not intend to honor Heaven (*to theion*) by offering and dedicating these gifts but to bribe Justice, which ye Gods will never allow, being perfectly righteous." Many such things as this Apollonios used to philosophize in this temple while he was still a young man.

I.12. The following story (*diatribē*) deals with his life at the temple in Aigai. The Cilicians were being ruled by an arrogant man who was also evil in the ways of love, and when word came to this man of the beauty of Apollonios he dropped the business he was doing—which was conducting a lawsuit in Tarsus—and dashed off to Aigai saying that he was sick and had need of Asklepios. Approaching Apollonios who was walking alone he said, "Introduce me to the God." But he replied, "And why do you need an introduction if you are good (*chrēstos*)? For the Gods welcome earnest men even without introductions." "By God that is true, O Apollonios," said the other, "but the God has made you his friend, and not yet me." "Well, as for me," said Apollonios, "noble goodness has been my introduction, being observed by me as much as is possible for a young man, so that I am both the servant and companion of Asklepios. If you also are concerned for noble goodness, advance confidently before the God and pray for what you wish." "By God I will," said the other, "if I can pray to you first!" "And what," said he, "would you pray to me?" "Only what must be asked for of the beautiful, namely, we pray them to share in their beauty and not to begrudge their youthful charm." As he was saying this, he affected an effeminate, moist-eyed manner, even undulating his body like the notorious pervert that he was. Apollonios glared at him angrily and said, "You are insane, you filthy scum!" When the governor heard this he not only became enraged but even threatened to cut off his head. Apollonios just laughed, shouting, "O fateful Friday!" naming the third day after that one. And sure enough on that Friday public executioners killed that arrogant man on the highway for conspiring against Rome with Archelaus, the king of Cappadocia. This and many such things are written by Maximus of Aigai, who was so well regarded as an orator that he was considered worthy of writing the imperial letters.

Apollonios' father dies and Apollonios goes home to settle his estate. He ends up giving away his share to relatives, since he had little need of money. At this point Philostratus also informs us that Apollonios decided never to have anything to do with sex either.

I.13. . . . Although Pythagoras was commended for saying that a man ought not to have sexual intercourse with any woman except his own wife, Apollonios said that this principle was intended for others by Pythagoras, but that he would neither marry nor ever participate in sexual pleasures. In this way he surpassed even Sophocles who said that he had escaped an uncontrollable and cruel master only when he had reached old age. But Apollonios through virtue and prudence was never overcome by lust even in his youth. Although he was still young, he controlled his bodily passion and completely mastered its mad craving.

Apollonios next enters on the customary Pythagorean vow of total silence for five years. Nevertheless, says Philostratus, his eyes and gestures were so eloquent that they alone sufficed to make his meaning clear, and he tells a story to illustrate this.

I.15. Now he spent some of the period of silence in Pamphylia and some of it in Cilicia, and even though he walked about among such luxury-loving peoples as these, he never spoke nor was induced even to mutter. Whenever he chanced upon a city filled with bitter wrangling, for there were many that used to bicker about their frivolous entertainments, he would step forward and show himself and, by expressing through his facial expression or with his hand the punishment about to strike them, he would instantly stop all disorder and they would fall silent as if at the Mysteries.

Of course, it isn't much to restrain people who are beginning to quarrel about dancers and horses, for those who are arguing about such things become embarrassed and get themselves under control and quickly come to their senses if they so much as see a genuine man. But a city in the grip of famine is not easy to communicate with in patient and persuasive speech in order to end the anger. However, for Apollonios even his silence was sufficient for those in such condition.

For instance, he once came to Aspendus in Pamphylia—this city is built on the river Eurymedon, the third largest of those there—where pea-vines were on sale and the people were eating them and anything else they could scavenge for food because the powerful men had shut up the grain and were holding it in order to sell it outside the country. A mob filled with people of all ages had seized the mayor and were just about to burn him alive even though he was clinging to the statues of the Emperors. At that time these statues were more feared and offered better safety from reprisals than even the statue of Zeus at Olympia, for there was a statue of Tiberius, of whom they say that a man was believed to commit treason against him simply because he hit his own slave while the latter happened to be carrying a silver drachma in his pocket with Tiberius' image upon it!

Anyway, Apollonios went up to the mayor and asked him by a hand sign what this was all about. He said that *he* had done nothing wrong but was being ill-treated along with the people, and that if he did not succeed in explaining the problem he would die with the people. Thereupon Apollonios turned to those standing there and beckoned that they must listen. They not only fell silent out of astonishment at him, but also laid their torches on altars that were there. Regaining his confidence, the mayor said, "Such-and-such and so-and-so"—naming many names—"are the real causes of the famine now upon us, for they have taken away the grain and are keeping it in different parts of the country." The citizens of Aspendus began to urge each other to go out to their estates, but Apollonios shook his head not to do this, but rather to summon those at fault and to obtain the grain from them with their consent.

When they arrive a little later, he all but breaks out in speech against them, so much does he suffer from the tears of the people—for children and women had gathered, and the elderly were groaning as if they would die of hunger at any moment. But honoring his doctrine of silence he writes the punishment down on a clay tablet and gives it to the mayor to read aloud. This was the punishment: "Apollonios to the corn merchants of Aspendus: The earth is mother of us all for she is just. But you are unjust since you have made her mother to you yourselves alone. If you will not cease, I will not permit you to stand on her." They were so terrified by these words that they filled the market place with grain and the city came alive again.

After the vow of silence was completed, he journeyed to "the great city of Antioch" (about 50 km. southeast of Cilicia). While there, Philostratus gives us this description of a "typical day" in Apollonios' life there.

I.16. At the rising of the sun, he would perform certain rites by himself which he explained only to those who had trained in silence for four years. Then after these things, at a suitable time if the city were Greek and the sacred ritual familiar, calling the priests together, he would philosophize concerning the Gods and set them straight if, perchance, they had deviated from the accepted ritual ordinances. But if the customary rituals were barbarian and strange, known only in that place, then Apollonios would investigate those who had established them and on what occasions they had been established and, upon ascertaining these things, he would seek to find ways in which he might improve them or suggest something wiser. Then he would hunt up his associates and command them to ask questions about anything they wanted to, for he said that philosophers needed at earliest sunrise to commune directly with the Gods, later to talk about the Gods, and after this to pass the time examining human affairs. After speaking with his companions and having enough of such fellowship, he would stand and spend the rest of the time talking to the crowd, not before noon but whenever possible right at the midpoint of the day. And when he felt he had carried on sufficient dialogue, he would have himself smeared with oil, given a massage and throw himself into cold water calling the warm public baths "man's old age."

A little after this, Philostratus gives the following description of Apollonios as a public speaker.

I.17. He would not give out a narrow, subtle discussion, nor talk on and on, nor did anyone hear him use the question-and-answer method like Socrates, as if he were ignorant, nor instruct his pupils like the Peripatetics. Rather, as if delivering divine truth, he would say when discussing, "I know . . ." and "It seems to me . . ." and "Where are you going?" and "It is necessary to know that . . ." And his sayings were short and hard as steel, authoritative words that went straight to the point. Indeed, his words sounded as if they were the ordinances of a king.

Once a heckler asked him why *he* never asked about anything. "Because," said he, "when I was a little boy I asked questions, but now I must not ask but teach what I have found out." "How, then, O Apollonios, will the wise man (*sophos*) speak?" he asked again. "Like a lawgiver," he said, "whatever the lawgiver has convinced himself about he must give as commandments to the people." This is the way he seriously discoursed while in Antioch, and he converted even the most vulgar people to himself.

I.18. Now after these things the plan occurred to him to make a longer journey, for he wanted to visit the Indian people and the wise men among them who are called Brahmans and Hyrcanians. He said that every young man ought to travel and seek foreign lands. An additional benefit would be the Magi of Babylon and Susa, for he would also learn their ideas on the way.

So he made his decision known to his followers, who were seven in number. But they all began trying to convince him to do other things so that he might somehow be drawn away from this intention. "I have been led by the advice of the Gods," he replied, "and have revealed my decision. I was testing you to see if you had the strength to do whatever I did. But since it is obvious you are too faint-hearted, stay well and philosophize," he said. "As for me there must be journeys. May Wisdom and my Guardian Spirit lead me!"

After saying that he departed from Antioch with the two servants whom he had inherited, one who could write quickly and the other elegantly.

We are here introduced to the first of several occasions when the disciples around Apollonios prove to be recalcitrant, cowardly and thick-headed. In fact, one suspects that this is actually a narrative trick by Philostratus to make Apollonios' bravery and determination stand out all the more sharply.

At any rate, Apollonios turns eastward toward India. This great journey Apollonios makes in stages. He first travels northeast to pick up the great trade routes, eventually coming to the ancient city of Nineveh. There he finds Damis who decides to join him on his trek as his disciple. It is Damis' notebooks that Philostratus allegedly is relying upon for most of his material. The first city they come to is the fabulous city of Babylon. However, Apollonios is not very impressed. Furthermore, as it turns out, it is the Babylonians who rejoice at the "good news" that a Greek sage has appeared.

I.27. As soon as he arrived at Babylon the official in charge of the great city gates learned that he had come for the sake of knowledge (*hyper historias*). He held out a golden statue of the king, which, if anyone does not bow down before it, he is not allowed to enter. Now this was not necessary for an emissary from the Roman Emperor, but anyone coming from one of the barbarian nations or just to learn about the country was disgracefully arrested if he did not first worship the statue. Such indeed are the ridiculous duties barbarians give their officials.

Now when Apollonios sees the statue, "Who," he says, "is that?" When he hears that it is the king, he says, "This man whom *you* worship will acquire a great reputation if he should be praised by me for being noble and good." And so saying he walks through the gates. The official is astonished at him and begins to follow and, taking hold of Apollonios' hand he—through an interpreter—asks him his name, his family, what profession he followed and his purpose for visiting. Writing all this down in a book along with a description of his clothing and appearance, he orders him to wait there (I.28) while he runs off to men whom they call "The King's Ears." Describing Apollonios he says that he neither desires to worship the king's statue nor seems to be anything like a human. They command Apollonios to come honorably and without doing anything violent. When he is present the eldest begins to question him as to why he would despise the king.

"I have not despised him," said Apollonios, "yet!"

"You might despise him?" asks the other.

"I certainly will," says Apollonios, "if, when I meet him, I find him to be neither noble nor good!"

"Indeed! And what gifts do you bring him?" When he mentioned Courage and Righteousness and other such Virtues, "Because," asks the other, "he does not have them?"

"Certainly not!" says Apollonios, "but so that he learns to use them, should he have them."

"But surely by using them," says the other, "he gained back the kingdom which you see after it was lost to him and restored this his house—something neither simple nor easy."

"And how many years have passed since he regained his power?"

"We are beginning the third year," says he, "some two months already."

At this, Apollonios says, with his customary determination to uphold his own view, "Mr. Bodyguard, or whatever it is proper to call you, Darius, the father of Cyrus and Artaxerxes, ruled these domains for sixty years, I believe, and when he suspected that the end of his life was near, it is said he sacrificed to Righteousness, saying, 'O Mistress, or whomever you may be,' as if he had long since desired Righteousness and even yet did not know her nor considered that he possessed her, for he educated his sons in such ignorance of her that they battled against each other, and the one was wounded while the other killed by his brother. But now you already consider this king to be equal, even though he does not know how to sit on the royal throne and you think he combines all virtues and you praise him, although it is you who would benefit, not I, if he were to become better."

At this the barbarian glanced at his neighbor and said, "What luck! One of the Gods leads this man here, for when a good man associates with a good man, he will make our king better, more moderate and gentler. I can see it in his appearance." And so they ran to spread the good news (*euangelion*) to all that a man was standing at the gates of the king who was wise and Greek and a good advisor.

Apollonios stays with the King of Babylon more than a year, which provides Philostratus with the opportunity to work in all sorts of anecdotes, including numerous rather pedestrian philosophical dialogues. The following are typical.

I.38. Once when the king showed him the tunnel which crossed under the Euphrates, he asked, "What do you think of this marvel?" Apollonios made light of the wonderful construction saying, "It would be a marvel, O King, if you walked on foot through a river as deep and impassable as this one is." And when the king pointed out the walls of Ecbatana and said they were a dwelling place of the Gods, he replied, "For the Gods it is not a dwelling place at all. Whether of true men, I do not know; the Spartans have no walls of any kind around the city where they dwell."

Another time after the king had decided a certain lawsuit between some villages and was boasting to Apollonios that he had carefully listened to the lawsuit for two whole days, Apollonios remarked, "You certainly are slow to find out what is just." Once, as vast amounts of tax money were pouring in from his subjects, the king opened his treasure room and showed Apollonios the money, tempting him to desire wealth. But he was not impressed with anything he saw, saying, "To you, O King, this is money. To me, garbage." "What then is the best use I may make of it?" he asked. "By spending it," he said, "for you are King."

Eventually, the two set off for India with the king's blessing. Book II opens with some strange geographical information. In fact, most of Philostratus' geographical references are quite inaccurate. By "Caucasus" mountains he might be referring to the mountain range lying along the east side of the Tigris River, called the Zagros Mountains. These mountains he had to pass over on his way to India. The real Caucasus Mountains are far to the north and lie on an east-west line between the Black Sea and the Caspian.

II.4. As they were passing over the Caucasus Mountains, they say they saw men eight feet tall, who were black, and others, when they crossed the Indus River, who were ten feet tall. But during the journey to the river they saw the following thing worth telling. They were going along at night by the light of the moon, when suddenly the ghost of a hobgoblin rushed upon them, changing from one horrible shape into another and even becoming invisible. But Apollonios recognized what it was and he shouted curses at the goblin and commanded those with him to do the same, for this is the remedy for such an attack, and the ghost took to flight in the shape of a bird, as specters often do.

II.5. (The next day) as they were crossing over the very highest peak of the mountain range and going slowly since it was so steep, Apollonios began to discuss the following with Damis:

"Tell me," he said, "where were we yesterday?"

"On the flatlands," Damis replied.

"And today, O Damis, where are we?"

"In the Caucasus Mountains," he said, "unless I have completely forgotten myself!"

"Were you down rather low, yesterday?" he asked again.

"That," said the other, "is not worth asking! For yesterday we were traveling down through the hollow of the earth, but today we are up next to Heaven."

"Are you sure then, O Damis," he said, "that yesterday the journey was low but today it is high?"

"Certainly," said the other, "unless I'm crazy."

"How do you think the roads differ from each other," asked Apollonios, "or what is better to you today than yesterday?"

"Well, yesterday I was walking where there were many people," said he, "but today, where there are few."

"What?" replied Apollonios, "Is it not possible, Damis, by turning aside from the thoroughfares in a city to walk where there are few people?"

"That's not what I said," he replied. "Yesterday we journeyed through villages and people, but today we have climbed up into a somewhat empty and sacred region, for you heard the guide say the barbarians consider it the home of their Gods," and as he said this, he gazed up at the peak of the mountain.

But Apollonios brought him to what he had been driving at from the beginning: "Can you tell me, Damis, what sort of communion with the supernatural there is if you walk close to Heaven?"

"None," he said.

"And yet surely you should now, having stood upon a mechanism so high and divine as this mountain, with new clarity expound teachings concerning Heaven and the sun and the moon, which you probably think you can touch with a pole standing this close to them!"

"What I knew yesterday about the supernatural," Damis replied, "I also know today. A new thought concerning it still has not hit me."

"Then, Damis," he answered, "you must still be low down, and have received nothing from the height, but you are as far from Heaven as you were yesterday. Thus what I asked you in the beginning was reasonable after all, only you thought it was a foolish question."

"Well, I certainly thought, Apollonios, that I would be wiser when I went down from this mountain, because I've heard that Anaxagoras of Klazmenion examined things in Heaven from Mount Mimas in Ionia and Thales the Milesian from Mount Mykale near his home, and they say some use Mount Pangaios for an observatory and others Mount Athos. But I myself, having now gone up on a height greater than all of these, am going down nothing wiser."

"Nor were they," said Apollonios, "for such vistas display a brighter Heaven and bigger stars and the sun rising out of the night, things already known to shepherds and goatherds. But in what way God cares for the human race and in what way he rejoices to be served by it, what true virtue is and what righteousness and moderation are, Athos will not show to those who climb it, nor the Olympus esteemed by the poets, unless the soul itself discerns them. And if it, pure and uncorrupted, can 'touch' *these* things, I would say it soars up much higher than this old Caucasus peak!"

From this point on, until Apollonios and his companions arrive at the imperial Indian city of Taxila, "the greatest city in India," and King Phraotes (a successor of King Porus who had fought Alexander the Great), Philostratus' narrative begins to read like the *National Geographic Magazine* as he describes the interesting regions and strange animals they encountered. Such "travelogues" were just as popular in Greco-Roman times as in our own and Philostratus plays this favorite theme to the hilt.

Before long, Apollonios arrives at another large mountain reputed to be the shrine of the Indian version of the Greek God Dionysos, and this allows Philostratus to discuss the conflicting claims made regarding the two Dionysoses, the Indian and the Greek. Then they finally reach the Indus River and see herds of elephants. A small boy riding an elephant provides Apollonios with an illustration for a tirade against slavery. Philostratus then offers some information of his own, and inserts a little treatise on different kinds of elephants, their uses in warfare, their incredible longevity, types of tusks, and how affectionate they are toward their young. This leads to a whole series of anecdotes telling of fierce animals' instinctive tender care for their young. Then Philostratus begins to describe the Indus River (about one kilometer wide where they cross), its periodic flooding, its similarities to the Nile, speculates as to why both India and Egypt (thought to be on the two edges of the earth) are peopled by dark-skinned races, and so on.

They finally arrive at Taxila, the royal city, "about the size of Nineveh," where they are welcomed by the king, Phraotes. Apollonios' first interest is in the monuments to the famous battle between Alexander the Great and the earlier Indian king, Porus. Alexander had defeated Porus, but found him such a gallant opponent that he returned his kingdom to him as a tribute to his bravery. When news of this astonishing gesture reached the Greek homeland, it caused widespread comment and resulted in a general curiosity about this Indian king for whom Alexander had shown such admiration. Thus, Philostratus pauses to recount a string of anecdotes about Porus revealing his character and wit.

II.21. My story (*ho logos*) will not let me pass by in silence what they write about this Porus. Once when Alexander was about to cross the Indus River and attack him and some were advising Porus to make allies of certain kings on his eastern boundary beyond the Hyphasis and the Ganges Rivers, saying that Alexander would never attack a coalition of all the Indians drawn up against him, Porus replied, "If the loyalty of my people is such that I cannot be saved without allies, then it were better that I should not rule!"

Another time when someone announced to him that Alexander had captured Darius the Persian king, he remarked, "Darius may have been king, but he wasn't a man!"

When the elephant groom had decked out the elephant upon which he was about to do battle, he said, "This one, O King, will carry you." Whereupon Porus replied, "I, rather, will carry him—if I still am the man I used to be!"

Advised that he should make sacrifices to the Indus River so that it would not accept the Macedonian rafts nor be easily crossed by Alexander, Porus said, "It is not right for those who can use arms to rely on magical curses."

After the battle when he seemed even to Alexander to be divine and beyond human nature, one of his relatives said, "If you had paid homage to him when he crossed over, O Porus, you would not have been defeated in battle nor so many Indians killed or yourself wounded." "But I heard that Alexander cherished honor above all," said Porus, "and I realized that if I abased myself, he would consider me a slave, whereas if I fought him, a king. And I thought his esteem worth more than his pity, nor was I deceived, for by representing myself such as Alexander saw, I both lost and gained everything in one day."

Such are the things they tell of this Indian, and they say he was the handsomest of all the Indians and taller than anyone since the Trojan men, but that he was quite young when he fought Alexander.

When Apollonios finally meets King Phraotes, he is surprised to find him living as ascetically as a Pythagorean philosopher despite his great wealth. They soon become close friends, as Phraotes tells Apollonios how young Indian boys are made into philosophers, while Apollonios helps him solve a difficult legal dispute. Following a very unphilosophical, enormous banquet, and an interminable debate concerning the effects of heavy drinking on the art of divination, King Phraotes sends Apollonios on his way toward the Brahmin sages living not far away.

This gives Philostratus the opportunity to resume his "travelogue," and so the reader hears about the great river Hyphasis. Many marvelous sights are to be seen along its banks: unicorns, cinnamon groves, pepper trees tended by trained apes, corn growing twenty feet high, fields of enormous beans, sesame, and millet, as well as other unnamed exotic fruits "sweeter than all the others the seasons bring." But most exciting of all was a dragon hunt that our travelers happened to see. Philostratus briefly digresses to inform the reader of the numerous varieties of dragons in India. For example, there is the small black marsh dragon not more than sixty feet long. Then there are the plains dragons, silvery, and "as fast as the swiftest river." But the real monsters were the mountain dragons. They had golden scales, eyes of fiery stone, bushy beards, could spit fire and made a horrible, brassy, clashing noise when they burrowed under the earth. This beast is so fearsome everything stays clear of it, although there are fabulous riches and magic charms inside its head for those who catch it. Thus the Indians have devised a secret method of capturing it, says Philostratus, and he proceeds to describe it.

III.8. They sew golden letters on a scarlet cloth and place it in front of its hole after placing a sleep-charm upon the letters so that they will overcome the irresistible eyes of the dragon. And they chant many forbidden mysteries over the letters which will cause it to stretch its neck out of its hole and sleep poised over the letters. Then the Indians fall upon the dragon lying there, striking its neck with axes, and when they have cut off its head, they ravage it for the stones inside, for they say hidden inside the heads of the mountain dragons are stones in the shape of flowers flashing forth every color in the rainbow and having a mystical force like the ring they say Gyges had which could make him invisible. But frequently *it* catches the Indian with his axe and secret art and carries him back into his burrow, all but shaking the mountain down. These are also said to live in the mountains around the Red Sea and they say they hear them hissing terribly and going down to the water and far out into the deep. How long these beasts live is impossible to know and unbelievable if I did say. This is what I know about dragons.

After traveling about a week, Apollonios and Damis reach the "heart of India" and the sacred mountain whereon the sages live, which the latter regarded as the "navel of the land"—i.e., the exact center. The travelers were met on the road by the sages' personal envoy, a youth who was "the blackest Indian of all" (III.11), who invites Apollonios up to the palace of the sages, asking the others to wait below.

The days following are spent learning about the fabulous qualities of the mountain, e.g., automatic robot tripods serving different dishes at meal time, large stone jars containing rain or winds and clouds which the sages release when the farmers need them, the mysterious weapons the sages have with which to defend their mountain fortress, and so forth. Just as marvelous is the daily life and religious ritual of the eighteen sages. Apollonios is astonished, for example, to find statues not only of Indian and Egyptian Gods but also of the older Greek Gods, Athena Polias and Apollo of Delos. He is gratified to see that the main part of their worship was devoted to the sun, to which they sang praises at noon and at midnight while suspended in midair several feet off the ground. Naturally there were no bloody sacrifices of any sort. Each day began with exercises followed by rubbing with a heat-producing ointment, and then a dip in a cold pool. After this, the rest of the day was passed in philosophical debate, settling the disputes of kings who came for advice, and healing the sick and afflicted.

Such well-thumbed philosophical topics as "knowing oneself," the nature of the soul, transmigration of souls, of what the cosmos was composed, whether there is more land or water on the earth, and so on, are related by Philostratus. The general tenor of these discussions is indicated below.

III.18. Thereupon he asked another question, namely, whom did they think themselves to be? "Gods," came the answer. When he asked why, the reply was, "Because we are good men." This answer seemed to Apollonios to be so full of sound education that he said it later about himself in his defense before the Emperor Domitian.

Philostratus periodically interrupts the philosophical discussions in order to liven things up. He first has a local king appear who exaggeratedly slanders the Greeks. Naturally Apollonios leaps to the defense and in the ensuing argument, the king is easily defeated and then reduced to tears. Of course, the whole thing is artificial, for Philostratus is just shrewdly playing upon his readers' prejudices. Then after more discussion, several sick are suddenly brought in to be healed. The contrived character of the whole outline should not escape our notice: (1) a series of debates concerning familiar themes of philosophy is interrupted by (2) a comic-serious dramatic confrontation with the visiting king (pointing forward to the deadly serious final clash with Domitian). This is followed by (3) a sumptuous, rather unphilosophical feast, (4) two more philosophical arguments, then (5) a cluster of healing accounts, followed by (6) more philosophical and natural-history discussions. After all this, Philostratus says in a final summarizing statement, "In such communion with the sages Apollonios passed four months there in discussion" (III.50). These are the healing stories.

III.38. In the midst of these words, the messenger of the sages appeared bringing in Indians needing help. And he led up a little woman pleading for her boy whom she said was sixteen years old and who had been possessed by a demon for the past two years, and she said that the character of the demon was that of a deceiver and a liar. When one of the sages asked why she said these things, she replied, "Because my boy is most beautiful, the demon has fallen in love with him and does not let him be in his right mind, or permit him to walk to school or to archery class or stay at home, but drives him out into deserted regions. And the boy does not have his own voice but speaks in a deep and hollow voice, like a man. And he looks at you with other eyes than his own. I constantly wėep because of these things and beat myself and chastise my son as much as is fair, but he does not recognize me. When I decided to come here—I decided to a year ago—the demon confessed himself using the child as a mouthpiece, and—would you believe it?—began telling me that he was the ghost of a man who died once in a battle, dying while loving his wife, but that she outraged their marriage by taking another after he had been dead only three days. And so, because of this he hated the love of women and changed over to this boy. But he promised, if I would not tell you about him, to give my child many good and wonderful things. I was really persuaded by these promises, but he has put me off for so long now, taking over my whole house, it's obvious he intends to do nothing reasonable or true."

Then the sage asked again if the boy were nearby, but she said he wasn't, although she had tried all sorts of things to bring him, "but the demon threatened to hurl me over steep banks and into pits and to kill my son if I brought him here for judgment, so I left him at home." "Be of good cheer," said the sage, "for he will not kill him after he has read these." And pulling out a certain letter from his robe he gave it to the woman, and indeed, the letter was addressed to that very ghost and filled with the most terrifying threats.

III.39. And someone limping also came up, who was already thirty years old, a mighty hunter of lions. Once a lion sprang and landed upon his back and he twisted his leg. But after they stroked his hip with their hands, the youth went away walking perfectly.

And someone who was flowing pus from his eyes went away completely cured of his disease, and another man who had a paralyzed hand departed with its strength returned.

The husband of a certain woman who had had seven painful pregnancies begged their aid in easing her birthgiving, and she was healed in the following way: they commanded the husband, when his wife was about to give birth, to carry a live rabbit under his shirt into the room where she was giving birth and, walking around her to release the rabbit at the same moment when she strained to push the baby out. Then the baby would easily come out, only they warned that the whole womb would be expelled together with the baby unless he shooed the rabbit outside the door immediately.

Philostratus concludes these stories by saying, "and the men were astonished at the manifold wisdom" of the sages. They resume their philosophical discussion, this time focusing chiefly on the art of predicting the future. Iarchus, the chief sage, assures Apollonios, "Those who delight in predicting, my friend, become divine from it and contribute to the salvation of mankind" (*pros sōtērian anthrōpōn*)(III.42).

There is a comical moment when Iarchus playfully asks Damis whether Apollonios' gift of foretelling the future has rubbed off on him a little after all this time. But Damis' answer is quite revealing. "It is not so much foretelling I am after," says Damis. Rather, since he is an Assyrian by birth, he hopes that by associating constantly with Apollonios and imitating everything he does, to learn Greek manners and philosophy and, in short, "mix freely with Greeks and *with his help become a Greek*" (III.43) [italics added]. There could not be any clearer evidence that Apollonios' gospel was in fact Greek culture and philosophy.

Finally Apollonios asks the sages about the fabulous animals living in India. That is, Philostratus is ready to interject some more of his "travelogue" material, and so he has Iarchus relate strange and marvelous accounts of huge man-eating porcupines, giant birds that quarry gold with their beaks, the immortal phoenix which sets fire to its own nest and then sings a funeral dirge to itself, only to come to life again as a worm, and so on.

When the time for parting came, after four months of such discussions, the sages embrace Apollonios and solemnly assure him that he "will seem to be a God to many not only after he is dead but even while living" (III.50).

He heads southwest toward the coast and boards a ship bound for Babylon. Philostratus relates bits and pieces of geographical and mythological lore as Apollonios sails along "the Red Sea" (=Persian Gulf) and then up the Euphrates River until he finally reaches Babylon. From there he retraces his steps to Ionia and Ephesus.

IV.1. Now when they saw Apollonios in Ionia entering Ephesus, even the artisans would not remain at their trades but followed him instead, some being astonished at his wisdom, others at his appearance, others his way of living, others his manner, others at everything at once. Oracles also circulated about him, some from the shrine at Colophon which announced that he shared its own wisdom, was absolutely wise and so on, others from Didyma, others from the temple at Pergamum, for God was commanding many in need of better health to come to Apollonios, for this was both what he wished and pleasing to the Fates.

Deputations also were coming to him from the cities considering him their guest and seeking counsel about life and the dedications of altars and images. Each of these he told the right thing to do by letters or by coming to speak to them.

Apollonios comes to Ephesus and immediately realizes that a terrible calamity is about to strike the city but its inhabitants are so frivolous and careless, they do not listen to his warnings. So he departs on a tour of Ionia intending to return when they are more receptive. He arrives in Smyrna where he gives a series of discourses on harmony within cities, of which the following *parable* is a part.

IV.9. As he was talking he saw a ship with three masts sailing away and the sailors on it doing different things in order to make it function properly. Turning around to those standing there, he said, "Do you see the crew of that ship? Some who are oarsmen are in tugboats, while others are pulling up and fastening the anchors, while others spread the sails out for the wind, and still others are watching from bow and stern. Now if any one of them left his post or did his nautical task ignorantly, they would sail badly and would themselves seem to be stormy weather. But if they compete with each other and strive to appear better than each other, then this ship will proceed excellently and their voyage will be entirely pleasant and peaceful and Poseidon the Protector will seem to be watching over them."

IV.10. With such words as these he restored harmony to the city of Smyrna. But when the plague struck the Ephesians and nothing could control it, they sent a delegation to Apollonios, asking him to become the healer of their suffering. He, thinking it unnecessary to be delayed by using the road, said, "Let us go," and was instantly in Ephesus— something Pythagoras also did, I believe, when he was once in Thurii and Metapontum at the same time.

Then, calling the Ephesians together, he said, "Be of good cheer, for today I will stop this plague," and so saying he led the whole body to the theater, where they later set up the statue of the Averting God Herakles in memory of the event about to happen. There they found an old man who seemed blind, craftily blinking his eyes, and carrying a sack with a piece of bread in it, wearing rags, and his face was very dirty. Standing the Ephesians around him, he said, "Gather as many stones as you can and throw them at this enemy of the Gods." But the Ephesians were amazed at what he said, and thought it a terrible thing to kill a stranger as wretched as this, for he of course was beseeching them and begging for mercy. But Apollonios vehemently urged the Ephesians to throw their stones and not to let him escape. And when some used their slings on him, he who seemed before to be blinking as if blind, suddenly glared around showing eyes full of fire. The Ephesians then realized it was a demon and showered him with their stones so that they heaped up a large pile on top of him. After a short wait, Apollonios ordered the stones removed and the beast which they had killed to be recognized. When it was uncovered of what had been thrown at it, it had disappeared! Instead the form of a dog was seen similar to those from Molottos, as big as the biggest lion in size, crushed under the stones. It had vomited foam like a mad dog. And so they erected the statue of the Averting God, that is of Herakles, over the place where the apparition was stoned.

"Having had enough of the Ionians," says Philostratus, Apollonios "set out for Hellas"—the Greek territory on the other side of the Aegean. On the way, Philostratus capitalizes on the popular interest in Homer's *Iliad,* by having Apollonios stop at the grave of Achilles and call up his ghost one midnight. When Achilles appears, he grows and grows until he is over twenty-five feet tall. Nothing daunted, Apollonios greets him in a friendly way and Achilles on his part seems glad to have someone to converse with at long last. In return for Apollonios' promise to have the customary offerings at his grave restored, Achilles agrees to answer any five questions about the Trojan War. These turn out to be cocktail-circuit bonbons, such as, was Polyxena, supposedly the lover of Achilles though never mentioned by Homer, really sacrificed to Achilles on top of his grave? And was Helen really abducted to Troy, i.e., wasn't the whole story simply invented out of whole cloth by Homer? And so on.

When he arrives at Athens, he is once again immediately recognized and acclaimed by one and all. The only sour note is a refusal by the chief priest of the mystery at Eleusis to initiate Apollonios during a current festival, on the grounds that he was a sorcerer and an associate of foul demons (perhaps word had come to him of Apollonios' conjuring up of the ghost of Achilles). Apollonios of course puts the priest down, to the delight of the crowd. On another occasion he is lecturing the crowd on the proper way to pour out libations to the Gods, when he is interrupted by a heckler—only Apollonios immediately perceives a deeper danger, i.e., the heckler is possessed by a demon.

IV.20. And when he told them to have handles on the cup and to pour over the handles—this being a purer part of the cup since no one's mouth touches that part—a young boy began laughing raucously, scattering his discourse to the winds. Apollonios stopped and, looking up at him, said, "It is not you that does this arrogant thing but the demon who drives you unwittingly," for unknown to everyone the youth was actually possessed by a demon, for he used to laugh at things no one else did and would fall to weeping for no reason and would talk and sing to himself. Most people thought it was the jumpiness of youth which brought him to do such things and at this point he really seemed carried away by drunkenness. But it was actually a demon which spoke through him.

Now as Apollonios was staring at him the phantom in the boy let out horrible cries of fear and rage, sounding just like someone being burned alive or stretched on the rack, and then he began to promise that he would leave the young boy and never possess anyone else among men.

But Apollonios spoke to him angrily such as a master might to a cunning and shameless slave and he commanded him to come out of him, giving definite proof of it. "I will knock down that statue there," it said, pointing toward one of those around the Porch of the King. And when the statue tottered and then fell over, who can describe the shout of amazement that went up and how everyone clapped their hands from astonishment! But the young boy opened his eyes as if from sleep and looked at the rays of the sun. Now all those observing these events revered the boy for he no longer appeared to be as coarse as he had been, nor did he look disorderly, but he had come back to his own nature just as if he had drunk some medicine. He threw aside his fancy soft clothes and, stripping off the rest of his luxuriousness, came to love poverty and a threadbare cloak and the customs of Apollonios.

Next Apollonios goes to Athens where he bitterly chastises the Athenians because of their lust for bloody gladiatorial shows. One is reminded of similar threats uttered by the Jewish prophets.

IV.22. He censured the Athenians for something else also. They would gather in the theater of Dionysos below the Acropolis and watch men butcher each other, enjoying it more than they do in Corinth today. For they would buy men for high prices, namely those who had committed crimes such as adultery or fornication or burglary or purse snatching or kidnapping, people who had received the death sentence, and, arming them, would command them to attack each other. Apollonios rebuked these practices and once when he was invited to the city assembly of the Athenians, he told them that he would not think of entering such a filthy place, filled as it was with the defilement of blood. Another time he said in a letter to them that it was amazing that "Athena had not already abandoned the Acropolis because of the blood you pour out there. For it seems to me that before long when you celebrate the sacred Pan-Athenian Festival, you will no longer use bulls but sacrifice hundreds of men to the Goddess. And you, Dionysos, will you continue to come to your theater now that it is filled with blood and gore? Do the sages of Athens perform religious ceremonies to you there? Go somewhere else, Dionysos! You are too pure for that!"

Apollonios then goes around the Greek temples of Dodona, Delphi, and others, correcting their practices. In Corinth he frees a young man from the clutches of a vampire masquerading as a beautiful young woman who was fattening him up for the kill.

Eventually he goes to Crete to worship on Mount Ida and from there he goes to Rome. Having landed in Italy, he receives word that Nero is terrorizing Rome, making a special target of philosophers. The famous

Stoic philosopher Musonius "second only to Apollonios" (IV.35) was already in prison. This news comes as a shock to many of the cowardly followers in Apollonios' train, and, as Damis observes, most of them found pretexts to turn back, thus "running away from both Nero and philosophy" (IV.37). But the eight remaining are ready to stick it out, "being unified by the encouragement of Apollonios, they desired both to die on behalf of philosophy and to appear better than those who had run away" (IV.38).

After he arrived in Rome, Apollonios' scorn at Nero's shameless posturing as a popular singer reaches the attention of the police and he is arrested and brought up for trial. However, he gets off because, for some mysterious reason, the scroll upon which the grounds for his arrest had been written is suddenly found to be blank. Apollonios is clearly superior to his foes and they are now afraid to attack someone with such mysterious powers. Not much later, he performs another even more miraculous feat.

IV.45. Here also is a miracle (*thauma*) of Apollonios. A young girl seemed to have died in the very hour of her marriage and the bridegroom was following the bier weeping over his unfulfilled marriage. Rome mourned also, for it happened that the dead girl was from one of the best families. Apollonios, happening to be present where they were mourning, said, "Put down the bier, for I will end your weeping for this girl," and at the same time he asked what her name was. The bystanders thought that he was going to give a speech like those which people give at burials to heighten everyone's sorrow. But he didn't; instead he touched her and saying something no one could hear, awakened the girl who seemed dead. And the girl spoke and went back to her father's house, just like Alcestis who was brought back to her life by Herakles. And when the relatives of the girl offered Apollonios 150,000 silver pieces as a reward, he replied that he would return it to the child as a gift for her dowry.

Now whether he found a spark of life in her which had escaped the notice of the doctors—for it is said her breath could be seen above her face as it rained—or whether, her life actually being completely extinguished, she grew warm again and received it back, no one knows. A grasp of this mystery has not been gained either by me or by those who chanced to be there.

Nero soon prohibits all philosophical activity throughout the city, and Apollonios decides to leave such an inhospitable locale and visit the "pillars of Hercules" at the western end of the Mediterranean Sea, i.e., the Straits of Gibraltar.

Summary

Book V

After passing several months in the region of Gibraltar, Apollonios and Damis voyage to Sicily and thence back to Greece. Once again he spends the next months touring Greece, reproving and correcting the priests in the various temples. Then, in the spring, he sets off for Egypt. As before, while Apollonios and Damis travel along, Philostratus uses this "travel" setting to provide Apollonios with little speeches or tirades on a number of conventional subjects, such as the folly of bloody sacrifices, the futility of greed, horse racing, and so forth.

He meets Vespasian in Egypt (it is the winter of 69)—after refusing to see him in Judaea, "a country which those who dwelt in it have polluted as much by what they do as what is done to them"—and assures him he should seek to be the next emperor. There then follows a lengthy debate on the popular question of how a sovereign ought to rule. Of course, Philostratus' speeches, put in the mouth of Apollonios, as well as speeches for the opposition, given to a rival, named Euphrates, contain nothing original or remarkable—in fact the way Apollonios is portrayed unabashedly playing up to Vespasian's ambitious desire for power is rather shocking. However, as we will see later, Philostratus has a very good reason for it.

Of interest to us, however, is another appearance of second-century Roman anti-Jewish hatred similar to the comment of Apollonios just mentioned. In the course of his argument Euphrates says—and the others readily agree—that Vespasian would have done better to use his army to invade Rome and depose Nero instead of wasting it in suppressing the Jewish rebellion. For the Jews, says Euphrates,

"have long since stood aloof, not only from Romans but from all men, they who seek an 'unspotted life'—to whom no fellowship with men at table or in libations or in prayers or sacrifices is welcome. Let them remove themselves from us farther than Susa or Bactria or the Indians beyond! There was certainly no good reason to punish this standoffish nation, whom it were better never to have taken over in the first place" (v.33).

This statement is significant as it documents the growth of the first stages of popular Roman anti-Semitism. This new phenomenon seems to have been provoked partly by Jewish exclusivism, as is clear from Euphrates' specific reasons why Gentiles resented this stubbornly aloof nation. With the rise of Christianity, however, a whole new religious dimension is added. But it is clear that there was already present a growing international hostility toward the Jews, triggered by the rebellion of A.D. 67–70 and A.D. 132–135, upon which Christianity could capitalize—as we can see it did in such virulently anti-Semitic writings as the Gospel of Peter and the Acts of Pilate.

Following the conference with Vespasian, Apollonios and his follow-ers depart for upper Egypt and the famous naked sages living in the desert.

Summary

Book VI

At this point, a geographical comment by Philostratus provides us with a fascinating glimpse of the way in which an educated Roman thought of "the world":

> "Ethiopia is the western end of everything under the sun just as India lies on the eastern and is bounded (on the south) by Egypt at Meroë and touching an unknown region of Libya, comes to an end at the sea which the poets call 'Ocean,' thus naming what goes around the entire mass of dry land" (VI.1).

It is a flat, roughly circular Earth having a rim of water ("Ocean") and three or four inland seas, lying beneath the curved bowl of Heaven to which were fastened sun, moon, and stars. Of lower Africa, or northern Europe, or central and eastern Asia, much less the Pacific and the New World, there is no awareness.

When Apollonios and Damis reach the territory where the Egyptian sages live, they find an unfriendly reception. It seems a stranger had come just before to warn that the Apollonios who would soon visit them is a sorcerer and an evil man. In this way Philostratus begins to weave into the plot the theme, which will reach a mighty crescendo in the final act when Apollonios, betrayed by this same stranger (it is actually the jealous philosopher Euphrates), at last must answer to charges of sorcery and treason before the Emperor Domitian himself.

This Euphrates, whom Apollonios bests in the debate on kingship with Vespasian mentioned above, was in fact one of the most famous philosophers in the first century. However, he is portrayed by Philos-tratus as a sinister, evil person. This suggests that Philostratus is not trying to give an unbiased portrayal of this conflict, but instead heightening their enmity to give his plot more excitement—just like the little erotic touches inserted here and there to spice up the story (e.g., the beautiful young boys Apollonios keeps meeting and virtuously refraining from seducing, although they are completely under his power). Details like these may have heightened his readers' interest in the story.

But we have gotten ahead of the plot. When the identity of the malicious stranger is revealed, Apollonios gives a lengthy defense of his way of life to the Egyptian sages. This is followed by several debates, one of which expresses the popular Greco-Roman scorn at the animal Gods of the Egyptians. Other typical discussions touch on the nature of the soul, the nature of justice and the structure of the cosmos.

But the visit is not a happy one and, before long, Apollonios and Damis and the rest decide to search for the fabled sources of the Nile, another popular bit of geographical lore. Proceeding upstream, says Philostratus, they finally came to the first of several huge, roaring cataracts or waterfalls. Then they pass two more, and with each one, the noise and confusion become more deafening and terrifying. Finally they find themselves in an incredibly dense, mountainous region, with giant geysers of water gushing forth out of the sides of sheer cliffs all around them. Fearing permanent deafness and nearly paralyzed with terror, because of the horrible demons which lurked all around (for all the demons and devils in the world gathered here, says Philostratus), they hastily retrace their steps.

After briefly recounting episodes in their stay among some "Ethiopian" villages, Philostratus abruptly drops the thread of the Egyptian journey and, using a common Hellenistic literary gimmick to speed up the passage of time and shift the scene of action, he suddenly describes the contents of some letters that passed between Titus, Vespasian's son, and Apollonios (cf. 1 Macc. 12, 14).

Using this change of subject as a springboard, Philostratus then jumps the story forward several years to an occasion when Titus and Apollonios meet each other in Tarsus, describing what they said to each other on that occasion. Before long Egypt and Ethiopia are forgotten and Philostratus, in rough summary fashion, fills the rest of Book VI with disconnected anecdotes of Apollonios' activities when he is back in the region of his boyhood—Cilicia. The main thing Philostratus wants to do is to hurry time along, i.e., both to introduce and get rid of the Emperor Titus, so that his wicked younger brother Domitian can then be brought onto the stage—and everything set up for the final clash between him and Apollonios that occupies so much of Books VII and VIII, which conclude Philostratus' tale.

Summary

Book VII

Book VII, which might be titled "The Martyrdom of Philosophers," contains Philostratus' efforts to set Apollonios' clash with the ruthless Emperor Domitian in the best possible light. First, Philostratus lists other examples where philosophers have faced death at the hands of a tyrant, e.g., Zeno, Plato, Diogenes, Crates. Then he finds fault with each one in such a way as to show that, not only was Apollonios' bravery, wit, and power superior to theirs, but he also confronted a tyrant who ruled the whole world, not just some petty island king or ruler of an obscure country.

Next Philostratus takes pains to show that Apollonios came to this clash quite voluntarily; he was not dragged thither by Domitian's superior might. Thus, when Domitian decides to arrest Apollonios (who is in Asia at the time), Philostratus says Apollonios knew of it by his powers of foresight, and immediately began his trip to Italy before the orders for his arrest had even reached the provincial governor of Asia.

Then Philostratus heightens the dramatic tension by emphasizing the base cowardice of even the closest of Apollonios' disciples. Meeting him when he arrives in Italy, they all try to dissuade him from throwing his life away. This, of course, provides "Apollonios" (=Philostratus) with several occasions to deliver ringing speeches on the duty of the philosopher to die unafraid for the sake of liberty, rather than cravenly preserve his freedom while tyranny makes slaves of everyone.

There is a curious ambiguity in Philostratus' portrait of Apollonios, however. On the one hand he is shown unceasingly pressing forward into danger, speaking of the need for bravery in the true philosopher, his patience under tribulation, his manliness, and the like. But on the other hand, there are places where Philostratus makes it equally clear that Apollonios is not really in any danger, either from the Emperor Domitian or anyone else. For example, on one occasion Apollonios says,

> "I myself know more than mere men do, for I know all things . . . and that I have not come to Rome on behalf of the foolish will become perfectly clear; for *I myself am in no danger with respect to my own body nor will I be killed by this tyrant* . . ." (VII.14) [italics added].

If this be true, what is the point of resounding phrases such as "it is especially fitting for the wise to die for the sake of the things they practice" (VII.14) and "death on behalf of friends . . . (is) the most divine of things human" (VII.14)? How can Philostratus have Apollonios say later on to an agent of Domitian's: "It will be enough for me to leave, having saved myself and my friends, on behalf of whom I am here *in danger*" (VII.38)? Either Apollonios is in danger or he isn't!

Well, as the outcome will show, he was not in any danger at all. But, then, what is the point of all these fine speeches about risking death at the hands of tyranny? Apparently, that is all they are—fine speeches; rather the rhetorical product of an author primarily concerned with their immediate effect, but who had not thought out their place in his story as a whole. For if all Apollonios' friends had had the same powers he did (such as being able to remove iron shackles at will), then obviously none of them would have been afraid of Domitian either.

Thus, when Philostratus describes Apollonios being led through the streets of Rome under heavy guard from the prison to the palace for trial, and how "everyone turned to see Apollonios, his appearance attracting admiration, for he seemed so god-like that those standing about were astonished, while his having come to risk danger on behalf of men made those who formerly slandered him now friendly" (VII.31). At this point it becomes clear that Philostratus' vanity and facile ability to conjure up a touching scene with his pen, regardless of its inconsistency with the rest of the story, has gotten quite out of control.

Summary

Book VIII

In any case, the grand climax to Philostratus' story is at hand. The final test has come; the vindication or collapse of everything Apollonios has trained for and practiced all his life will now be revealed. Either he will "be true to himself" now, in the moment of supreme crisis, or all will brand him a coward and a traitor to philosophy.

There is a preliminary hearing at which the Emperor Domitian becomes enraged when Apollonios will not buckle under his threats. This is followed by a period of solitary confinement and the shaving off of his hair, intended to soften Apollonios up. During this time, various soldiers or spies, secretly sent from Domitian, harass Apollonios in the midst of his seeming helplessness. But Apollonios withstands it all, seeing through all the stratagems to intimidate him.

Finally the day of the public trial dawns. The audience hall is jammed with people as the procedure begins. There is a brief preliminary skirmish with some minor official (a skillful touch to delay the action, thus heightening the suspense), and then his old enemy, the philosopher Euphrates, who is now his chief accuser, loudly demands that Apollonios stop ignoring the king and give his full attention to the "God of all mankind." Thereupon, Apollonios who had been insultingly standing with his back to the emperor, ostentatiously looks up towards the ceiling (i.e., towards Zeus). This bold affront so enrages Euphrates that he begs the king to get on with the accusations so that they could end the trial and begin the torture Apollonios so clearly deserves.

Domitian accordingly reads out the first charge: Apollonios dresses differently than everyone else. He does not wish to bother the animals to get wool or skin, Apollonios replies skillfully. Then Domitian reads the second charge: Why do men consider Apollonios equal with the Gods? This, declares Apollonios, is simply because they see in him a good man (lifting a line from the Indian sages). Third, how could he predict the plague that struck Ephesus if he were not a sorcerer? Apollonios explains that his light diet enables him to sense harmful pestilences in the air before other men do.

Finally, the accusation of sedition comes up. Domitian asks whether Apollonios had plotted to help Nerva overthrow the government, and to this end had he not sacrificed a young boy and examined his entrails for the signs of a favorable omen for the plot? What of that? Apollonios scornfully rejects the whole accusation as a blatant lie, and dares anyone to come forward with proof that he did any of these things. The gallery unexpectedly applauds loudly and—wonder of wonders—the emperor seems to be impressed himself! But suddenly, something totally unexpected happens. (*End of summaries.*)

VIII.5. When Apollonios had said these things, the crowd indicated its approval more loudly than was customary in the court of the king. Thereupon, Domitian, considering those present to have borne witness together in Apollonios' favor, and being somewhat influenced himself by his answers—for when questioned he seemed to have given logical answers—declared, "I acquit you of these charges! But, you must stay here so that we may meet you privately." But Apollonios took courage and said, "I thank you, O King, but because of these sinful courtiers here, the cities are being destroyed, the islands are full of fugitives, the mainland full of weeping, your soldiers are cowardly, and the Senate is suspicious. Give me my freedom, if you will, but if not, then send someone to imprison my body, for it is impossible to imprison my soul! Indeed, you will not even take my body, 'for you cannot kill me since I am not a mortal man,'" and, saying this, *he vanished from the courtroom!*—which was a smart thing to do at the time, for it was obvious that the tyrant was not going to question Apollonios sincerely but just detain him by various pretexts. For he boasted later in not having killed the sage. But Apollonios did not want to be dragged into further confinement, and anyway he considered it more effective if the king were not ignorant of his real nature, that he could never be taken captive involuntarily!

> And so, Apollonios suddenly appears out of the blue to Damis and a friend in a small town by the sea, where he had sent Damis several days before the trial.
>
> At this point, however, Philostratus breaks the narrative in order to present a very long speech that he claims Apollonios had composed to give before the king—but, due to his sudden departure, he didn't have an opportunity. So Philostratus gives it for Apollonios in its entirety (it runs to more than 800 lines!).
>
> It is clearly intended to be Apollonios' final *testament,* summarizing and

defending his whole life's work. (In fact, this may be what Philostratus is referring to above, at the end of I.3.) Its artificiality can scarcely be doubted. Otherwise, what is the meaning of Apollonios' earlier word to Damis that he was *not* going to prepare just such an oration in defense of his life, but speak extemporaneously (VIII.30)? Philostratos, following the time-honored methods of Hellenistic historiography, has here simply fabricated the speech Apollonios *ought* to have given on this momentous occasion—with all the rhetorical skill he can muster.

In fact it is a skillful forensic declamation taking up each of the four accusations and completely demolishing them. Of particular interest, therefore, is a passage in the section dealing with Apollonios' (=Philostratus') rebuttal of the accusation of sorcery: i.e., why do men worship him as a God? As part of the reply, Apollonios (=Philostratus) sets forth very explicitly what sort of being he (=Philostratus) thought Apollonios was. In other words, here we have Apollonios (=Philostratus) state the abstract concept itself of "divine man" which actually underlies this whole writing from beginning to end.

Philostratus starts off the passage by having Apollonios compare the Egyptian sages' view of God with that of the Indian sages.

VIII.7.7. As for the Indians and the Egyptians, the Egyptians condemn the Indians for various things and find fault with their teachings about conduct, but as for the explanation which is given about the Creator of all things, in this they more or less agree with them, because, in fact, the Indians taught it to them. This explanation of the origin and existence of all things recognizes God as Creator, the cause of this creating being his yearning for the good. Since these things are interrelated, moreover, I go on to say that those who are good among men have something of God in them. Now of course it is thought that the order (*kosmos*) which is dependent upon God the Creator includes all things in Heaven, in the sea, and on the land, in which there is equal participation by men—but according to Fortune. Then there is also another order (*kosmos*) dependent upon the good man which does not transgress the limits of wisdom; and you yourself, O King, say that it needs a man formed like a God (*theō eikasmenos*).

And what is the character of this order? Well, anyone can see that all around us there are deranged souls insanely grabbing for every passing fad, our laws obsolete to them, having no common sense, their piety toward the Gods sheer disgrace, loving idle chatter and luxury from which springs wicked laziness as the advisor of their every act. Other drunken souls rush in all directions at once, nothing restraining their frenzy even if they should take every pill thought to bring sleep.

Therefore, what is needed is a man who will care to instill order in their souls—a God sent to mankind by Wisdom. Such a man as this is able to urge and to lead people away from the passions by which they are so violently carried off in their everyday behavior, as well as from their desire for material possessions, because of which they will tell you they have nothing as long as they can't hold their mouths open under the stream of wealth pouring down. However, to curb them from committing murder is perhaps not impossible for such a man, although to wash away the guilt of a murder once committed is not possible, either for me or for the God who is Creator of All.

In view of the likelihood that this entire speech has been created by Philostratus himself, this brief description of a "God-man sent to the world by Wisdom" is all the more significant as indicating precisely what Philostratus wanted to convey to his audience about Apollonios. And, even more important, it corresponds exactly to the savior concept enunciated by the Christian church father Eusebius, quoted in the Introduction (pp. 19–21), as well as Philo's conception of Moses (see pp. 253–55.). This is clear evidence that, beneath the cultural and religious variations, there was a widely-shared concept of the Savior God, appearing among men for a time to heal and save.

In fact, Apollonios (=Philostratus) goes on to say this explicitly a few lines later: "I do all things for the salvation of men" (VIII. 7.10). Just before this passage, "Apollonios" explains why the cities he has visited think that he is a God, and it forms a good summary of his whole "mission" on behalf of the salvation of men: "Indeed, I have been worthy of much honor in each of the cities which needed me, performing such things as healing the sick, making more holy those being initiated into the Mysteries or offering sacrifice, rooting out pride, and strengthening their laws" (VIII.7.7).

After giving his version of Apollonios' self-defense at his trial (shades of Socrates!), Philostratus tells how he suddenly appears to Damis in Dicaearchia, the small town on the seacoast where the other was waiting for him. So Apollonios emerges from the hour of peril unscathed. Indeed, says Philostratus, he made "the tyrant a plaything by his philosophy" (VIII.10). Where is all the talk of danger and risk now?

Damis is naturally startled to see him and asks if he is a ghost. "Apollonios put out his hand saying, 'Touch me and if I escape you I am a ghost come from Persephone's realm'" (VIII.12). Damis is overjoyed to see it is really his master, though completely mystified how he came from Rome so quickly.

Apollonios decides to leave Italy that same day for Greece, and so they set sail for Sicily and thence to the Peloponnese. Upon arrival they settle in the temple of Zeus at Olympia. Instantly word gets around that Apollonios is not at Rome in prison, or dead, but has just arrived at Olympia. At this, "the whole of Greece came together to see him as never before for any Olympic festival" (VIII.15). The question on everyone's lips was, how had he gotten away from Domitian? Apollonios would only say that "he had given his defense and was saved." But when several Italians arrive, they tell the whole story of what happened in the courtroom. "At this Greece was moved to near worship of him, believing him to be a *divine man (theios aner)* for this reason above all—that he did not indulge in loud boasting about any of his deeds" (VIII.15, italics added. Cf. *Letter* 48: "even the Gods have spoken of me as a divine man [*theios aner*]"; *Epistles of Apollonios*).

After forty days of discussions and debates at Olympia, Apollonios proclaims to all that he will now depart and "converse with you in each of your cities, in the festivals, the religious processions, Mysteries, sacrifices, libations—for they have need of a knowledgeable man" (VIII.19). He then visits a shrine of Apollo where, after staying in its sacred cave seven days (longer than anyone ever had before), he emerges with an authentic book of the teachings of Pythagoras, which, Philostratus adds, is preserved to this day at Antium in the palace of Hadrian.

A large band of disciples now follows Apollonios everywhere. The Greeks call them "Apollonians," and Philostratus describes one of his sermons to them, an attack on lawyers who are willing to argue any case before the judges for money, calling them "people who welcome enmity; indeed their vocation is the same thing as selling hatred" (VIII.22).

After two years, Apollonios sails for Ionia, and while staying in Ephesus, he suddenly sees a vision—while giving a lecture—of the assassination of Domitian taking place in Rome at that very moment. No one is willing to credit Apollonios' vision, although they would like to. But before long envoys come with the news that the Emperor Domitian has in fact been murdered and Nerva is now on the throne. A sudden wave of awe sweeps the city at Apollonios' prevision. The Emperor Nerva then sends for Apollonios to come assist him in ruling the empire, but Apollonios refuses (for the curious reason that he knew Nerva would die in less than two years!). Sending Damis to Nerva with his letter of apology, Apollonios himself "dies" not long after. Of the circumstances surrounding Apollonios' passing, Damis preserves no mention (because he was in Rome), but Philostratus says he has found three other accounts of it and he relates all three.

VIII.30. Some say he died in Ephesus while being served by two slave women, the two male slaves I mentioned at the beginning having died already. He freed one of them but not the other, having a reason in mind, for Apollonios said, "If you serve her you will benefit from her, for it will be the beginning of a good thing for you." Thus, after he died one served the other until one day, on a whim, the latter sold her to a merchant and then someone else bought her from him even though she was not goodlooking. But he was in love with her and being quite wealthy he both made her his wife and inscribed in the public archives the children he had by her.

But others say he died in Lindos; that is, they say he entered the temple of Athena and just disappeared once he got inside. But those who live in Crete say he died in a more remarkable way than the way the people of Lindos tell.

For they say that Apollonios lived in Crete, an object of greater veneration than ever before and that one day he came to the temple of Dictynna (Artemis) at a deserted hour. Dogs are kept there as a guard for the temple, keeping watch over the riches inside it and the Cretans consider them as fierce as bears or other wild beasts. But when he comes up, they do not bark but come up to him wagging their tails, something they would not do even to those very familiar to them. The temple attendants thereupon arrest and bind Apollonios on the grounds of being a wizard (*goēs*) and a thief, claiming he had thrown the dogs something to soothe them. But around the middle of the night he freed himself and after calling to the men who had tied him up so as. not to be unobserved he ran up to the gates of the temple, which immediately opened by some unseen power, and when he had gone inside, the gates closed together again as they were shut originally. Then the voices of young women singing came forth from inside the temple and the song was "Come from earth, come to Heaven, come."

By the time the temple attendants get the locked door open again, Apollonios has disappeared; i.e., he is in Heaven. One is reminded of the "Empty Tomb" story in the gospels; it also is a "translation" account. To prove that he is not dead, Philostratus finishes his biography with a story of a doubting disciple who refused to believe that Apollonios really was still alive. One day Apollonios appears to him, and removes all of his doubts.

VIII.31. This young man would never agree to the immortality of the soul. "I, my friends, am completing the tenth month of praying to Apollonios to reveal to me the nature of the soul. But he is so completely dead that he has not even responded to my begging, nor persuaded me that he is not dead." Such were the things he said then, but on the fifth day after that they were busy with these things and he suddenly fell into a deep sleep right where he had been talking. Now the rest of the youths studying with him were reading books and busily incising geometric shapes on the earth when he as if insane suddenly leaped to his feet, still seeming to be asleep, the perspiration running off him, and cried out, "*I believe you!*"

When those present asked him what was wrong, he said, "Do you not see Apollonios the Wise, how he stands here among us listening to the argument and singing wonderful verses concerning the soul?"

"Where is he?" they said, "for he has not appeared to us even though we wish this more than to have all mortal wealth!"

But the youth replied, "It seems he came to discuss with me alone

concerning the things which I would not believe. Hear therefore what
things he prophesied about the doctrine (*logos*):

> "The immortal soul is not at thy disposal
>   but belongs to divine Providence.
> Thus, when thy body dies,
> Like a swift horse freed from its bonds,
> The soul leaps lightly forth
> Mingling with the gentle air,
> Shunning its harsh and dreary servitude.
> As for thee, what benefit to know this now?
> When thou art no more,
> Then thou wilt know this well enough.
> So why learn of such things among the living?"

Now this clear teaching of Apollonios on the mysteries of the soul was
given as an oracle in order that we might be encouraged and know our
own natures as we go to the place the Fates assign us.

I do not remember finding a tomb or epitaph of Apollonios anywhere,
even though I have traveled over most of the earth hearing everywhere
supernatural stories (*logoi daimonioi*) about him. There is, however, a
temple at Tyana built at the emperor's expense, since even emperors
considered him worthy of the honors they themselves received.

For Caracalla's dedication of a shrine to Apollonios at Tyana, see Cassius Dio LXXVII
18.4.)

Poimandres
The Hermetic Tractates

Introduction: This writing comes from a large, heterogenous collection of writings known as the *Corpus Hermeticum,* so-called because some of them have to do in one way or another with the God Hermes. The meaning of the title of this writing is uncertain. The two most commonly accepted interpretations are: (1) the title is Greek and may mean, "shepherd of man" or "shepherd"; (2) the title derives from the Coptic (*p.eime.n.re*) and means "the knowledge of the Sun-God (*Ra*)." The second alternative better fits the document's contents. The author is unknown and opinions differ as to the date of the writing. But the second century A.D. is a likely date.

Part of the reason for the uncertainty as to Poimandres' date is the puzzling character of the writing itself. Although the author clearly relies on the Jewish creation account in Genesis, chs. 1–2, the writing as a whole comes from a very different context. Is *Poimandres* a Greco-Egyptian mystical revelation of the creation of the world, which dips from time to time into the narrative of Genesis? Or is it a product of esoteric Jewish mysticism, well assimilated to mystical traditions of other religions? In either case, *Poimandres* is an excellent example of the religious syncretism that flourished during the Greco-Roman age, that is, the process in which religious traditions mix and appropriate symbols from other traditions.

Poimandres gives expression to a profound pessimism regarding life, a deep rejection of the tangible world. Human beings are not at home in this world; they are "strangers in a strange land." They are "in the world" only because they have somehow gotten themselves subjected to a terrible demonic Power which rules the physical universe.

The corollary to this deep disenchantment with the world is the view that authentic human existence may only be restored by enlightenment, enlightenment in the form of secret, saving knowledge (*gnosis*). This knowledge brings to a few elect humans the realization of their predicament in the world and the message that they really do not belong here, but are destined to return to the heavenly realm from whence they came. In short, humans are presented in *Poimandres* as heavenly souls entrapped in this evil and unredeemable creation.

So humans are dual creatures; they are divine, immortal souls which have somehow gotten ensnared in filthy physical bodies. *Gnosis* frees the divine element from the trap of the body, so that the souls may ascend through the heavenly spheres back to their true heavenly abode.

There are three parts to *Poimandres*. The first section (chs. 1–19) speaks of the creation of the world and of the entrapment of the divine in physical nature. The second section (chs. 20–26) tells of redemption, the ascent of souls to the heavenly home, and their mystical union with the Father. In the last part (chs. 26–32), the enlightened hearer of *Poimandres'* gospel is instructed to preach the gospel of enlightenment to his fellow humans. This instruction is concluded with a lyrical final prayer.

---

1. Once when my thoughts were turned toward the existence of things, and my mind was greatly uplifted, my bodily senses were subdued as in those who are weighed down by sleep after overeating or from physical weariness. It seemed a great being of unmeasurable size began to call my name. It said to me, "What do you wish to hear and to see, and when you have understood, to learn and to know?"

2. I said, "Who are you?" "I am Poimandres," he said, "the True Mind; I know what you wish; I am with you everywhere."

3. I said, "I want to learn about the existence of things, and to understand the nature of these things, and to know God. Oh, how I want to hear these things!"

He replied, "Hold in your mind whatever you want to learn, and I will teach you."

4. He had no sooner said this than he changed his appearance, and in an instant all things were opened to me, and I saw a boundless vision. Everything became shining light, pleasing and happy; when I saw this, I loved it. After a little while there was a downbearing darkness which came on bit by bit; it was terrifying and hateful. It twisted and coiled down, it seemed to me, like a [snake[1]]. Then the darkness changed into a kind of wet substance (or, nature), indescribably shaken, and it gave off smoke as from a fire. The darkness gave off a kind of sound, continuous and inarticulate. Then it gave out a formless cry, which seemed like a voice of fire.

5. From the light . . . a holy Logos came down and assailed the substance (nature), and unmixed fire leaped up from the wet substance (nature) into the heights above. The fire was light, sharp, and, at the same time, active, and the air which was light followed to the spirit (perhaps, "the ether"), going up as far as did the fire from the earth and water, so that it seemed suspended from the fire. But the earth and

[1]cnj.—See A. D. Nock and A.-J. Festugière, *Hermès Trismégiste* (Paris: Société d'Edition, 1960) I, p. 7.

water remained mixed together, so that one could not tell the earth from the water. The mixture was in motion, stirred by the order of the spiritual Logos which was carried over it.

6. Poimandres said to me, "Do you know what this vision means?" "Well," I said, "I shall know." "That light," he said, "is I, Mind, your God, who is before the wet substance which appeared out of the darkness. The shining Logos coming from the Mind is the Son of God." "What does this mean?" I said. "Know this. The (capacity) in you to see and hear is the Logos of the Lord, and the Mind is the Father, God. They are not to be distinguished from each other. Their union is life." "I thank you," I said. "But now consider the light and know this."

7. When he said this, he regarded me for a long time, so that I was afraid at his aspect. But he looked up, and then I saw in my mind the light which is in unmeasurable powers, and it became a boundless, ordered cosmos. The fire was enclosed by a great force and was held static. That is what I discerned in the vision, because of the Logos of Poimandres.

8. As I was astounded, he spoke again to me. "You see in the Mind the archetypal form, the primal beginning of the beginning which never ends," Poimandres said to me. "These elements of nature," I said, "from where did they spring?" Again he said concerning these things, "They are from the will of God which received the Logos and saw the beautiful cosmos and imitated it, as the world was made through its own elements and begotten souls (or, "according to its own elements and its own products, the souls," so Nock-Festugière).

9. But the Mind, God, was both male and female; it was life and light, and it begot by Logos another Mind, the world-creator *(demiurgos)*. The demiurge, a God of the fire and spirit, crafted seven governing powers which orbited the sensible world. Their governance is called fate.

10. At once the Logos of God leaped from the downbearing elements (of God) into the pure creation of nature and became one with the world-creator Mind; they were of the same being. The elements of the downbearing substance were left without Logos so that they were merely stuff.

11. However, the world-creator Mind, together with the Logos, surrounded the circles and made them spin around. He also spun his creatures around and let them spin from an indeterminate beginning to an unbounded end; their rotation begins where it ends. This spinning of things, just as the Mind willed it, brought forth from the downbearing substance arational, living beings, arational because they did not have the Logos. The air bore flying creatures, and the water bore swimming things. Earth and water were separated from one another, just as the

Mind wished. And the (earth) produced from herself living things which she held in her, four-footed animals and snakes, wild and tame beasts. 12. The Father of all, Mind, who was life and light, brought forth a Man in his own likeness whom he loved as his own child. For the Man was very beautiful, having the image of the Father. God truly loved his own image, and he made him lord of all creatures.

The above section is based upon Genesis 1:1–26.

In the Greco-Roman world the most popular model of the cosmos was the human being, in a macrocosm/microcosm analogy. As the human mind was considered the governing and essential part of a human being, analogously the cosmos was thought to be ordered and controlled by Mind (God), whose reasoning order (*logos*) gave structure to existence. This analogy meant also that any connection between God and man came through mind (R. G. Collingwood, *The Idea of Nature* [New York: Oxford University Press, 1960], pp. 3, 29ff.).

What the author of Poimandres sees in the first part of the vision is an archetypal creation of the cosmos (like an architect's model) in the mind of God. A secondary creator-God (demiurge) which is begotten from God (who is both male and female) is the shaper of creation, because the high God cannot have anything to do directly with (evil) creation. This is a common, gnostic viewpoint (Gospel of Philip 63,99). The stuff from which creation is formed is a kind of cosmic soup; the water and earth are mixed together (Gen. 1:1–2).

The Demiurge (ch. 9) creates the planets, which control destiny. Fate was a popular *bête noir* in Hellenistic thought and symbolized human helplessness. The planets' orbits are the juncture between the earthly and heavenly regions of the cosmos. (See the *Dream of Scipio* 17–19). When the Demiurge and the Logos start the planets spinning in their orbits (ch. 11), the cosmos takes on form and order, based on the archetypal model of the cosmos which is in Mind. The force of creation is like a great centrifuge; the planets' spinning causes a separation of earth and water and spins out the creatures (ch. 11).

So far, so good, but trouble is at hand with the creation of the archetypal Man (ch. 12) who is given power over all this creation (cf. Gen. 1:28).

13. When he (i.e., the Man) considered the world-creator's creation, which was made in the fire (or, "which was in the Father"), he wanted to create also, and the Father gave him permission. He entered the world-creator's sphere, having full power, and he considered the creations of (his) brother. They (the governing powers) were pleased with him, and each one shared power (or, "jurisdiction") with him. He learned well their essence and partook of their nature, and then he wished to break out of the orbits and to know the power of the one who rules over the fire.

14. The Man who had full power over the world of mortal beings and

arational animals peered down through the joint (i.e., between the heavenly and earthly realms which are bounded by the orbits of the spheres), having broken through their borders, and he showed to the downbearing nature the beautiful form of God. When (nature) saw that he had in him all the boundless beauty and energy of the governing powers combined with the form of God, she smiled with love, for she had seen reflected in the water the image of the Man's beautiful form and his shadow on the earth. He saw the likeness of his form in her, reflected in the water, and he loved it and wished to dwell there. The will and the action were one, and he came to inhabit an arational form. Nature received her beloved, wholly embracing him, and they were united; they were lovers.

15. For this reason, alone of all beings which live on earth, man has a double nature; he has a mortal body and is immortal on account of a common essence with the Man. Being immortal, he has power over all things; but he still suffers, being mortal and under the rule of fate. Though he is above the line between heaven and earth (lit., "above the joint," see ch. 14), he has become a slave to the cosmic system. Though he is bisexual, being from a bisexual father, and sleepless, from the sleepless one . . . he is overcome. [Here, the text is unreliable. It is usually assumed that the end of the sentence indicates that humanity, because of the Fall depicted above, is now a heterosexual animal, and one who must sleep. See below, ch. 18.]

16. And after this: "[. . .] O, my Mind. For indeed I also love the Logos." Poimandres said, "This is the mystery which has been hidden to this day. Nature had intercourse with the Man and brought forth a most astonishing marvel. (The Man) had in himself the nature of the combination of the seven powers, which as I told you were from the fire and spirit (or, "wind"). Nature, then, could not delay, but immediately gave birth to seven men corresponding to the seven ruling powers; these men were bisexual and inclined toward Heaven." And after this (I said), "O Poimandres, I have now come to a great desire to hear more. Do not drop the subject." Poimandres said, "Be quiet, for I have not even come to the first point." "Behold," I said, "I am quiet."

17. "As I was saying, it happened that the birth of the seven first men took place in the following way. The earth was female; water was the impregnating element; fire was the nurturer. From the ether, nature received the breath (or, "spirit"), and she brought forth the bodies according to the image of the heavenly Man. The heavenly Man was of light in soul and mind; the soul was from life, the mind from light. Thus, everything in the sensible world remained this way until the end of one period and the beginnings of the (origin of) species.

18. "Hear the rest of the explanation which you wanted to hear. When

the period was fulfilled, the bond uniting all creatures was broken by the will of God. All creatures, being bisexual, were divided into males and females; humans (were divided) also, at the same time. God immediately said by a holy word (*logos*), 'Increase in increasing, and multiply in multiplying, all creatures and things. Let anyone who has a mind know himself as immortal and that the cause of death is love, and let him understand all beings.'

19. "When this was said, Providence, through fate and the conjunction of the spheres, caused living things to have sexual intercourse and established generations, and all things were fulfilled, each according to its species. Thus, he who knows himself has come into the good which is above all else, but he who loves the body through the error of love remains erring in the darkness, suffering in his senses the pangs of death."

> The heavenly Man causes a crisis in the God-head, in the heavenly sphere. He and Nature mix. (14). The language in this section contains many sexual innuendos; Man and Nature have become "lovers."
>
> Thus (15) humans become immortal, heavenly beings trapped in mortal bodies. From the intercourse between Nature and the Man, the human race is begotten (17). But there is more trouble. The heavenly Man is androgynous (bisexual); so were his children. But they split into male and female and from this split comes sexual activity, sin and guilt. Note how this differs from the story in Genesis. In Genesis 3 it is after the first act of rebellion (eating from the forbidden tree) that sex is made a curse (Gen. 3:16). In Genesis, sex does not cause sin. In *Poimandres,* it is the act of sex which brings about the fall of the whole cosmos. *Poimandres* thus reflects here an interpretation of Genesis 1—4 which we find in other Jewish and Christian writings from this period.
>
> In the following sections *Poimandres* describes human redemption. What is required is spelled out in the final sentence of ch. 21. In ch. 24., the process by which humans became entrapped in this world is reversed. There comes, with redemption by *gnosis,* the ascent of the soul to mystic union with the God-head: "This is the good goal of those who have knowledge, to become God" (ch. 26).

20. "What great sin have they committed," I said, "those who are ignorant, that they should be deprived of immortality?" "You appear not to have duly considered what you have heard. Did I not tell you to pay attention?" "I am thinking, and I remember, and I am grateful, too." "If you comprehend, then, tell me why those who are in death are deserving of death?" "Because the source of the individual body is the hateful darkness, from which comes the moist substance, from which the body is made in the sensible world, and from which death is watered."

21. "You have it correctly, Man. Now, why is it that 'he who

understands himself departs to him,' as the Logos of God has it?" I said, "Because the Father of everything is comprised of light and life, from whom the Man is begotten." "You speak well. Light and life are God and the Father, from whom the Man was begotten. If then you learn he is from life and light and that you, too, come from these, you will go again into life." Poimandres said these things. "But tell me more. How shall I go into life, O my Mind?" I said.

"Let the man with a mind recognize himself."

22. "Do not all men have a mind?" "Watch your tongue, friend. I, Mind, stand by those who are holy and good and pure and merciful, the pious. And my presence gives help. They immediately know everything, and they lovingly worship the Father, blessing and singing regularly to him in filial love. And before they give the body to its proper death they despise the senses, knowing their workings. What is more, I, the Mind, will not permit the assaulting work of the body to prevail. I, the guardian of the gates, bar the door against the entry of evil and shameful deeds, cutting off short the imaginations.

23. "But I am far away from the foolish, the bad, the evil, the wicked, the greedy, the killers, and the impious; I have given up my place to an avenging demon who applies to such a man the keenness of fire, pierces his senses, and arms him for more lawless deeds in order that he will have more punishment. The man thus does not cease having desire for his boundless appetites; he remains insatiably battling in the dark. This torments him, and causes the fire upon him to blaze more."

24. "You have taught me all these things well, O Mind, but now tell me about the ascension which takes place." In response to this Poimandres said, "In the dissolution of the material body, you deliver the body to be changed, and the form you have, becomes unseen. You deliver your now inactive character to the demon. The body's senses return to their sources, becoming part of them and again being restored to the Energies. Anger and lust go away to the arational nature.

25. "And thus man eagerly rushes upward through the junction (between the earthly and heavenly realms). At the first zone he gives up the power to increase and decrease; at the second (zone) the workings of evil and ineffective deceit; at the third, ineffective deceitful lust; at the fourth, the ostentation of arrogance is deprived of its effect; in the fifth, unholy boldness and rash daring; in the sixth, the evil appetite of wealth, now ineffective; and in the seventh zone, ensnaring falsehood.

26. "Then, stripped of the powers at work in the junction, he comes upon the eighth nature (the ogdoad); he has his own power and sings, with the Beings, hymns to the Father. Those already there rejoice at his arrival, and having become like his companions he hears certain powers above the eighth nature singing a kind of sweet song to God. Then, in

good order they go up to the Father, and they surrender themselves to the powers. Indeed, having become powers themselves, they are in God. This is the good goal of those who have knowledge (*gnosis*), to become God. Why do you wait? As you have now received everything from me, should you not be a guide to all those who are worthy, so that through you the human race may be saved by God?"

27. When he had said this to me, Poimandres mingled with the powers. I gave thanks and blessed the Father of all. Then I was sent forth after having received power from him and having been taught the nature of everything and the great vision. I began to preach to men the beauty of piety and knowledge (*gnosis*): "O people, earthborn men, you who have given yourselves to drunkenness and sleep and ignorance of God, be sober; cease your debauchery, you who are enchanted with arational sleep."

28. Those who heard gathered around me unanimously. And I said, "Earthborn men, why have you given yourselves to death, when you have the power to change to immortality? Repent, you who wander around in error and cohabit with ignorance. Free yourselves from the dark light, change to immortality, put aside corruption."

29. Some stood apart and mocked me, giving themselves to the way of death. But some begged to be taught and threw themselves at my feet. I raised them; I became the mystic guide of the human race. I taught them doctrines (*logos*) of how and in what manner they should be saved; I sowed among them the doctrines of wisdom (*sophia*), and they were nourished from the ambrosial waters. When it was evening and the sun's rays began to dim completely, I charged them to give thanks (*eucharistein*) to God, and when they had completed the thanksgiving (*eucharistia*), each returned to his own bed.

30. I wrote down the benefaction of Poimandres in myself. I was filled with what I wanted and I rejoiced. For (to me) the sleep of the body was the wakefulness of the soul, and the closing of the eyes a true dream, and my silence a gestation of the good, and the speaking of the word (*logos*) a begetting of good things. All this happened, by reception from my Mind, that is from Poimandres, the Logos of complete authority. I came to men because I was divinely inspired. Therefore, I give a blessing to God the Father from my soul and whole strength:

31. "Holy is God and the Father of all.
　　Holy is God whose will is fulfilled by his own powers.
　　Holy is God who wishes to be known and is known by his own.
　　Holy are you who established all by the Logos.
　　Holy are you of whom all nature has produced the image.
　　Holy are you whom nature did not form.

Holy are you who are mightier than all power.
Holy are you who are greater than all authority.
Holy are you who are better than praise.
Receive pure, rational (*logikas*) worship from a soul
and heart held out to you, O inexpressible, indescribable
one, you who are named in silence.

32. Incline to me and empower me in my beseeching you
that I may never fall from the knowledge (*gnōsis*)
which is proper to our being and that I may enlighten
with this grace those of humanity in ignorance,
my brothers, your sons. Indeed, I have faith, and I
witness. I go forth into life and light. Blessed be
you, Father. Your man wishes to share your sanctifying
works, as you have given him all authority."

The Life of Moses
Philo of Alexandria

Introduction: Philo of Alexandria (c. 30 B.C.–A.D. 50) was born into one of the wealthiest and most influential Jewish families in Alexandria. The family undoubtedly enjoyed the rights of Roman citizenship, even though they were Jews by descent and religious observance. While serving as a judge in the large Jewish community in Alexandria, Philo found time for extensive writing and set forth his notion of the religious heritage of Israel in terms of a variety of Greek philosophical concepts. As such, he is often referred to as an excellent example of that period during which the interpenetration of Greek and Jewish modes of belief and culture were at a peak in Alexandria. It is within this upper-class, educated, cosmopolitan context that Philo addressed his Greek-speaking Alexandrian friends about the revered Lawgiver of the Jews: Moses.

Philo did not portray Moses in a manner strictly identical with the biblical portrait of Moses. It is certain that he considered the Five Books of Moses as totally divine and Heaven-inspired. This high estimation led him to paint an extremely exalted portrait of Moses himself—i.e., *as a divine/human savior God.* Consider the following quotations:[1]

> "But there are others whom God leads higher, preparing them to soar above every species and genus (on earth) to position them near himself. Such an One was Moses about whom he says, 'But you stand here with Me' (Deut. 5:31). This is what is indicated by the fact that when Moses was about to die he was not, having been abandoned, 'added to his fathers' like the other (patriarchs) nor, as if he were changeable, was anything added or taken from him, but he was bodily removed (from earth to Heaven) 'through the Word' (*dia rhēmatos*) of the First Cause (*aitia*; Deut. 34:5), that is, through the same Word by which the entire universe was created.
>
> From this you may learn that the God who works in all things considers the wise man (*sophos*) to be worthy of honor equal to the Word (*logos*) itself, for he lifts up the perfect man (*teleios*) from earthly things to himself.
>
> For not even when God permitted Moses to associate as a loan to earthly creatures did he confer upon him merely ordinary virtue (*aretē*), like that of a ruler or king, to master the passions of his soul. Rather he elected him to be God and Leader, showing thereby that the whole region of the body and the mind that rules it were his subjects and slaves. 'For I give you,' said he,

[1]We are indebted for the following discussion and references to E. R. Goodenough, *An Introduction to Philo Judaeus,* 2nd ed. (New York: Barnes & Noble, 1962), pp. 145–51.

253

'to Pharaoh as a God' (Exod. 7:1). But God (i.e., Moses) cannot accept any decrease or increase, being fully and completely identical to himself.

This is why we are told that no one knows his grave (Deut. 34:6) for who would be capable of observing the removal of a perfect soul (*psychē teleia*) to Him Who Is (*ho ōn*)?" (*Sacrifices of Abel and Cain* 8–10).

What Philo has done in this statement is to cast Moses in terms Greeks would readily understand, viz., as the perfect God-king and Savior. For, to Philo, Moses' kingship really is cosmic. As he says at one point in his *Life of Moses:* "God thought Moses to be worthy to be made known as a partner in His province. Thus Moses was given *the entire cosmos* as a possession fit for His heir. Consequently, each of the elements obeyed him as its master, taking on other qualities at his commands" (*Moses* I.155f., italics added).

For Philo, the main reason for the exalted stature of Moses is the biblical account of Moses' encounter with God on Mt. Sinai. For although Philo clearly thought of Moses as already semi-divine at birth, he refers to the Sinai encounter as the moment of God's total self-revelation to Moses, which in turn reveals the latter's semi-divine status. For it was here that:

"Moses entered into the very same darkness within which God was, that is, into the formless, invisible, noncorporeal and original Pattern of Being of existing things, where he perceived what is forever invisible to natural, mortal sight. Then putting himself and his life among us like a beautiful work of art, he set up this wholly noble and divinely formed work as a model for those who wish to imitate it. Blessed indeed are they who stamp his pattern into their own souls, or desire that it were so stamped! For the mind especially should bear the perfect form of virtue, but if it cannot do that, at least let it have the resolute desire to do so" (*Moses* I.158).

However, Moses as the Savior and incarnation of the Logos of God is not merely the perfect model to be imitated, according to Philo. As the ever-present divine Savior, Moses also comes to the aid of each soul yearning for his perfection. Moses is thus the saving Mediator between God and man:

("Moses, as the truly righteous man) brings everything he has into the common stock and gives it without stint for the benefit of those who will use it. What he himself lacks he asks from God who alone has unlimited wealth. God thereupon opens up the heavenly treasure and pours down a torrent of good things like rain and snow, so that all the earthly channels are filled to overflowing. And God is accustomed to give these things and not turn away *the pleas of his own Logos.* For when Moses on one occasion besought him with entreaties, it is recorded: 'I am compassionate upon them according to thy word' " (*Migration of Abraham* 121, italics added).

Thus Philo can actually pray to Moses to lead his soul into the deep mysteries of his saving revelation—the Five Books:

"O Thou Revealer (*hierophantēs*), though the eyes of our soul are closed because we do not desire to see, or cannot do so, still do Thou uphold us and help us and do not cease to anoint us until Thou has initiated us into the hidden meaning of the Sacred Oracles and revealed those locked beauties that are invisible to the uninitiated. This it is meet for Thee to do" (*Som.* I.164f.).

These quotations (many more could be added) should indicate to anyone familiar with the Gospel of John or the letters of Paul that Philo unmistakably belonged to the same Hellenistic-Jewish thought world. Of course, there is no evidence that Philo was familiar with the earliest Christian writings. Nevertheless, what Philo says in regard to Moses as a Savior God is strikingly similar to New Testament writers' application of this concept to Jesus Christ.

A second major point should be mentioned, which has to do with *Philo's use of sources.* There is considerable debate as to what type of writing the Christian gospels are; indeed, whether they are all the same type of writing. One of our purposes has been to include evidence that may serve to throw further light on the question, by transliterating the Greek terms in our texts which give the ancient genre of the writing in question. These are especially likely to occur in prefaces, such as those given earlier.[2] However, one significant term, which has not been mentioned yet, is the name of the speech the defendant (or his lawyer) would give during his trial to convince the judge of his innocence. It was called (among other things) an *encomium.* Consider the following observation by the Church Father Origen:

" '. . . Then Pilate said to Jesus, "Do you not hear how many things they witness against you?" And he did not answer him a word so that the governor was greatly astonished' (Matt. 27:13–14). It was worthy of astonishment, even to those with a small measure of intelligence, that one who was accused and against whom false witness was brought, although he was perfectly capable of proving himself not guilty of the charges and *although he could have related in detail the praises of his life and his powers (enkōmia tou heautou biou diexelthein kai tōn dynameōn)*—that they were in fact from God—in order that he might reveal to the judge a way toward a

[2]See pp. 121–27.

kinder attitude towards him, in fact did not do this but instead he despised and nobly ignored his accusers. If he had made a defense, it is obvious that the judge would have released Jesus without hesitation. This is clear from what is written about him where he said, 'Which of the two do you wish I should release to you, Barabbas or Jesus, the so-called Christ?' Further, the Scripture continues, 'For he knew that they delivered him on account of envy' " (Matt. 27:17–18).[3]

Now the "praise (*encomium*) of his life and his powers—that they were from God" (and not from Satan), is precisely one of the main points of rebuttal that Philostratus composed in defense of Apollonios for his trial before the emperor Domitian.[4] As the educated of that time well knew, Aristotle had defined an *encomium* as having one purpose: to *praise* the achievements of the person in question, beginning with "noble birth and education . . . virtuous parents (and) all attendant circumstances" (*Rhetoric* I.ix.33). A record of noble achievements reveals the man's noble character. Therefore the encomiast's duty is to stress these to the complete exclusion of everything else—especially questionable or derogatory events or traits.

Thus considered, the prefaces of both Philo and Philostratus take on new significance. Each author clearly states that it is his intention to portray the achievements of his hero to a hostile or indifferent audience of outsiders. This being so, each author naturally recounted the "life" of his hero in the most impressive way possible. We may therefore surmise in the case of Philostratus what we know is true of Philo, that any negative or objectionable aspects were intentionally glossed over or carefully explained so as to appear in a favorable light.

We mention this because of the well-known fact that the early Christians also faced ridicule and mockery in their attempts to portray Jesus of Nazareth as the "savior of mankind." One recalls the famous remark of Paul, that he preached "Christ crucified, a scandal to Jews and foolishness to Gentiles" (1 Cor. 1:23). Less familiar, perhaps, but saying exactly the same thing, is the observation of the Christian philosopher Justin Martyr in his open letter to the Emperor (c. 140): "People think we are insane when we name a crucified man as second in rank to the unchangeable and eternal God, the Creator of all things, for they do not discern the mystery involved" (*Apol.* I.13). There can be little doubt, therefore, that the gospel writers faced a situation that called for an encomium for Jesus.

This suggests, in other words, that it is not inaccurate to regard Philo's *Life of Moses*, Philostratus' *Life of Apollonios* and the gospels as

[3] *Contra Celsum,* tr. and ed. H. Chadwick (Cambridge: Cambridge University Press, 1965), Preface 1-2; italics added.
[4] See above pp. 237–39.

different kinds of *encomia*. This would certainly account for two striking features of all of these writings: first, the great lengths to which the writers have gone in praise of their subjects, and second, closely related to it, none of these writers ever narrates any event, from birth through youth to young manhood to middle-age and finally to the all-important circumstances surrounding the death, that in the slightest degree might seem less than totally praiseworthy and admirable.

These two features stand out all the more sharply in Philo's case because here we are in the extraordinarily fortunate position of knowing what most of his source material was—namely, the original Five Books of Moses in the Bible. With them on one side and with Philo's writing on the other, it is possible to reconstruct to a considerable extent—always taking into account of course the oral traditions about Moses that Philo also said he laid under contribution—the precise changes Philo made when writing his own account. In other words, we can virtually "track" Philo as he works through the biblical stories about Moses, and, in effect, observe him actively at work, shaping, molding, and transforming his central character into one who would be impressive to Alexandrians.

For example, the biblical stories that Philo silently passes over fairly cry out of the biblical text: Aaron's leading role in the Golden Bull debacle; the cowardice of the Jews at the prospect of having to fight the inhabitants of Canaan; above all, God's punishment of Moses so that he never entered the Promised Land. Other events of a questionable character Philo retains but carefully justifies, such as Moses' murder of the Egyptian, or his reluctance after seeing the Burning Bush to obey the command of God to be his agent in freeing the Jews.

Many of these will be commented on more fully in the notes accompanying the text. This much can be said here, however. On the one hand, while Philo has clearly omitted a great deal, especially the legal material (which he treats at length elsewhere), the material he did use he has expanded considerably. At no point can we say he has followed his source slavishly. This was not his way of retelling the sacred story. Both in minor as well as in major aspects, Philo clearly felt entitled to edit, rearrange, and revise his source material. Yet, at the same time, he did remain largely faithful to his source. Only occasionally did he bring in what appears to be totally new material (Moses' education, the translation of his laws into Greek), and here we know Philo relied on substantial, authoritative oral tradition. In general, therefore, his changes consisted mostly of what he *omitted*. What is really new and different is the basic portrait itself, i.e., the divine/human savior concept.

Secondly, we should remember that Philo's use of the term "Life" (*bios*) as a description of his writing does not apply only to Book I, but to all *four* parts of his account: Moses as the ideal God-king, High Priest, Lawgiver and Prophet. In other words, the entire writing is not a biography in our sense of the word; rather it is more like a formal portrait. Events and anecdotes are selected and narrated so that each one will shed some new light on Moses' divine character, someone whom Philo believed to be at least potentially, the savior of the whole human race.

Book I

1. I have decided to write the life of Moses, whom Gentiles know to have been the lawgiver of the Jews while the Jews acknowledge him to be the interpreter of their sacred laws, a man in every respect the greatest and most perfect, to make him familiar to those who deserve not to remain ignorant of him. 2. For even though the fame of the laws which he left behind has already gone out through the whole world, ranging even to the uttermost corners of the earth, what sort of man he himself really was is not known to many people since the historians among the Greeks did not consider him worth remembering, no doubt out of jealousy and because not a few of the commandments of the lawgivers of their cities are the opposite of his. 3. Instead they waste the talents they have acquired through education in composing poems and long-winded narratives that are supposed to be funny, filled with voluptuous licentiousness, and notoriously shameful. Rather they should have used their natural abilities for the sake of the instruction to be gained from telling about good men and their lives, lest anything that is good whether ancient or recent, once it is consigned to silence, be deprived of the light it might give. If they had done this they would not seem so constantly to ignore noble things in order to turn our attention to things not worth hearing about, telling wicked stories elegantly just for the sake of revealing something disgusting.

4. But I for one will ignore their insulting disregard of Moses and will myself make known the facts concerning the man, namely what I have learned both from the sacred books which he left behind as marvelous memorials of his wisdom and also from some of the elders of the Jewish people. By combining the oral tradition with the written I think I know more accurately than others the facts concerning his life.

Several points in this preface are worth noting. First, there is the injured air Philo adopts when he mentions the way Greek historians have passed over Moses in silence, and he insults them in return for their presumed slight.

Second, he has combined oral with written materials to produce his account (not that he ever identifies either in the body of his work—but that, too, is customary). Third, he gives as the justification for his own undertaking of this task the fact that, through his preparation, he will give the most accurate account. Both of the latter are also to be found in the preface to the Gospel of Luke 1:1–4.

Moses the King

5. I will begin at the point where one must begin. Although Moses was Chaldean by race, he was born and raised in Egypt because his ancestors had migrated there during a time when a protracted famine was destroying Babylon and the neighboring peoples. They and their families had moved to Egypt to find food, since it was a broad and verdant land, most productive of everything human nature requires, especially grain. 6. The river of this country, during the hottest part of the summer when other rivers whether caused by springs or rainfall begin to dry up, increases and overflows, flooding the fields and turning them into lakes. Without needing any rain they produce bountiful crops of all kinds year after year unless perchance the wrath of God interrupts on account of the irreligiousness that abounds among the Egyptians.

7. For a father and mother he obtained the best there was, although belonging to the same clan his parents were drawn together more by likemindedness than by race. Moses was the seventh generation from Abraham, the original settler and founder of the whole Jewish nation.

8. Moses was honored with a royal upbringing through the following circumstances. The king of the Egyptians feared that as the Jewish race was constantly increasing in number, the immigrants might become more numerous than the native people and might wrest the supremacy from them, so he devised wicked schemes to diminish their strength. He ordered the Jews to continue to raise the female babies born to them, since a woman is weak by nature and afraid to fight, but to kill all the male babies lest they continue to multiply in every city. For the power of an abundance of good men is a stronghold in enemy territory hard to conquer or overthrow.

9. When the child was born he immediately seemed more beautiful than normal, so it is said that his parents ignored the proclamations of the tyrant as much as possible and actually kept him at home for three whole months while his mother breastfed him unknown to anyone. 10. But since in most monarchies there are always people prying into things hidden away and eager to carry some new report to the king, his parents began to fear that in their concern for saving one, more should perish instead, namely, they themselves with him.

And so weeping bitterly they put Moses out to die beside the riverbank and departed groaning in anguish, pitying themselves because of what they were compelled to do, calling themselves murderers and child killers, and pitying their child also for so pointless a death. 11. Moreover as often happens in terrible situations they began to condemn themselves for being the cause of an even greater misfortune. "Oh why," they said, "did we not put him out to die as soon as he was born? Most people think that a baby who does not partake of the first day's food is not human. But we wonderful parents actually nursed Moses for three whole months, thereby bringing greater grief upon ourselves and torture upon him, since he is now able to experience pleasure and pain and will die fully conscious of this grievous evil." 12. And so, ignorant of what was about to happen, they departed, mourning and filled with sadness.

But a sister of the abandoned child, still young herself but compelled by familial devotion, stood a little way off anxiously watching to see what would happen. All of this was taking place, it seems to me, in accordance with God's providence concerning the boy.

13. Now the king of the country had one beloved daughter. They say she had been married a long time but could not bear children although as usual she especially longed for a male offspring who would receive the fortunate inheritance of her father's dominion, which was liable to fall into a stranger's hands for want of a male heir. 11. Always sad and sighing, on this day especially she sank under the weight of her anxieties and although she habitually remained at home and never even crossed the threshhold, today she went out with her maids to the river where the child was lying. And just as she was about to begin using the sprinkling vessels and prayer libations she perceived Moses lying in the very densest part of the marsh and commanded him to be brought to her.

15. After she had examined him from head to foot she rejoiced at his beauty and good health and, seeing him begin to cry, began to pity him, her soul already having been turned within her toward motherly affection as if he were her own baby. Then realizing that it was a child of the Hebrews who had been terror-stricken by the king's decree, she began to consider what she might feed him for she thought it not safe to take him immediately to the palace.

16. While she was still uncertain what to do, the baby's sister, guessing as if from a watch tower the meaning of her hesitation, ran up and asked if she wanted the baby nursed by a Hebrew woman who had been pregnant not long before. 17. When the princess said that was what she wanted, the girl's and child's mother was brought as if she were a stranger, and she very quickly and gladly promised to nurse him on the pretext that she needed the wages. And so, through this strategy, God brought it about that the child's first nourishment should be from his

own mother. Then the princess gave him the name Moses (Greek: *Mōüsēs*), which she did because he was actually taken up from the water, for the Egyptians call water *mōü*.

18. When Moses began growing steadily and filling out, not even more quickly than might be expected, he was weaned and his combined mother and provider of nourishment presented him to the princess since he no longer needed to be nursed but had become a princely, beautiful boy. 19. And she seeing him more perfect to the eye than others of his age took a liking to him even greater than before and made him her son, having already beforehand artfully fashioned some padding for her body in order to seem pregnant so that everyone would think the child was really her own and not a substitute secretly brought in. For God makes whatever he wills easy to do, even things hard to accomplish.

20. Now, although he began to be provided with the kind of food and servant-help customary for a prince, Moses did not give himself up completely to childish habits, teasing and mocking and infantile behavior, even though those who had been appointed to care for him were quite lenient and not at all strict. Instead he displayed a precociously serious and respectful attitude, paying attention only to those things which he heard or saw that were likely to benefit his soul. 21. Different teachers immediately appeared from everywhere, some of their own accord from the districts of Egypt and neighboring regions, while others were summoned from Greece at high salaries.

Philo's desire to show how Moses mastered all the wisdom of the world of his, i.e., Philo's, day is responsible for this glaring anachronism. Of course, in Moses' day, Greece did not even exist, much less have an international scholarly reputation. Although we may be surprised at this remarkable departure from his source (Exod. 2:10), it would be incorrect to conclude that Philo is simply inventing this out of whole cloth. Rather, he is relying, to some extent, on the oral traditions he referred to earlier, as we can see from their appearance elsewhere, in Josephus, *Antiquities* II. 232–237, in the Tannaitic midrash on Exod. 2:10 (see quote in H. St. J. Thackeray, *Josephus*, Loeb ed., Vol. IV. 265, note c), and in Christian literature, Acts 7:22, "he was instructed in all the wisdom of the Egyptians."

Thanks to his superbly gifted nature his powers soon excelled theirs, and he began to discover things by himself before they could be taught, as if he were just remembering and not learning for the first time, 22. even thinking up difficult questions himself. For great natures discern many new things in the field of knowledge and just as the bodies of wrestlers which are healthy and agile in every part need no special attention from their trainers, or at any rate, very little, and as the farmer devotes little care upon plants growing vigorously and becoming well-formed, improving by themselves, in the same fashion a well-formed soul begins to flourish by itself and benefits more from things said beforehand by itself than what is said by its teachers. Taking its own starting point in intellectual inquiry, it plunges forth eagerly, as the proverb says, "like a duck to water."

23. The scholars of the Egyptians instructed him in arithmetic and geometry, both rhythm and harmony, the theory of meter and the whole of music, both as to the use of instruments as well as textbooks on the simpler techniques and more advanced treatises. Besides this, they taught him their philosophy contained in the symbols displayed in their so-called sacred hieroglyphic writing and through the adoration of animals which they even worship as Gods. But the other course of education the Greeks taught, while those from the neighboring regions taught Assyrian letters and Chaldean astrology. 24. This branch of mathematics he also learned from the Egyptians who especially pursue such things. Thus accurately learning everything from both where they agreed as well as where they disagreed, his mind rose above their rivalry as it sought for the truth. Indeed his mind was incapable of accepting any falsehood, as so often happens with the quarrelsome philosophical schools which will support and contend for any doctrine whatever without questioning to see if it is really true or not, the same as lawyers do who argue cases for the money without a thought for justice.

25. But as Moses was already passing beyond the limits of childhood he increased his judgment, not letting his youthful lusts run unchecked as some do, even though there were the numberless provocations abundantly available that palaces offer. Instead, he bound them by self-control and patience as by reins to restrain their impetuous force. 26. Each of the other passions also which are by nature frenzied and riotous he made gentle, taming and civilizing them, and if somehow one only so much as began to stir or flutter awake he would provide a harsher remedy in punishment than mere verbal scolding. All in all he carefully watched for the first attempts and impulses of the soul as if it were a wayward horse, fearing lest it run away from the rationality (*logismos*) which ought to hold the reins, turning everything into chaos. For these passions are the causes of both good and bad; good when they are obedient to the leadership of reason (*logos*), but the opposite when they turn from regular paths to anarchy.

27. Of course, those associating with Moses and all others were continually amazed as if astonished by a new marvel and closely examined what in fact it might be inhabiting his body or what sort of imprint is in his mind, whether human or divine or a mixture of both, for it is in no way like a common man's but stands above that, being lifted up toward more majestic things. 28. For he would give his stomach

nothing more than the minimum amounts nature decreed and as for the region below the stomach, he did not even think of it except to conceive his children. 29. He undertook an unusually austere way of life holding luxury in greater contempt than anyone else, for he yearned to live for the soul alone, not the body, displaying through his actions each day the teachings of philosophy, as he would state what he knew and then do those things which accorded with what he was saying, so that there was a harmony between reason (*logos*) and life. Whatever reason dictated, his life reflected, and whatever his life was, it was shown to be rational, both harmoniously blending together like a musical instrument.

At this point Philo digresses to assert that when Fortune exalts other men to a much lower level of prosperity than that which Moses now enjoyed, they quickly forget their friends and ancestral ways, becoming cold and arrogant as if they themselves were somehow the cause of their newfound wealth.

32. But Moses, having already reached the pinnacle of human good fortune and indeed being considered the son of the present king's daughter and being expected by almost everyone to accede to his grandfather's dominion, all but being named "the new king," nevertheless Moses remained loyal to his own ancient, native culture. The benefits of his adopted family, even if temporarily more brilliant, he considered false, but the virtues of his natural parents, even if at the moment they were not very evident, were at any rate a genuine part of his heritage. Like an impartial judge he fairly repaid both his family and his foster parents, the former with kindness and devoted loyalty, the latter with gratitude for all they had provided, and he would have gone on being grateful thenceforth had he not noticed a grave new sin begun in the country by the king.

The king singles out all Hebrew men to be forcibly enrolled in state-controlled building projects. Philo digresses to recall for the reader's sake that the only reason the Hebrews were in Egypt in the first place was the great famine long before and now the king was wickedly beginning to treat the Hebrew people, who were really guests and refugees, like slaves and enemies of the state.

37. Then the king gave orders for impossibly heavy tasks, piling up labor upon labor on the Hebrews, and the iron fist was ready for those who sank down due to weakness, for the king appointed as overseers of the tasks merciless, savage men who had no compassion toward anyone, men who earned the label "slave drivers" by what they did. 38. The Hebrews were put to work, some shaping clay into bricks,

others bringing straw from everywhere to mix in and strengthen the bricks. Others were set apart to rebuild houses, city buildings, town walls, and irrigation canals, carrying building materials themselves every day and night without a break, given no chance to rest, not even being allowed to sleep but forced to do everything at once, fetching the materials as well as building, so that before long their bodies became exhausted since their souls had already yielded to despair. 39. Naturally, scores upon scores died as if under the onslaught of a terrible plague but their corpses were just thrown aside and left unburied outside the cities. They were not allowed even a little dust to cover them up or relatives and friends to come and mourn those so pitiably destroyed. And even the unconstrained passions of the soul, which nature has made more nearly free than anything else, these impious men sought to crush under more powerful tyrannical pressure.

40. Witnessing these things, Moses became alternately depressed and then angry, since he was not in a position either to punish the wrongdoers or to help those being wronged. He did what he could verbally, such as it was, advising those in charge to be more lenient, to give up or at least abate such excessively harsh commands, while he exhorted the Hebrew workers to bear their present condition nobly, to take it like men, not to let their souls have any sympathy for their bodies but to hope for better things from such evils, 41. since everything in the world sooner or later changes into its opposite: clouds into empty air, violent winds into quiet breezes, stormy seas into tranquility, while human affairs are even more changeable since they are least stable. 42. Repeating such things as these, Moses sought like a good doctor to ease their heavy affliction. But after a brief respite the Egyptians only returned with vigor renewed from their pause, laying wholly new outrages upon the people more intolerable than before. 43. For some of the overseers were exceptionally harsh and unrestrained, no better than savage, carnivorous beasts or venomous reptiles, animals in human form, treacherous beasts in human bodies appearing deceptively civilized but underneath more hard-hearted than iron or steel.

44. One of the most violent of these taskmasters, a man who had mercy on no one, whom entreaty made even harsher, flogging those who didn't obey him with breathless haste, tormenting them to death, outrageously torturing his workers—this man Moses did away with, justifying his action as the right thing to do. Of course it was right that a man who lived to destroy others should himself be liquidated.

All this from two verses in Exodus: "One day when Moses had grown up, he went out to his people and looked on their burdens; and he saw an Egyptian beating a Hebrew, one of his people. He looked this way and

that, and seeing no one, he killed the Egyptian and hid him in the sand"
(Exod. 2:11–12).

45. Now when the king heard of it he became very angry, not because
someone had killed or destroyed unjustly or justly, but because his
grandson did not agree with him and did not have the same enemies and
friends as he. Instead Moses hated the people he liked but loved those
whom the king detested, showing concern for those toward whom the
king was indifferent and inexorable. 46. Given this opportunity, various officials who had long been suspicious of the youth and who feared
that in due time he would remember the evil and injurious things they
had done in the past and avenge himself on them, these courtiers began
pumping thousands of rumors into the king's open ears, some on one
side, others on the other side, trying to instill in him the fear that Moses
was planning to seize power and saying, "He will attack you! He will
stop at nothing! He is forever hatching new schemes because he wants to
be king before the proper time! He flatters some, threatens others, kills
without a trial and despises especially those who are friendly toward
you. What are you waiting for? Cut the ground out from under him and
his plots! Any delay on the part of the victim gives the advantage to the
attacker!"
47. Because such slanders were circulating everywhere, Moses withdrew into the neighboring country of Arabia where he would be able to
live safely. At the same time he cried aloud to God to deliver the
Hebrews from their helplessness as well as deservedly to punish those
who let no opportunity pass by to insult them, and, moreover, that he
double his gift by permitting him to see these both take place.

God heard his prayers, noting Moses' characteristic love of the good
and hatred of evil, and not long after he brought judgment upon Egypt
as it was proper for him to do. 48. Before this came about, however,
Moses was exercising in the contests of virtue, having as a trainer his
own special rationality under whose guidance he was being trained for
the best of careers, the theoretical and the practical. He regularly sought
to disentangle the doctrines of philosophy, easily resolving them with his
soul and depositing them indelibly in his memory, then bringing his own
personal, wholly admirable actions into conformity with them in
everything. Nor did he allow mere appearances to deceive him but held
only to the truth, keeping one guide before himself, namely, the right
reason of nature (*ho orthos tēs physeōs logos*) which alone is the source
and fountain of virtues (*aretē*).

At this point, Philo illustrates his argument by introducing a story based on
Exod. 2:15–22. The difference between the story as told in Exodus and as

Philo tells it is most instructive of Philo's methods. Once in Arabia, says Philo, Moses did not merely hide nor did he seek to ingratiate himself with local officials for the sake of protection, should the Egyptians come after him. Instead, he fearlessly intervened in the affairs of others when the "healthy impulses of his soul," namely, "his love of the good," prompted him to do so.

51. I will describe something he did at this time and although it might seem a trivial thing nevertheless it did not spring from a trivial spirit. The Arabs raise cattle and appoint as shepherds not only men but also women, youths, and maidens among them. Nor are these only of the less important, lower classes, but even members of the very best families. 52. So it was that seven maidens whose father was a priest had led their flock of sheep beside a certain fountain and, having tied buckets to the draw-ropes, were taking turns in pulling up the water, quickly filling the drinking troughs which lay nearby. 53. Now there were other shepherds also who constantly came and took advantage of the weakness of these young maidens, driving them away with their flock in order to bring up their own animals to the already prepared water, benefiting from the labors of others. 54. This happened once when Moses was nearby, and when he saw it, he ran over and stood nearby saying, "Will you stop doing wrong, even though you think you can take advantage of the desert? Are you not ashamed to let arms and elbows remain idle? You are long hair and flesh—not men! These girls work like youths, willingly doing whatever needs to be done while now you mince around like girls! Will you not go away? 55. Will you not give way to those who came here first, to whom the water belongs? Should you not have filled the troughs for them in order that the water be more plentiful? Yet here you are trying to snatch what has already been prepared! But by the Heavenly Eye of Justice, you will not get away with it, for it sees even in the most deserted places! 56. In fact, it has appointed me their unexpected ally and I assuredly am a cofighter with the Great Hand of Justice on behalf of these who are being wronged! It is not fitting for the greedy to see that Hand but you will suddenly feel it strike out of the blue unless you change!"
57. While he was delivering this ultimatum, they became terrified of him because as he was speaking his appearance was transformed into a prophet's because of the inspiration of the Holy Spirit. They feared that he was about to cast a spell (*chrēsmos*) or utter an oracle (*logion; scil.*, that would kill them), so they gave in and led the flock of the young maidens back to the troughs having first moved their own aside.
58. The girls returned home exceedingly jubilant and related events beyond expectation to their father, which created in him an ardent

desire to see the stranger. He therefore upbraided his daughters for their ingratitude, saying such things as: "What is the matter with you? You should have brought him back with you immediately, and if he was reluctant, insisted on it! Or did you suspect that I would be inhospitable? Or do you think you will not run afoul of evil men a second time? He who forgets favors must soon lack allies! But never mind; your transgression can still be healed. Quickly run back and invite the stranger both to visit us and to accept a reward for thanks is owed to him." 59. The girls run back and overtake Moses not far from the well. Explaining the message from their father, they beg him to return home with them. Their father is immediately struck by his beautiful appearance and a little later by his character, for great natures are conspicuous and need little time to be recognized, and so he gives Moses the prettiest of his daughters as a wife, through this one deed giving evidence of all the qualities which exhibited his noble goodness. Now only goodness is worthy of our love since it does not need support from the other virtues, for goodness carries within itself sufficient self-authentication. 60. After the wedding, Moses took charge of the herds and as he was herding sheep he was receiving the first instruction in leadership, for practice in shepherding is also a preliminary exercise in the expected rule Moses was one day to exert over the herd of men.

> Philo expands considerably on this theme, arguing that "the only perfect king is one well-versed in knowledge of sheep herding". Then, realizing that this might sound a little ridiculous to the reader, he sternly warns: "laugh if you want," it is still the truth. Then Philo proceeds to describe how Moses' phenomenal skill led to daily improvement in the size and quality of his flocks to the astonishment and envy of his neighbors. After this, Philo turns to the story of the Burning Bush.

65. One day as Moses led the flock to a place with plenty of water and grass which was especially abundant in sheep fodder, while he was in a certain glen he saw a most astonishing marvel. A bramble bush, the sort full of thorns and exceedingly frail, suddenly caught on fire by itself and became wrapped in a ball of flame from roots to branchtips as if it were spewing up from some fountain. Nor was the bush burnt up but it remained whole, seeming as it were to use the fire for food instead of itself being fuel for the fire. 66. Suddenly in the midst of the flame there appeared a certain form of the most wondrous beauty unlike anything ever seen, a most divine image flashing forth light more brilliant than the fire itself. Some might suspect it was the very form of Him Who Is (*ho ōn*), but let it be called a herald (*angelos*), because through a marvelously fashioned vision it was heralding (*diangellō*) in a silence more eloquent than speech events very soon to happen.

Philo is uneasy about the Gentile reaction to the scripture which says, "*God* called to him out of the bush," Exod. 3:4, but cf. v. 2. Philo explains that the burning but not consumed bush is a symbol of the persecuted but not destroyed Hebrew people, while the angelic being in the center is a sign of God's imminent deliverance. Philo then briefly digresses to give an allegorical explanation of each point of the vision, concluding with a rousing exhortation to the captive Hebrew nation. He then resumes the account.

71. Now after God showed this wondrously fashioned portent to Moses, a most distinct disclosure of events about to be accomplished, he also through oracles (*chrēsmoi*) begins to urge him to hurry back to care for his people, not only in order to be a cause of their freedom but also to be the leader of their settlement elsewhere, which would take place not far away, promising to assist him in all things. 72. "For since they have suffered much evil and endured intolerable arrogance," God said, "there being no one among men to relieve nor have mercy on their misfortunes, I myself have had pity on them. For I know that each by himself and all with one accord have turned to prayers and supplications in hopes of assistance from me, and I am kind by nature and favorable to genuine prayers.   73. Go therefore to the king of that country and have no concern about anything, for the former king from whom you fled through fear of a plot has died and the country has been entrusted to another who remembers nothing of your deeds. And taking with you the elders of your people, tell the king that the Hebrew nation has been summoned by me through an oracle to make a three-day journey outside the country in order to sacrifice according to the rites of their fathers."
74. But Moses, not ignorant that his own people as well as all others would disbelieve the things told them, said, "If however they inquire what the name is of him who sent me and I myself am not able to tell them, will I not seem to deceive?" 75. God said, "First, tell them that I Am He Who Is (*egō eimi ho ōn*) in order that, having learned the difference between what is and what is not, they may be taught in addition that absolutely no name applies to me literally, to whom belongs being as such (*to einai*)."

Philo here gives a Platonizing interpretation of this famous verse in Exod. 3:14, the first of a long line of similar interpretations in Christian exegesis. However, it must also be said that the door was at least partially opened for him in the Greek translation of the Hebrew text that he used (called the Septuagint, see on this further below, pp. 281–84). It reads here, "And God spoke to Moses, saying, 'I am The Being' (*egō eimi ho ōn*)" (Bagster translation).

But if their natures are too weak to be satisfied with that and if they still seek some further designation, explain only this much to them: I am God: God, that is, of the three men named after a virtue, the God of Abraham, the God of Isaac, and the God of Jacob, of whom the first is the standard of wisdom gained by teaching, the second is the standard of wisdom acquired by nature, and the third is the standard of wisdom achieved through training.

> This brief reference is the only indication that Philo gives in this entire writing that, in fact, this portrait of Moses is not an isolated, independent writing. It actually is part of a four-volume series, dealing with Abraham, Isaac, Jacob—and Moses. Nor are these other writings any more biographical in our modern sense than this one is. What Philo actually has in mind is something quite different: a four-part *allegory* using the biblical figures as protagonists. All four together comprise the sum and substance of the Jewish religion. Each represents a different path toward the ultimate divine self-disclosure: Abraham is the soul which succeeds through education, Isaac stood for the perfect soul born from the union of the seeker (Abraham) and Wisdom (Sarah), and Jacob symbolized the soul which finally wins through to the divine vision by arduous struggle. Of all, Moses is Philo's favorite as the perfect pattern of rational virtue; see further E. R. Goodenough, *Introduction to Philo Judaeus* (New York: Barnes & Noble, 1953), pp. 140–151.

But if they should still disbelieve, after they have been taught further by three signs which no man has ever seen or heard of before, they will change their minds.

77. Now the signs were the following: the rod which Moses was carrying God commanded to be cast to the ground where it instantly came alive by itself and turned into the largest of reptiles; a full-grown enormous snake. At this Moses quickly retreated from the animal and out of fear was desperately looking for a way to escape when God called him back and ordered him to pick it up by the tail, at the same time giving him the courage to do so. 78. It was writhing about but at Moses' touch it stood straight up, stretched out to its full length, and immediately transformed its essential nature by itself back into a staff, so that his soul marveled at the double change. It was unable to decide which of the two was more astonishing since it was equally impressed by the two marvels (*phantasia*).

79. That was the first and not long after another miracle was performed. He orders Moses to conceal one of his hands in his tunic and a little later to bring it forth. As he does what was commanded, the hand suddenly appears whiter than snow. When he places his hand back in his tunic and brings it forth again, it changes back to the same color it was, regaining its proper appearance.

80. These things he was taught while alone with God, like a teacher with a friend. In these cases Moses had with him the instruments for the miracles, namely, his hand and the staff with which he was provided. 81. The third miracle was neither portable nor could it be taught beforehand but it was to be just as astonishing, having its occurrence in Egypt. It was this: "When you have drawn some water from the river," said God, "pour it upon the earth and it will become the reddest of blood, being changed both in appearance and potency into something entirely different."

82. Apparently this also seemed believable to Moses not only because of the undeceitfulness of the speaker but also because of the miraculous deeds that he had already been shown, the hand and the staff.

83. Now although he believed, nevertheless Moses begged God concerning the mission, saying that he stuttered and was slow of tongue, especially since he had just been hearing God speaking, for he considered human eloquence to be speechlessness by comparison with divine. At the same time Moses was cautious by nature, shrinking back from overly grandiose things, judging that such exceeding great tasks were not for the likes of him. Instead, he urged God to choose another who could easily accomplish each of the things commanded him. 84. But God, although approving of his modesty, said, "Come now, are you ignorant of Who it is that gives man a mouth and fashions the tongue and throat and the whole mechanism of rational speech? It is I Myself! Therefore fear nothing. At my indication everything will be strengthened and transformed into good working order so that the streams of words will flow beautifully and smoothly from a clean fountain with nothing still hindering it. And if there be need of an interpreter, you will have for a subordinate speaker your brother in order that he might announce to the people your messages while you repeat the divine messages (*ta theia*) to him."

And so, Moses starts on his way back to Egypt with Aaron, prepared for a showdown with the pharaoh. Needless to say, Philo does not mention the strange little episode in Exod. 4:24–26, where the Lord inexplicably tries to kill Moses. As is familiar to us all, the Egyptian monarch only reacts to Moses' announcement with angry contempt, so that Moses unleashes the ten plagues upon Egypt. For some reason, Philo here rearranges and considerably expands his source material (Exod. 7:14—12:50) so that Aaron performs three plagues (Nile into blood; frogs; gnats), Moses performs three (rainstorms; locusts; darkness), both do one (boils), and God does the last three alone (horseflies; death of cattle; death of firstborn). The Egyptian king is totally crushed and has no choice but to permit Moses and the Hebrews to leave. At this moment of victory when they are finally about to set off for the Promised Land with Moses at their head, Philo intersperses a long lyrical passage emphasizing the dominant motif of this whole first book: Moses the Perfect Leader, Moses the Divine King.

148. Moses was appointed the leader of all the Jewish refugees, having received dominion and kingship not in the way those do who force their way into royal office by means of soldiers and armed cavalry and infantries and navies, but because of his virtue and noble goodness and consideration for all, which he never failed to exhibit. 149. Furthermore, the God who loves virtue and goodness granted it as a prize worthy of him since Moses had given up the Egyptian leadership even though he was the son of the daughter of the previous king. But because of the injustices occurring throughout the country, he bid good riddance to hopes of succeeding those in office, due to his nobility of soul and greatness of spirit and natural hatred of evil. Thus it seemed fitting to him who is the President and Manager of all things to repay Moses with the kingship of a more populous and powerful nation which was soon to be made holier than all others so that it might forever offer prayers on behalf of the race of men for the prevention of evil and participation in good things.

A reference to Exod. 19:6, "You (Israel) shall be my own possession among all peoples; for all the earth is mine, and you shall be to me a kingdom of priests and a holy nation" (RSV). Noteworthy is the way Philo understands this to mean that Israel will have an *intercessory* role.

150. Once Moses had received the dominion, however, he did not do as some would, namely desire to exalt his own household and promote his own sons, although he had two, to greater power so as to display them as his partners in the present and successors thereafter, for his mind was guileless and pure toward everything, small as well as great. Thus he conquered his natural tender affection toward his children like a good judge by the impartiality inherent in his rationality (*logismos*). 151. For he had set one supremely necessary goal for himself, namely, to help his subjects, taking in hand everything whether by word or by deed which might be for their benefit, overlooking no opportunity in his endeavors for the common prosperity. 152. Only he of all those who had ever acted as leaders did not treasure up gold or silver, nor levy taxes nor acquire houses or possessions or cattle or servants or public revenues or anything else conducive to an expensive and luxurious life, even though he could have. 153. Instead, he considered the effort to acquire wealth of material possessions a reflection of a poor soul and scorned it as a kind of blindness. On the other hand, he held in high

esteem that natural wealth which is not blind, being more zealous for it than anyone else I ever heard of. He would not worry about his clothing or food or other things pertaining to daily life for the sake of living in greater pompous conceit. Instead, he lived with the thrift and simplicity of a common citizen.

154. But as for those things in which a ruler *ought* to be lavish in his desires, Moses truly was—namely, in continence (*enkrateia*), patience, moderation, shrewdness, judgment, understanding, industry, suffering hardship, scornful of pleasures, righteousness, advocating excellence, lawfully censuring and punishing wrongdoers, praising and honoring the upright, again according to the Law.

155. Consequently, having bid good riddance to great wealth and to the riches mankind pants after, God honored him in return with the greatest and most perfect of riches, that is, the wealth of the entire earth and sea, rivers, and all other things, the elements and their combinations. For inasmuch as God thought him worthy to be made known as a partner in his province, Moses was given the entire cosmos as property prepared for his heir. 156. Consequently, each of the elements obeyed him as its master, taking on other qualities in obedience to his commands. Nor should we be surprised at this, for if, as the proverb says, "Friends share all things in common," and the prophet is said to be the friend of God, it follows that he would participate also in his possessions, as much as is needful. 157. Since God possesses everything, He needs nothing, and while the good man rightly possesses nothing, not even himself, yet he receives a share of the treasures of God, as much as he may. And is that not only fair? For he is a citizen of the world (*kosmopolitēs*), not a citizen of any of the individual cities found in the inhabited world, and as such, necessarily has as his "estate," not some piece of land in this or that country, but the whole world! 158. Is that not true? And was it not still grander than being partner with the Father and Maker of All to have the joy of being considered worthy of His own Name? For Moses was in fact called God and King of the whole nation!

Once again, Stoic ideals come clearly to the fore. Here he portrays Moses as the Stoic "king": the man who needs nothing and is not bound by ties of loyalty to any one particular city, but through self-renunciation, is ruler over all. On the other hand, the title "God" seems strikingly out of place, but here Philo has scriptural warrant, see Exod. 4:16.

It is said that Moses entered into the very same darkness within which God was; that is, into the formless, invisible, noncorporeal, original pattern of being of existing things, where he perceived what is forever invisible to natural, mortal sight.

Philo is referring to the momentous meeting between Moses and God on Mount Sinai, an event he will refer to again several times. Because the text is so important at this point, we will give the Greek at some length: *aeidē kai aoraton kai asōmaton tōn ontōn paradeigmatikēn ousian.* The "pattern of being" which Moses somehow perceived is not God, but the Logos, a term Philo uses to refer to the rational, moral order underlying all of nature.

Then, putting himself and his life among us like a beautiful work of art, he set up this wholly noble and divinely-formed work as a model (*paradeigma*) for those who wish to imitate it. Blessed (*eudaimonos*) indeed are they who stamp His pattern (*typos*) into their own souls, or desire that it were so stamped! For let the mind especially bear the perfect form of virtue (*to eidos teleion aretēs*), but if it cannot do that, at least let it have the resolute desire to acquire that form.

Philo here clearly enunciates one of the fundamental notions of Hellenistic sacred biography: by relating the *acts* of someone dear to the Gods and more than human, lesser mortals could see reflected the pattern or form of a life truly pleasing to the Gods, and imitate it so as to be fortunate in this life, and heir to a blessed existence in the hereafter. In a sense, the lives of Moses or Apollonios or Pythagoras or Jesus were written as handbooks of moral perfection.

On the other hand, readers of these writings felt great consolation from the way these "divine/human Saviors" were always selflessly giving of themselves for the betterment of the human condition, even after their "death." Philo says that Moses made helping others his supreme goal, toward which he devoted every effort. Philostratus says nearly the same thing of Apollonios; see p. 239. For these reasons, such writings served to arouse love and gratitude toward the central figure, coupled with a new desire to mend one's ways and live according to the example of the Savior.

Philo continues his portrait of Moses as the resourceful Leader, the wise General, the loving-yet-stern Father of his erring children; in short, as the ideal King, "the Living Law."

Note the place names that are used: all are in the current Greco-Roman usage. This is just one more clue that this writing was meant for non-Jews.

162. Since he was about to be a lawgiver, he himself long before became a rational and living law (*nomos empsychos te kai logikos*) by divine Providence which had already appointed him the future lawgiver even though he did not know it. 163. And so, having received sovereignty over a willing people, God directing and approving, Moses set off for their new home in Phoenicia and lower Syria and Palestine, which at that time was called the land of the Canaanites, the boundaries of which used to stand at a distance of three days' journey from

Egypt. 164. But he did not lead them up by the short way for on the one hand he feared that the local inhabitants might attack him to prevent being disturbed or enslaved and would force him to turn around and take the same road back to Egypt, thus exchanging enemy for enemy, new for old, being mocked and scoffed at, finally being captured and subjected to worse and more grievous injury than before. On the other hand, Moses desired to lead them through a long stretch of desert to test their obedience when their daily needs were not abundantly available but slightly wanting.

165. So he immediately turned off onto an oblique road thinking it might extend to the Red Sea and began to travel along it. At that very moment, they say, a marvel came to pass, a portent of nature which no one remembers happening before. 166. A cloud shaped into a good-sized pillar appeared and went before the caravan, shining by day with light like the sun, at night like fire, in order that they might not wander off the road during their march but follow the inerrant Guide along the way. Perhaps it was one of the subordinates of the Great King, an invisible angel, a guide concealed in the cloud, whom it were not lawful to look upon with the eyes of the body.

167. Meanwhile, the king of Egypt, as soon as he saw them turning off into what he thought was an impassable desert, walking into the rocky and trackless wilderness, was delighted at this false step in their journey, believing that they were hemmed in with no way out. Then he became sorry that he let them go in the first place and made ready to pursue them, intending to force the multitude to return out of fear and enslave them or just to kill them on the spot, obliterating them from the youths on up.

> The King of Egypt pursues them with his whole army and "six hundred of his finest scythed chariots," hoping to trap them beside the sea. The Hebrews, suddenly caught unprepared and unarmed, panic and loudly bewail their fate, accusing Moses of leading them by deceit into a fate worse than slavery, namely, certain death. But Moses rises to the occasion.

173. When Moses heard their desperate cries he excused them, having remembered the oracles. And dividing his mind from his speech he was simultaneously interceding silently with God to deliver them from this helpless predicament while at the same time he was cheering up and exhorting those who were bewailing their fate, saying, "Do not be dejected! God's method of defense is not like man's! 174. Why do you leap to merely probable or likely conclusions? God's assistance has no need of advance preparations! When there is no way, God finds his own way. Things impossible to all else are possible for him alone and easy."

175. He said these things, still in a calm way, but soon he paused, and then, becoming possessed by God (*enthous*), inspired by the Spirit which customarily often visited him, he uttered this prophetic oracle (*thespizei prophēteuōn*): "Those fully armed troops which you now see you will see no longer drawn up in battle formation, for they will all fall headlong and disappear into the ocean depths, so that no remnant of them will still appear upon the earth—and this not in a long time, but in this very night!"

And sure enough, at sundown a mighty wind began to blow and under cover of pitch darkness, pushed back the waters of the Red Sea. Moses then struck the sea with his staff and miraculously the waters parted, piling up in two high, sheer walls on either side. The Hebrews quickly passed through as if on dry ground, but when the Egyptians attempted to pursue them, the great walls of water suddenly buckled and came tumbling down upon them, drowning them all (cf. Exod. 14:5–31).

180. This great and marvelous work astonished the Hebrews, who thereby gained an unexpected bloodless victory. Seeing their enemies destroyed in a moment, once and for all, they set up two choirs there on the beach, one of men and the other of women, and sang hymns of thanksgiving to God, Moses leading the men and his sister the women.

Freed of their Egyptian menace at last, the Hebrews set out toward "Phoenicia"—Philo regularly uses the Greco-Roman designation so that his Gentile readers would understand (see above I:63). Next come various adventures in the desert, as the Hebrews successively ran out of fresh water (Exod. 15:22–26), food (Exod. 16), and water again (Exod. 17:1–7; cf. also Num. 20:1).

Using the last episode as a springboard, Philo jumps over a great portion of his source material to Num. 20, which contains the same story as Exod. 17:1–7. Philo uses the rest of Exod. 17 in the first of the battles he recounts, then switches to Num. 20ff. for the successive episodes to the end of Book I.

This manner of mechanically reducing a larger source by stringing together little sections of it and expanding them, or weaving together incidents into a different order than that of the original, all without any warning or indication of what is going on, was perfectly acceptable Hellenistic "history" writing. For example, Philo skips over the entire Mount Sinai account, probably because he wants to focus on it later in Book II. But here in Book I, it is as though it never happened, and Moses is simply portrayed as going in a round-about way from Egypt through the desert to Phoenicia.

Besides omitting as irrelevant great sections of legal and cultic material in Leviticus and Exodus, it is also clear that Philo is quietly covering up some dirty linen. For example, nothing whatever is said about Aaron's leading role in the Golden Bull debacle (Exod. 32:19–35), or the Lord's angry decree that neither Moses nor Aaron may enter into the Promised Land (Num. 20:12). In fact, Philo skillfully tells the story in Book I in such a way that the ignorant reader ends up with the definite impression that Moses actually did enter the Promised Land in the triumphant conclusion of Book I. To be sure, it should be noted that chapters 319–333 describe the possession by Moses of *trans*-Jordan lands, which are taken over by the tribes of Reuben and Gad. But the way Philo goes on to omit any mention of the fact that it was Moses' *successor* who conquered the rest of the territory on the other side of the Jordan creates the impression that Moses successfully completed this great task as well.

But we are getting ahead of the story. After these trials in the wilderness, the Hebrews reach the "Phoenician" regions, and immediately are attacked by the forces of Amalek (Exod. 17:8–16). As will be remembered, according to Exodus this battle was won because Aaron and a friend held up Moses' arms over the battlefield long enough for the Hebrews to win. That version was apparently not acceptable to Philo, who tells the story this way.

216. (Having sent his fighting force into battle under Joshua), Moses sprinkles himself round about with his customary purification rituals and then quickly runs up to a nearby hill where he beseeches God to shield and preserve victory and dominion for the Hebrews, whom he had already delivered from more grievous battles as well as other evils, namely, catastrophes threatened by men but also from the revolutionary alterations of the natural elements in Egypt and the constant famine during their travels. 217. Then when they are about to join in battle, something extraordinarily marvelous takes place affecting his hands, for they are first very light and then very heavy, and when they are lightened and taken up on high, his fellow fighters are strong and fight gloriously like stout men, but when they are weighed down the enemies are strong, God thereby recalling through symbols that the earth and all the nether regions are the proper portion of the one group, while the most holy air belonged to the other, and just as Heaven reigns and rules the earth in all things, so also this nation will conquer all its opponents. 218. As long as his hands like balances continue first to get lighter and then heavier, during this time the contest is undecided. But suddenly they become weightless, the fingers fluttering like wings, and they are lifted up on high into the air like the winged creatures that fly through the air and they remain lifted up until the Hebrews win a total victory, their enemies being slaughtered from the youths on up, which indeed was brought about so that they justly suffered what they wrongly desired to inflict on others.

Next Philo turns back to Numbers 13—14 and recounts the story of the spies sent into Canaan. Moses wanted a more exact description of the "Phoenician" countryside, so he sent out twelve men to survey the land, in order to decide what to do next. When the spies came back, ten of them told fearful tales of the gigantic size of the inhabitants and their huge walled cities, while Joshua and another man described a bountiful land, easily to be taken. However, the ten cowardly scouts persuaded the people not to try an invasion and so the whole people turned away to do some more wandering in the desert. Philo does not mention the biblical explanation of this additional forty years' wandering, namely, the anger of the Lord at the disobedience of the people (see Num. 14:26–35). According to Philo, the cause is totally human: the people cravenly decide not to invade Canaan for the time being.

When they eventually do try again, of course, more conflict awaits them. Their first battle is against the Edomites (Num. 20:14–21), and then another king, whom Philo mistakenly names "Chananes,"[1] rushes into battle against them, only to be resoundingly defeated like his predecessors (Num. 21:1–3). In each case, Moses makes nice set speeches to rouse his men for battle—in typical Hellenistic "history" fashion.

After this, Philo skips over the story of Moses and the bronze serpent (Num. 21:4–9), and picks up the brief account of the stop at a certain well in the wilderness, where the Lord had promised to give water to them (Num. 21:16–18). Of this minor story Philo skillfully makes a glorious event, indeed a sort of joyous, anticipatory celebration of the conquest of the whole Promised Land itself.

255. A little later, the Hebrews discovered a spring of sweet water which bountifully provided enough drink for the whole multitude, for the spring was in a well on the borders of the country. They drank it not as if it were water but pure wine so that their souls overflowed. In their festivity and joy, the choirs dear to God formed a circle around the well and sang a new hymn to the God who apportions land in a foreign country, to the true Leader of settlers, because here for the first time since they had left the long stretch of desert and were about to take possession of inhabited territory, they had found abundant water and felt it appropriate not to pass by the spring unnoticed.

Book I concludes with the telling of two more battles; a minor conflict with the Amorite King, Sihon (Num. 21:21–26), and, finally, the great battle against Balak, king of the Moabites, who had hired the "far-famed Mesopotamian prophet, Balaam" to help him. Of course, the Lord thwarts all of Balaam's spells, and makes him prophesy against Balak (Num. 22–24). In the process of rewriting this material, Philo converts the contents of Numbers 25, an unrelated account of certain Hebrew men who

[1]See *Vit. Mos.* I:250; cf. Num. 21:1 *LXX.*

cohabited with the Moabite women and the resultant wrath of the Lord, into a devilish plot suggested by Balaam to Balak, which he tried after everything else had failed. Balak carries it out with terrible consequences to the Hebrews until Phinehas leads a purge of the offending Hebrews, slaughtering them wholesale. After this Moses goes into battle against Balak and utterly defeats him, capturing immense booty (cf. Num. 31). It is an excellent example of Philo's method of conflating two different and unrelated narratives into one unified account.

Finally, as in Numbers 32, two of the tribes, Reuben and Gad, decide to settle down where they are and not cross the Jordan River. This causes immediate suspicion since the other tribes conclude that these two will not help in the fight to conquer the main part of the land and Moses has to quell the dissension and reach a compromise satisfactory to everyone. With this, Book I ends, i.e., with the successful prospect of the full-scale invasion directly in view. The reader has the pleasant impression of Moses' resiliency and resourcefulness as Leader of his people and Philo closes Book I thus.

334. The matters pertaining to Moses' kingship have now been recalled, and it is right to speak next also of the things he did through his high priesthood and lawgiving, for he was granted these powers as especially most appropriate to his kingship.

Book II

It is possible that a portion of Book II has disappeared, namely after ch. 65. The treatment of Moses as Lawgiver is disproportionately short, so a considerable amount of material could be lost from that part of his writing.

The contents of Book II which remain are far more complex than Book I. The chronological narrative is given up completely, and facets of the Sacred Books of Moses are treated under three heads: legislative, high-priestly and prophetic. It should be emphasized that all three are still understood as illustrative of Moses' supernatural character, as was the case in Book I.

1. The first composition (*syntaxis*) is about the birth and upbringing of Moses, about his education and rulership in which he ruled not only blamelessly but very commendably and about the things done by him in Egypt and on the journeys, both beside the Red Sea and in the desert—things which surpass all power of words to describe. Furthermore, it deals with the hardships which he underwent and the allotment of the foreign districts which he partly divided up among his soldiers. That which is here composed concerns things which came after and are related to them. 2. For some say, and they are not wrong, that cities advance toward excellence only if the kings practice philosophy or if philosophers are kings. Now Moses appears to have displayed to an

uncommon degree not only these two qualities within himself, namely, the kingly and the philosophical, but also three others, of which the first is his activity concerning lawgiving, the second concerning the high priesthood, and the last concerning prophecy.

3. I have decided to speak now concerning these three, necessarily supposing them to be quite appropriately combined in the same person, for by the providence of God he became King and Lawgiver and High Priest and Prophet and in each he carried off first prize. 4. But why all are to be combined in the same person must be made clear. It befits kings to command what is necessary and to forbid what is wrong, but the ordination of things to be done and the prohibition of things not to be done is a property of the Law so that the King is immediately a living Law (*nomos empsychos*) and the Law a just King. 5. Further, the King and Lawgiver should be in charge not only of human affairs but also divine, for without divine protection the affairs of kings and subjects will not prosper. For this reason such a person needs to be foremost in priestcraft in order that, on the basis of perfect rituals (*teleioi hieroi*) and perfect understanding of the worship of God (*epistēmē teleia tēs tou theou therapias*), he might seek the prevention of evils and the bestowing of good things, both for himself and for his subjects, directing such petitions to the Gracious One who responds to prayers. For how can he who is favorable by nature, who considers worthy of privilege those who sincerely serve him, not bring their prayers to fruition?

6. Nevertheless, myriads of human and divine matters are unclear to King and Lawgiver and High Priest. Likewise, although Moses was all these things he was also mortal, so that in addition to having such a bounteous heritage of good things, he needed to obtain prophecy in order that whatever could not be discovered by rational means could be learned from the foreknowledge of God. For those matters which surpass the mind, prophecy anticipates beforehand.

7. How beautiful and harmonious is the union of these four qualities! Intertwined and sharing in each other, they dance in rhythm, receiving and repaying benefits, imitating the Virgin Graces whom an immutable law of nature ordains shall never be disunited, concerning which it is right to say what one often hears pertaining to virtue: to have one is to have all.

8. To begin with, let us speak of the virtues belonging to the context of giving laws. Now I am not ignorant of the fact that it is fitting for him who is to become the best of lawgivers to be in full and complete possession of all virtues. But since, as in households, there are some who are the most closely related members of the family, while others are more distantly related although all are relatives of each other, so also some virtues are understood to be rooted in certain matters while others

are not so directly involved. 9. In the legislative context, we may distinguish four brothers or relatives: love of mankind, love of justice, love of the good, and hatred of evil. Each of these is demanded of everyone into whom enters the zeal for giving laws: love of mankind, or presenting to the public an exposition of one's maxims (*gnōmai*) concerning the common good; righteousness, or honoring equality and distributing to each according to his worth; love of the good, or approving everything naturally noble and unrestrainedly providing them to all worthy of their abundant use; and, finally, hatred of evil, or rejecting those who dishonor virtue and regarding them with suspicion as enemies of the human race.

10. It is a great thing indeed if someone obtains even one of the virtues here described and certainly marvelous if anyone can grasp them all at once, yet it seems Moses alone succeeded in doing this, plainly displaying all the above-mentioned virtues in the things he ordained. 11. Those who read the Holy Books moreover know they would not be what they are unless he had grown up such as he was, for he wrote under the guidance of God and handed them on to those worthy to use them as the most beautiful of their possessions; duplicates and copies of the rational pattern (*paradeigma*) enshrined in the soul. The laws which Moses revealed became the clearest manifestations of the above mentioned virtues.

12. The following consideration will make especially believable our contention that Moses became the best of all the lawgivers anywhere, whether among the Greeks or the barbarians, and that his laws are the best and are truly divine (*alēthōs theioi*) since they omit nothing that is needed. 13. If anyone rationally (*tō logismō*) surveys other nations' customs, he will find them continually changing due to all sorts of causes: wars, tyrannies, and numerous other undesirable things heaped upon them by ill fortune. Oftentimes excessive affluence brought about by an overabundance of money and possessions has overthrown the laws, the masses being unable to bear "too much of a good thing," and as a result of intemperance they become arrogant. Well, arrogance (*hybris*) is the adversary of law.

14. Only the laws of Moses have remained as steadfast, unshaken and immovable as if they had been enacted with the seals of Nature herself (*sphragisi physeōs autēs*) stamped on them, remaining firm from the day he wrote them until now. Hopefully they will continue to endure throughout all eternity as if immortal—as long as the sun and the moon and all heaven and earth exist. 15. For even though our nation has experienced various changes of good fortune and the opposite, nothing—not even the least of the commandments—has been altered, for it seems that everyone highly honors their majestic, godly character.

Philo goes on to assert that there is yet something still more wonderful about them. Peoples the world over, who care little enough for each others' laws, are unanimous in their sincere and profound admiration for the laws of the Jews. These have attracted the "attention of all, barbarians, Greeks, inhabitants of the continents, of the islands, of the nations to the East, those to the West, Europe, Asia, the whole inhabited world (*oikoumenē*) from end to end" (II. 20). As evidence, Philo points to the widespread Gentile concurrence in the Jewish custom of the Sabbath and reverence for their annual Passover festival. To understand how Philo could assert this bold claim without fear of ridicule, it is necessary to remember the extremely privileged position the Jews as a nation actually occupied in Imperial Roman policy during this period. See further V. Tcherikover, *Hellenistic Civilization and the Jews* (Philadelphia: Magness Press, 1961), pp. 306–308.

He then goes on to relate a story which is not in his main source for the life of Moses, the point of which is to prove the fully inspired character of the *Greek translation* of the Hebrew Scriptures. This is a rather strange idea when you stop to think about it, but we should remember that Philo and many other Jews in the Diaspora could not read Hebrew (or "Chaldean" as foreigners called it), and therefore cherished this Greek translation as their Holy Word, much as modern fundamentalist Protestants still cherish the King James Version.

Although the origin of this story is a fascinating question in itself, let it suffice to say that the chief reason Philo repeats it here is because the story tells how the translation of the Hebrew Scriptures was eagerly sought by a famous *Gentile* king. This king actually existed: Ptolemy II Philadelphus, the second of the post-Alexander Greek rulers in Egypt. He ruled from 285–246 B.C., and may well have encouraged the enterprise here described. The earliest version of the story Philo tells here is a writing called *The Letter of Aristeas,* which appeared approx. 175 B.C.

25. The sacred quality of Moses' legislation has seemed marvelous not only to the Jews but also to all others. This is evident from what has already been said and from what I am about to relate next.
26. In ancient times, the laws were written in the Chaldean language, and they remained for a long time in the same dialect without changing, as long as their beauty had not appeared to other men. 27. But when, due to the careful and continuous observance every day by those using them, others also became aware of them, and their fame spread in all directions—for although excellence can be hidden for a short time by envy, in due time it will shine forth once again thanks to the benevolence of Nature. Eventually, some thought it a shame that the laws had been drawn up only for half of the race of mankind, namely the barbarians, while none of the Greeks had any share in them, and so they turned to the task of translating them.

It is a bit startling to see Philo here adopting the Greek outlook, according to which the whole world was divided into two groups: Greeks and everyone else (called "barbarians"). Incidentally, the term "barbarian" was originally not so much a derogatory term as it was a generic, like "Gentiles."

28. Since this was an important task for the common good, it was not entrusted to private citizens or public officials, of whom there were a great number who would have done it, but to kings, namely the most highly regarded of kings. 29. Ptolemy, called Philadelphus, was the third in succession from Alexander the Great who had conquered Egypt. As far as virtues in leadership are concerned, he was the best, not only of his contemporaries but also of those who ever were in ancient times. Even today, so many generations later, Ptolemy's fame is still sung for the many evidences and memorials of genius that he left behind in cities and countries, as the proverb shows when deeds of great distinction and large public buildings are called "Philadelphian" after him. 30. In short, just as the dynasty of the Ptolemies flourished more grandly than all other royal dynasties, so also Philadelphus stood out among the Ptolemies. The praiseworthy things this one man achieved were more than all the rest put together, so that just as the head is the leader of a living body, he became in a way the head of kings.
31. Such a man as he had a zeal and longing for our legislation and decided to adapt the Chaldean to the Greek language. He immediately sent off ambassadors to the High Priest and King of the Jews—they were the same person—explaining his plan and urging him to choose some according to merit who might translate the Law.

This last sentence is one of the clues that this Greek translation only included the Torah, the Law or first five books of the Hebrew Scriptures. Of course, by Philo's time all the rest was translated as well.

Although Philo claims in ch. 32 that the High Priest was receptive to King Ptolemy's proposal, later orthodox Jews were by no means inclined to agree. They ordained a mourning fast to commemorate this tragic event, claiming that when the Torah was translated into Greek, God sent darkness on the earth for three days; see G.F. Moore, *Judaism* (Cambridge: Harvard University Press, 1962), vol. II, p. 68.

32. The High Priest was naturally pleased and considering that the king would not have been eager to undertake such a task without the prompting of Divine Wisdom he carefully sought out the most highly approved Hebrews, who in addition to their native also had a Greek education, and joyfully sent them off.
33. When they arrived they were hospitably received with courteous

and warm speeches and as their host sumptuously entertained them they entertained him in return. For he tested the wisdom of each one by proposing new instead of the customary problems and they cleverly and precisely solved them, not falling back on lengthy speeches but just as the occasion required with brief, pithy aphorisms (*apophthegmata*).

34. Thus gaining his approval, they immediately began to complete their noble mission. Reckoning the task of translating laws divinely uttered in oracles (*thespisthentas nomous chrēsmois diermēneuein*) to be extremely difficult since they were required neither to subtract nor add nor alter anything but to preserve their original form and image in the translation, they sought out the purest of the places in the region around the outside of the city to perform the task. For inside the city walls there was every kind of unclean animal, disease, death, and unhealthy behavior of healthy citizens. Thus they looked elsewhere.

35. Now Pharos island lies near the city of Alexandria. It is a long narrow strip of land pointing toward the city, surrounded not by deep water close to shore but many shallows, so that the roaring and noisy splashing of the waves is spread out over a long distance and becomes soft and indistinct. 36. This made the island seem still and quiet and so they decided it was especially suitable as a place where they could, with the soul alone, commune with the laws. Thereupon they set up their lodgings and taking the sacred books they stretched them and their hands up toward Heaven asking God that the project not fail. And he assented to their prayers in order that the majority or even the whole race of mankind might benefit by making use of these philosophical and wholly noble commandments for the improvement of life.

The explanation in the next sentence that the Book of Genesis begins with an account of the creation of the world is another obvious clue that this *Life of Moses* could hardly have been intended for Jewish readers.

37. Now after each one found a secret place to sit where there was no one else present except the four parts of nature: earth, water, air, and heaven, the creation (*genesis*) of which was about to be given sacred exposition (*hierophantein*)—for the creation of the world is described at the beginning of the laws—as if possessed by God they began prophesying, not many different things but each one the very same words and sentences as if all were being simultaneously dictated to by an invisible prompter.

38. Now who does not know that every language and especially Greek has many words and that the same thought can be shaped in many different ways by changing the wording of the sentences, each expression being appropriate to the matter at hand? However they say this did

not happen to this legislation but that the words corresponded exactly, the Greek with the Chaldean, each one perfectly corresponding to the thing it indicated . . .

40. The clearest argument for this is the fact that if Chaldeans know the Greek language or if Greeks have learned Chaldean and they read both copies, the original and the translation, they are astonished, revering the two as sisters or rather as being one and the same in contents and in words. Furthermore, they regard these men not as mere translators but as expounders of sacred mysteries (*hierophantēs*) and prophets (*prophētai*), to whom God granted an encounter, through their sincere rationality (*logismos*), with the most pure spirit (*katharōtatō pneumati*) of Moses himself.

41. For this reason, to this day a feast and a celebration is held every year on Pharos island to which not Jews only but all kinds of other people cross over in order to magnify the place where the splendor of that translation first shone forth, and also to give thanks to God for his good service in times past but ever anew . . .

43. This is why the laws of Moses are seen to be blessed and are eagerly desired by all, common citizens and rulers alike, and this even though our nation has not prospered for a long time, for things cannot blossom into their prime if somewhat over-shadowed. 44. But if some new start toward better times would take place, how much progress there would no doubt be! I believe that every man would abandon his own customs and, bidding good riddance to his ancestral ways, would change over to honor these laws alone! For if our nation should prosper, our laws would shine out once again darkening all others just as the rising sun does the stars!

This story which Philo has gotten from the oral tradition is a priceless gem from the brief but dynamic period (c. 200 B.C. down to c. A.D. 50) when Hellenized Judaism, especially in Alexandria, transformed itself from a nationalistic into a confident, universalistic religion inviting converts from all nations and regions. Philo stands out as one of the chief spokesmen for this new Judaism, a Judaism whose outlook and basic convictions are not unlike those of modern Reform Judaism. Early Christianity itself is a direct outgrowth of this outward-looking, universalistic Judaism. It would be interesting to speculate what might have happened to Philo's type of Judaism if it had continued to develop and flourish.

For example, his treatment of Moses' laws is exceedingly interesting. He points out that all other nations' lawgivers have one thing in common: they gave their laws for their own city only. But Moses, asserts Philo, precedes *his* legal code with a history of the creation of the universe, in order to show that these laws are far superior since they come from the Creator himself and are intended for all men everywhere.

"(Moses) considered that to begin his writings with a description of the foundation of a man-made city was below the dignity of the laws. Rather, he surveyed the greatness and beauty of the whole code with the exceptional accuracy of his mind's eye, and saw that it was too excellent and too divine to be confined within the circle of any city on earth. So he prefaced them with an account of the origin of the Great City (*megalopolis*), thinking that the laws were a very faithful image (*eikōn*) of the government (*politeia*) of the universe."

And then Philo gives in one succinct sentence the basic idea which guided him in all of his voluminous commentaries on the law of Moses:

"Thus, whoever desires to examine carefully the meanings of the different parts of the commandments will find that they aim at the harmony of the universe (*hē tou pantos harmonia*), and are in accord with the rational principle of eternal nature (*tō logō tēs aidiou physeōs*) (II. 51–52). This amazing statement should give some idea how Philo viewed Moses as the Lawgiver *par excellence*.

Next, Philo takes up the third of his four-part portrait, and begins to describe Moses' priestly activities. As before, Moses stands out in every way. This time the exceptional status of Moses' priestcraft is explained by the fact that Moses received all of his instructions regarding worship directly from God on Mount Sinai. What other High Priest could make that claim?

66. We have already fully recounted two parts of the life of Moses, namely the royal and the legislative; the third, concerning his priestcraft is to be added to these.

The greatest and most necessary quality of a High Priest is piety (*eusebeia*). Moses practiced this one especially, at the same time making use of the other gifts given him by Nature which philosophy took over like good soil, making it even better by the attention he paid to her wholly noble teachings; nor did it cease before the fruits of virtue were completely formed in word and deed. 67. For this reason Moses came to love God and be loved by God as few others, becoming inspired by the love of Heaven, to a remarkable degree honoring the Ruler of All and being honored by him in return. Now wisely serving him who truly exists is appropriate to honoring, and it is the practice of priestcraft to serve God. It was this privilege, than which there is no greater good in existence, which Moses was considered worthy of, being taught through oracles each of the rituals and sacred duties.

68. However, first of all he had to be pure in soul and in body, having nothing to do with the passions but keeping himself pure from all things whatever pertaining to mortal nature: eating and drinking and intercourse with women. 69. This last in particular he despised for a long time, almost from the day he first began to prophesy and to be possessed by God, thinking it proper always to keep himself prepared for oracles from God. On one occasion he disregarded food and drink for forty

successive days, doubtless because he had better food coming from Heaven above through his soul's contemplation. This fast made him better first in mind, then in body, advancing in each one to such strength and health that those seeing him later did not believe it. 70. For in obedience to divine commands Moses had ascended the loftiest and most sacred mountain in that area where it was unapproachable and impassable and remained there for the period just mentioned while partaking of none of the necessary benefits of food. Then forty days later it is said that he descended with an appearance much more beautiful than when he went up, so that those who saw him were amazed and astounded, their eyes being unable to long withstand the assault of the sun-like brightness flashing forth from him. 71. While he was up on the mountain, he had been inducted into the mysteries (*mystagōgeō*), being taught all things concerning priestcraft, the first being instructions about the temple and its furnishings.

With this build-up one might wonder what Philo can say that would demonstrate the alleged supernatural beauty and significance of the priestly cultus inaugurated by Moses. The continuation must have seemed impressive by ancient standards. Philo enumerates the high points of the priestly instructions in Exodus (taking up the material according to his own order from ch. 26, 27, 25, 30, 28 and 38). He describes the structure and lay-out of the tent of meeting, the ark of the covenant, the High Priest's vestments, the sacred vessels and utensils, and much more. However, none of these items is left without Philo's inimitable allegorical explanation. For example, the reason Moses ordered an altar of incense in the exact center of the tent of meeting was to symbolize the thankfulness of the earth, which occupies the exact center of the universe. The seven-branched candlestick represents the sun and the six planets. The table of show bread located on the north side of the sacred tent signifies the North wind which provides the most beneficial weather for growing wheat, and so on and so on. Consider this passage.

118. (The robe of the High Priest) is a representation and copy of the world, a part of it corresponding to each part of the world. Beginning with the full-length robe, this gown is completely violet in color which is a counterpart of the air, for air is by nature black and is after a fashion a robe all about us, being stretched out from above near the region of the moon down to the earth and spreading out everywhere. Whence also the gown spreads from the chest to the feet all around the body. 119. Around the hem, knobs shaped like pomegranates and flowers and bells are embroidered. The flowers are a symbol of the earth, for flowers and all things grow from it. The pomegranates symbolize water because of their flowing juice, while the bells symbolize the harmony and sympho-

ny of these things, for nothing at all could begin if the earth were without water or the water without earth but only if they come together and form a mixture of both. . . .

122. Reason (*ho logos*) suggests that the ephod (shoulder cape) is a symbol of heaven by the following likely conjectures. First of all, the two emerald stones carried on the points of the shoulders recall, as some think, the major leading stars of day and night, the sun and the moon, although one might argue, coming somewhat closer to the truth, that they are each one of the hemispheres . . . (The twelve stones fastened) on the breast plate, not alike in color and being divided up into four rows of three, what else do they indicate but the twelve signs of the zodiac? . . .

131. Such are the riddles that Moses hints at through the sacred vestments. By placing a turban instead of a crown on his head, he thinks it right that while the one consecrated to God is worshiping, he surpasses all men, not common citizens only but even kings. 132. On top of the turban is the gold plate (*petalon*) on which is carved the marks of four letters said to recall the name of Being Itself (*to on*), meaning that without invoking God's aid, nothing of what exists will be sustained, since it is his good and gracious power which brings about the harmonious existence of all things.

133. Dressed in this fashion, then, the High Priest is sent to the sacred tasks in order that whenever he enters into the temple to offer the traditional prayers and sacrifices, the whole world goes in with him, being carried in by these likenesses: the robe, the air; the pomegranates, water; the flowers, the earth; the scarlet (thread in the ephod), fire; the ephod, heaven; the emeralds carried on the shoulders, the two hemispheres; the twelve stones on the breast in four rows of three, the zodiac; and (the *petalon*) is the cosmic rationality (*to logeion*) connecting and administering the whole. 134. For it were necessary for him who is consecrated to the Father of the world to make use of his Son, the most perfect advocate of virtue (*paraklētos teleiotatos tēn aretēn huios*), in order to obtain forgiveness of sins (*amnēstia hamartēmatōn*) and provision of abundant good things.

The thought is that the High Priest appears before God, the Father of All, as *his Son*, i.e., dressed as a "miniature world" (*brachys kosmos* II.135). And since God's Son is the "perfect advocate" (*paraklētos*), God can hardly deny his pleas. Needless to say, although the symbolism is different, this conjunction of "Son-Advocate" language is strikingly similar to early

Christian terminology.

Next Philo describes how Aaron, Moses' brother, was chosen as the first High Priest through a miraculous sign. After this, he narrates the story in Exodus 32 which tells how God chose the first temple attendants, namely the tribe of Levi. But here Philo must have experienced some difficulties, for in the Bible this is the story of the Golden Bull, i.e., a story of mass idolatry led by none other than Aaron, Moses' brother, the newly appointed High Priest. It requires a delicate laundering job of major proportions, but Philo is equal to the task. His Greek readers never know that Aaron had anything to do with it.

161. After Moses had ascended the mountain nearby and was alone with God for many days, some men of unstable natures, thinking his absence to be a perfect opportunity for causing anarchy, unrestrainedly rushed headlong into impiety and utterly forgot their reverence for Being Itself (to on), becoming zealous worshipers of Egyptian idols. 162. Having fashioned a golden bull, a replica of the animal considered to be the most sacred in that country, they offered sacrifices not fit to be offered; they set up ill-suiting choirs; they sang hymns in no way differing from dirges, and were completely carried away, being over-powered by a double drunkenness, the one from the wine and the other from foolishness. They caroused and dallied the whole night long unaware of what was about to happen, cohabiting with pleasurable wickedness, while unforeseen Justice which sees what is not seen and what is worthy of punishment was getting ready to strike.

163. When the continuous shouting in the camp, because of the crowds of people carousing together, began to spread over a great distance so that the echo even reached the top of the mountain and struck the ears of Moses, he was at first undecided what to do. His love for God made it impossible for him to abandon the fellowship with God in which he conversed privately with him one to one, while his love for man meant that he could not ignore the multitude below filled with the evil results of anarchy. 164. For he understood that awful din, perceiving in the confused and indistinct noise what is unclear and unapparent to others, namely, the typical passions of the soul. The continual uproar had become a drunken melee, intemperance begetting gluttonous satiety, and satiety insolence. 165. Pulled this way and tugged that way toward each side, Moses remained still, being at a loss what to do.

While he was thinking it over, the following was uttered in an oracle to him: "Go there quickly. Descend. The people are hurrying into lawlessness and are worshiping and sacrificing to the form of a bull fashioned by hands as to a God—which is not God—having utterly forgotten all the things which they have seen and heard tending towards piety." 166. Astonished and necessarily believing these unbelievable events, like an arbitrator or mediator Moses did not immediately rush off, but first made an appeal and pleaded on behalf of the nation asking for pardon of their sins. After the guardian and intercessor had reconciled the Ruler, he went down simultaneously rejoicing and downcast for he was full of joy that God had accepted his supplication, but he was plunged into anxiety and sorrow upon seeing the lawlessness of the multitude.

167. Arriving in the middle of the camp and being amazed at the sudden change of habits of the multitude and how great a lie they had exchanged for so great a truth, he observed that not everyone had been infected by the disease but that there were some healthy people still possessed of a passionate hatred of evil. Desiring to distinguish those who were incurable sinners from those who despised the things being done and to see if any sinners would repent, he announced a proclamation (*kerygma*)—it was in fact an accurate test of each mind to determine its degree of holiness or the opposite— 168. which said, "If anyone is for the Lord, let him come to me!" Little enough said but it was great with meaning! For this is what was being made clear: "If anyone considers nothing made by hand nor any creature to be Gods but that there is One Ruler of all that is, let him come to me."

169. Out of all who were there, some who were the rebels devoted to the Egyptian vanity did not pay any attention to what he said, while others, out of fear of punishment perhaps, likewise did not draw near, either fearing something from Moses or from the mob, for the mass always attacks those who do not agree with it. 170. One tribe out of all of them, called the Levites, as soon as they heard the proclamation, eagerly ran up to him as if given a signal, their swiftness displaying zeal and their haste, their souls' eagerness for piety.

> Moses orders the Levites to slaughter immediately all of the offending Hebrews, and before long, 3,000 have been killed. As a reward for their zeal, they became Aaron's assistants. And that ends the Golden Bull episode; not a word about "And Aaron received the gold from their hands . . . and made a molten calf" (Exod. 32–34; RSV).
>
> Finally, Philo tells the story of Aaron's Rod, a rather brutal account in Numbers 16–17 which describes how the Lord destroyed Korah and his followers, by having the earth swallow them and their wives and children alive, while fire burnt up the rest, all because they protested Moses' favoritism in choosing his brother as High Priest. None of that appears in Philo's account however. Rather there is only the miracle of Aaron's Rod, which is divine confirmation of Moses' choice.
>
> This concludes the description of Moses' activities as the perfect High Priest, and Philo is ready to proceed to the last part of his work: Moses the Prophet.

187. Since we have said that it is necessary to include four things in the world's most perfect leader (*teleiotatos hēgemonos*), namely kingship, lawgiving, priestcraft and prophecy, in order that through lawgiving he might ordain what is necessary and forbid what must not be done, through priestcraft he might manage not only human affairs but also divine, and through prophecy whatever cannot be comprehended by rational processes he might announce through oracles—having fully treated of the first three and shown that Moses was the world's best king, lawgiver, and High Priest, I come to the final section in order to show that he became the most highly approved prophet also.

188. Now I am not ignorant that all the things which are written in the sacred books are oracles (*chrēsmoi*) delivered through Moses, but I will speak here of those more especially his own. But first I should explain that some of the oracles (*logia*) came from the presence of God through a prophet as the interpreter of God; others were uttered in response to questions as answers, and others were from Moses himself when he was possessed by God and carried out his mind.

Philo here enumerates three kinds of divine utterance (*logion*) in the sacred writings: those where Moses is simply God's mouthpiece (or interpreter, *hermeneutēs*), and two other kinds, in which he is, strictly speaking, a prophet (*prophētēs*). Of these, one kind involves questions put to the Deity which are answered in oracles, and another kind occurs when the prophet is filled with the divine spirit and gives an oracle foretelling some future event. Philo says he will restrict himself to examples of these latter two kinds of "prophecy."

Of the first sort, where Moses was confronted with a difficult situation and had to inquire of God what to do, Philo gives four examples. The first concerned a man who cursed God (Lev. 24:10–16); the second, a man who profaned the Sabbath rest (Num. 15:32–36); the third, a complicated problem concerning conflicting ritual obligations (Num. 9:1–14); and the fourth, a knotty legal question concerning seven orphaned girls (Num. 27:1–11). In the first two cases, God orders a stern, inexorable punishment of the miserable offenders. In the last two, his boundless mercy and great wisdom are revealed. Indeed, as Philo tells the story of the poor orphaned daughters and God's tender concern for them, he suddenly bursts into an unusually exalted passage of praise.

238. He who is the Maker of All, the Father of the world, holding together and controlling earth and heaven, water and air and whatever comes from each of these, he who rules Gods and men, did not disdain to give an answer to orphaned girls. And having given an answer, he added something more than a judge would, . . . he who is kind and gracious, who fills all things everywhere with his benevolent power—he expressed praise of the lowly maidens! 239. O Master, how may one

hymn Thee? With what mouth, what tongue, what instruments of speech, what sort of reason—the authoritative part of the soul? If the stars should become a single choir, could they sing a worthy hymn? If the whole of Heaven should resolve itself into one voice, could it describe a single part of Thy virtues?

> For examples of Moses' accurate prediction of future events while under divine inspiration, Philo goes back to the events narrated in Book I and repeats four cases, in order to show that Moses' predictions actually did come to pass: (a) announcing to the Hebrew people by the Red Sea that they would soon see the oncoming Egyptian forces totally annihilated; (b) warning the people not to store the heavenly manna, for it would rot; (c) calling the Levites to slay everyone worshiping the Golden Bull; and (d) predicting the horrible death to befall all those who dared to question the selection of Aaron as High Priest.
>
> In each case, Philo is careful to emphasize that Moses made the prediction while out of his normal mind, i.e., "no longer being in himself, being carried away by God and prophesying (*thespizō*)" (II. 250); or, again, "He no longer remained his own self and *utterly* changed both in form (*eidos*) and mind (*dianoia*), he said, prophesying . . . etc." (II. 272). It was clearly a major aspect of Hellenistic religious experience that human beings could become "filled with the God(s)" and, in that condition, speak divine truth inaccessible under normal conditions.
>
> This concludes Philo's lengthy and substantial account of Moses, "the greatest and most perfect man who ever lived." All that remains is to describe Moses' ascension to Heaven, that is, to describe how the divine part of Moses *returned* to Heaven. For it is clear that Philo understands the hint in Deut. 34:6: "no man knows the place of his burial to this day" as indicating that there may be a memorial somewhere over there in the land of Moab, but *Moses himself didn't stay there, but ascended to Heaven.* This is Philo's version of the Empty Tomb account as found in the Christian narratives about Jesus Christ. The fact that Deut. 34:6 says, "And (the Lord) *buried him* in the valley in the land of Moab" (RSV) did not disturb Philo's view in the slightest, as we can see in the passage following, because what really occurred was a resurrection and transmutation of Moses' earthly body/soul duality into "a single nature . . . a pure sun-bright mind" (*eis monados physin . . . noun hēlioeidestaton*), immortal forever.

288. After a long time, when he was about to be sent to the other colony in Heaven and, abandoning mortal life, to be immortalized, having been called back by the Father, with his dual being of body and soul finally transmuted into a single nature, wholly and completely transformed into a pure sun-bright mind, at this point Moses was again carried away by the Spirit and no longer uttered general oracles to the whole nation but spoke to one tribe after the other, foretelling the things about to happen which thereafter would come to pass. Some of

these have already occurred while others are still expected, since belief in things about to be is confirmed by what has occurred before. . . .

290. . . . (These oracles are) marvelous enough but especially marvelous is the conclusion of the holy writings which, as the head is to a living animal, this is the chief part of the whole legislation. 291. For when he was already rising up into the air and standing as it were at the starting line in order that he might fly straight up the race course to Heaven, Moses was inspired and possessed by God so that while still living he prophesied shrewdly concerning his own death: how he died, although not yet dead, how he was buried, while no one was present—obviously not by mortal hands but by immortal powers, how he was not given last rites in a tomb of his forefathers but obtained a memorial of special honor which no man has ever seen, and how the entire nation was saddened, mourning him for a whole month, displaying their sadness individually and collectively on account of his indescribable kindness and solicitude toward each one and toward all.

292. Such was the life and such also the death of the King and Lawgiver and High Priest and Prophet Moses, as commemorated in the sacred writings.

Alexander the False Prophet
Lucian of Samosata

Introduction: For our final selection, we have included a parody of the whole Savior concept. In fact, that is precisely why this writing is significant: it contains the same basic Savior image, only now it has been inverted and made into a vehicle for satire.

Lucian of Samosata, the author of this writing, was a second-century B.C. precursor of H. L. Mencken. A prolific and popular writer, he looked at his world with sharp, satirical eyes. Very few elements of Greek society from bedroom to the marketplace to the philosophical academy escaped Lucian's keen and debunking wit. However, most of his satires are not bitter in tone, such as this one is. One senses that this "Life of Alexander" was not entirely in fun; he thoroughly despised Alexander and his kind.

There is not much question that this Alexander was an actual cult leader, whose religious charade survived his death for some time. Of course, as Lucian is virtually our only source of information about Alexander, it is not possible to evaluate the accuracy of his assessment very well. According to Lucian, Alexander was a pious fraud (*goēs*) of a type not uncommon in the Hellenistic world, or any other time, for that matter. Lucian's Alexander is an early Elmer Gantry.

Scathing as it is, Lucian's story nevertheless employs the form of a Hellenistic biography (*bios*), such as we see in the accounts of Moses and Apollonios. As we have pointed out with regard to them, the subject is set forth as a model of moral perfection, so that the author emphasizes the achievements of the subject and often launders his shortcomings. Lucian does just the opposite: he makes everything about Alexander look as vile and despicable as possible. Since the *bios* contains an account of the unusual ancestry, birth, education, and exploits of the hero, ending with the hero's exemplary death and ascension to Heaven, Lucian follows this whole format, but turns it inside out!

You, dear Celsus, probably think it a small and petty thing to ask me to set down for you in a book the life of Alexander, the charlatan (*goēs*) of Abunoteichos, all his cleverness, boldness, and trickery. But if someone wished accurately to examine each item, it would not be less a job than to write the deeds of Philip's son, Alexander. One was as great in evil as the other in excellence.

However . . . I will attempt the task for you and will try to clean out that Augean stable, if not completely, at least as much as I can, carrying out a few buckets full, so that you may mark how great, how inexpressible, was the bullshit that three thousand head of cattle were able to create in many years.

I am ashamed, actually, for both of us—you and me—that you want to hand down in memory and writing a thrice-abominable man, and I spend my energy concerning such a story (*historia*) and the deeds of a man who is not worth having educated people read about. It would be better to have the mob see him ripped apart in a great amphitheater by foxes or apes . . .

First, I will draw a portrait of him in words, making as good a likeness as I can, although I am not much of an artist. His body—see if I can portray him to you—was large and handsome to see, truly godlike. He had fair skin, a light beard—his hair was partly his own and partly false, but it was well matched, so that many did not see that some was false. His eyes glowed with fervor and spirit; his voice was sweet and clear at once. As a whole, from this standpoint, no one could fault him.

Such was his appearance, his form; but his soul and mind—O Herakles, our protector, and Zeus, our guardian, and the Dioscuri, our Saviors—our attackers and enemies should fall in with him and have such a one as an ally!

Lucian continues to describe Alexander's qualities. Alexander is bright, sharp, quick-witted, and thoroughly decadent.

On the whole, imagine with me and picture in your mind a many-colored mixture of soul, concocted from lying, guile, perjury, and malice, a soul reckless, bold, adventurous, meticulous in scheming, persuasive, believable, a consummate actor playing at doing good, and looking just the opposite of its purpose. No one on a first meeting could go away without praise for him as he seemed the most wonderful, straight, simple, and above-board of all men. More than all this, he had a greatness of purpose—he made no small schemes but always kept his mind on the grandest goals.

Lucian now recounts Alexander's "education," as one did in writing the "life" of a famous man. Alexander, however, had a "street" education; because he was so handsome he sold himself as a boy prostitute to men who would take care of him and whom he could bilk.

Among others, a certain lover who was a charlatan (*goēs*) took him, a man who promised miracles, divine charms, and charms for lovers, "sendings" (of malignant spirits) upon enemies, discoveries of treasures, and inheritances of estates.

This man saw that Alexander was a talented boy, quite ready to help him in his work, and that the boy did not love his (master's) evil less than he loved the boy's beauty. So he educated him and employed him as helper, servant, and deacon. He himself claimed to be a physician to the people, but as it is said about the wife of Thon, the Egyptian, he knew "many drugs that were good when mixed, and many bad ones" (*Odyssey* 4.230). Alexander inherited and took over all of these. This teacher and lover was from Tyana, one of those who had been a companion of Apollonios and who knew all of his ploys. You now see from what school this man about whom I speak comes.

> Lucian now tells us about Alexander's deeds. This is also customary in the "life" of a "divine man." We will limit ourselves to an example or two. In the first story, Alexander and his company make their first major flimflam. It is on Alexander's home town, Paphlogonia; Alexander considered its people to be particularly stupid and gullible.

Alexander . . . played at madness, causing his mouth to fill with foam. He did this easily by chewing the root of soapwort which the plant dyers use. To the people the foam seemed divine and awesome. Long before this, they made and fitted, from linen, a snake's head which had an anthropomorphic look. It was painted and looked lifelike. By using horsehair threads, one could open and close its mouth, and a forked, black tongue like a snake's, also controlled by threads, would dart out. The serpent of Pella was prepared and cared for at home. At the proper time it would reveal itself to the townspeople and be an actor in their show; what's more it was to be the protagonist.

But now, it was time to start. He designed a scheme. He went during the night to the foundations of a temple which were just being dug—water was standing there which had gathered by seepage or fallen from the sky—there he hid a previously blown goose egg, which held a new-born snake. He buried the egg in the mud and went back.

In the morning, he ran out naked into the town square, wearing a loin cloth which was also gilded, carrying his falcon, and shaking his loose hair like a possessed devotee of the Magna Mater. He climbed up on a high altar and, speaking to the people, he blessed the city because it was immediately to receive a manifestation of the God.

Those who were there—most of the city, with the women, old men, and children had come running pell-mell—marvelled, prayed, and fell down in worship. He shouted some gibberish, like Hebrew or Phoenician, and astounded the folk who did not know what he said, except that in everything he mixed in Apollo and Asklepios.

Then he ran to the temple under construction, went to the excavation and the prepared fountain of the oracle, entered the water, singing hymns and praises to Asklepios and Apollo in a loud voice and called upon the God to come with good fortune to the city. Then he asked for an offering vial. When someone gave him one, he quickly immersed it and brought up, with the water and mud, that egg in which he had hidden "the God." He had closed the seam from which the liquid was blown out with white wax and white lead. Taking the egg up in his hands, he said he now held Asklepios!

The crowd stared unblinkingly to see what would now happen; they already marveled greatly at the discovery of the egg in the water. But then he broke it and took the embryonic snake into the hollow of his hand, and those present saw it moving and winding around his fingers. They cried out at once and welcomed the God, blessed their city, and greedily they glutted themselves with prayers for treasures, riches, health, and every other benefit from him.

Then he ran home at once, taking the newborn Asklepios, "twice-born, when other men are only once born" (*Odyssey* 12.22), fathered not from Koronis by Zeus, nor a crow, but from a goose! The whole crowd followed in a religious frenzy and mad with hopes.

> Alexander stays at home to set up the "sting." The news of his miracle spreads, and, when the folk finally see Alexander, he is in a sumptuous room, clothed as a God, and with a big snake (the Pella serpent) draped around him as he lies on a couch. This convinces the folk of the marvelously fast growth of the tiny snake Alexander had extracted from the egg; he used, of course, two different snakes. The snake's head was firmly held—Alexander does not want to be bitten—and the linen serpent's head is made to look as if it were the snake's real head. Of course Alexander may now promise oracles to predict the future, healings, and cures—for a healthy fee.
>
> Another of Alexander's "miracles" was to accept sealed scrolls which contained questions put to the God. Alexander took the scrolls into the temple sanctuary. They were returned, still sealed, but with the God's answer miraculously inscribed on them. "This trick would seem to a man like you, and, if it is not gauche to say so, like me, obvious and easily exposed. But to those idiots full of snot it was miraculous and close to incredible," comments Lucian.
>
> Alexander, according to Lucian, now establishes an international oracle corporation and a very lucrative, central shrine at which, if we believe Lucian, the main worship is the debauching of men, women, and boys.

He established mystery rites with torch-light processions and priestly offices. The celebration was to be held three days each year, forever. And on the first day was a proclamation, as at Athens: "If any atheist or

Christian or Epicurean has come to spy on the rites, let him flee; let those who believe in the God do the mysteries under a good fortune."

Then immediately, at the beginning, there was a purging ceremony; he led the act, saying, "Outside, Christians!" And the whole crowd chanted, "Outside, Epicureans!"

Then there was the childbirth of Leto, the birth of Apollo and the marriage to Koronis, and the birth of Asklepios. On the second day was the Epiphany of Glycon and the birth of the God. On the third day was the marriage of Podaleirios and the mother of Alexander; it was called Torch Day, and torches were burned. Finally, there was the "eros" of Selene and Alexander, and the wife of Rutilianos was born. The Endymion (Alexander!) bore the torch and acted the priest. While he lay in full view, pretending to sleep, a certain very pretty woman came down to him from the roof, as if from Heaven, not Selene but Rutilia who was the wife of one of the emperor's stewards. She really loved Alexander, and he her, and before the eyes of her ruined husband there were kisses and embraces. If there had not been many torches, perhaps there would have been actual intercourse . . .

He warned everyone to refrain from homosexual intercourse, saying that it was impious. He himself invented a certain kind of propriety: he ordered the cities of Pontus and Paphlagonia to send choirboys for a triennium to sing hymns to the God for him; they were to send those tested and judged exceptional in nobility, youth, and beauty. He kept these boys locked up and treated them as if they were bought, sleeping with them and treating them disgustingly in every way.

He made it a law not to greet anyone over eighteen years old with his lips, nor to greet with a kiss. But he kissed only the young, to the others he stretched out his hands to be kissed. They were called "those within the kiss."

He made sport of the fools in this way continuously, corrupting women heedlessly and cohabiting with boys. It was a great thing, pleasing to each, if he should look at someone's wife. If she was worthy of a kiss, each man thought that good fortune would immediately run through his house. Many women bragged that they had given birth by him, and their husbands testified that they spoke the truth.

Lucian's catalog of Alexander's trickery is long. Finally, as is the custom, Lucian describes the death and the order of "succession" of the "divine man."

Alexander predicted by an oracle concerning himself that he was destined to live one hundred and fifty years and then die by a lightning bolt. But he died horribly; he had not reached the age of seventy . . .

his leg became infected to the groin and seethed with worms. It was then that his baldness was revealed; he let the physicians pour water on his head on account of the pain. They could not do this unless they removed his wig.

Such was the end of Alexander's heroic play; it was the climax of the drama. It seemed to be providential, if indeed it happened by fate. And it was necessary for his funeral games to be worthy of his life—so there arose a struggle for the shrine. Those who were the chiefs of his conspirators and of his fellow charlatans gave the decision to Rutilianos as to which of them should be judged worthy to inherit the shrine and to be crowned with the garland of hierophant and prophet. Paitos was one, a physician by trade, an elder, who did things befitting neither a physician nor an elderly man.

But the judge, Rutilianos, sent them off uncrowned and kept the office of prophet for himself after Alexander died . . .
